Police on Screen

ALSO BY M. RAY LOTT

The American Martial Arts Film
(McFarland, 2004)

Quicksand Jesus
(CGP, 2006)

Police on Screen

Hollywood Cops, Detectives, Marshals and Rangers

M. Ray Lott

McFarland & Company, Inc., Publishers
Jefferson, North Carolina, and London

LIBRARY OF CONGRESS CATALOGUING-IN-PUBLICATION DATA

Lott, M. Ray, 1960–
Police on screen : Hollywood cops, detectives, marshals and rangers /
M. Ray Lott.
p.   cm.
Filmography : p.
Includes bibliographical references and index.

ISBN 0-7864-2577-6 (softcover : 50# alkaline paper)

1. Police films— United States— History and criticism.
2. Detective and mystery films— United States— History and criticism.
3. Western films— United States— History and criticism.   I. Title.
PN1995.9.P57L68   2006   791.43'6556 — dc22   2006010758

British Library cataloguing data are available

©2006 M. Ray Lott. All rights reserved

*No part of this book may be reproduced or transmitted in any form
or by any means, electronic or mechanical, including photocopying
or recording, or by any information storage and retrieval system,
without permission in writing from the publisher.*

Cover photograph ©2006 Brand X Pictures

Manufactured in the United States of America

*McFarland & Company, Inc., Publishers
Box 611, Jefferson, North Carolina 28640
www.mcfarlandpub.com*

Officer Tommy Scott,
killed in the line of duty,
29 April 2005.
Never forgotten.

Table of Contents

Preface 1

    I. Law Enforcement in Cinema 3
    II. Easy Streets 10
    III. The New Deal Hero 26
    IV. Cold Warriors 34
    V. Sci-Fi Cops 42
    VI. The Professional 63
    VII. Wanted: Dead or Alive 72
    VIII. Film Noir, Feminism and Private Heat 97
    IX. Workin' for the Railroad 111
    X. Vigilantes with a Badge 119
    XI. Bad Apples 129
    XII. Keystone 141
    XIII. The O.K. Corral 150
    XIV. Gunsmoke 161
    XV. One Riot—One Ranger! 174
    XVI. Walkin' the Beat ... Cruising the Street... 187
    XVII. End of the Trail 194

Filmography 203
Sources 211
Index 213

Preface

Celluloid Lawmen is among the first books of its kind, a critical-historical analysis of law enforcement in cinema. It examines the police in their various and many incarnations, from the officers on the street handling social anomie and cultural blight, to the detectives picking up the pieces of the brutally murdered, and sometimes being the only ones who care about justice for the corpse in front of them. We see sharpshooting bounty hunters and two-fisted private eyes who support the men and women wearing the badge. We watch sci-fi cops. New Deal cops. Cold War cops. Even the "Professional," who only knows and does one thing. We study the vigilante cops. Railroad cops. Crooked cops. There are the legendary Texas Rangers, and even Wyatt Earp and the famous shoot-out at the O.K. Corral.

To accomplish this, I viewed scores of police films, or films involving police activities, to provide a comprehensive examination of the material in question. Any strength this study possesses is shared with the filmmakers and performers who do their best in every movie; any deficiencies are my own.

I'm sure many readers wonder about the acknowledgments that most writers include in their books. The reader doesn't know these people, right? But I do. The significance of thanking those who helped or inspired me is *not* so the readers know who they are, but that they know *I* know who they are — and how they contributed in no small way to my getting the job done. With that said, I'd like to thank God, my wife, Ivy, and my family, and the circle of trust which has stood by me in trying times. Hey, I'm still standing.

One more thing. When the director yells "Cut," the celluloid lawman turns back to actor, and whether he has fallen off a 12-story building or has been shot a hundred times, he's up and about with the rest of the cast and crew. Things are not so easy in real life. I spent almost 23 years as a police officer, but the very nature of the job is *not knowing* what the shift in front of you holds. Los Angeles Airport Police Officer Tommy Scott was killed in the line of duty, April 29, 2005, the first to be lost in that department's history.

Officer Scott had been a peace officer for four years, but already he was training personnel; his promotion was thoroughly deserved. Tommy worked harder than anyone on the force. There wasn't a radio call he wouldn't answer or an officer he wouldn't assist. He had become that consummate professional we all wish we were — but most never are. He had risen through his own merit to a position where he tried to make a difference.

This book is dedicated to Officer Tommy Scott and law enforcement personnel everywhere who went down fighting, giving their lives to keep the rest of us safe and protected.

I

LAW ENFORCEMENT IN CINEMA

The history of law enforcement officers stretches back thousands of years, though many of us could not recognize those past incarnations today. What we identify as modern policing began at the beginning of the twentieth century, at the same time cinema developed from a novelty to an art form — and big business. In many ways, the two are linked by content, yet separated by the very same thing, the fiction often bearing little resemblance to the reality it purports to represent. Put simply, film portrayals of the police generally strive for entertainment, not authenticity, and have provided audiences with a rich vein of myth.

As John Ford's characters recount in *The Man Who Shot Liberty Valance* (1962), when the legend becomes fact, print the legend!

Law Enforcement

Prior to the Roman Empire, Mesopotamian and Greek cities often used African slaves to protect the marketplaces and royalty. Their different appearance distinguished them from the citizenry; this can be seen as one of the first stabs at making law enforcement personnel stand out. Most attempts at using slaves, however, were short-lived or outright failures. At the time Octavius took power after Julius Caesar's assassination, he created a special police-bodyguard force called the Praetorian Guard who protected him and rooted out trouble. One-third of the Guards operated undercover, watching civilians. The Praetorians were eventually disbanded for becoming too involved in politics and organizing assassination plots themselves. One of the concepts that still survives from the time of Octavius' reign is the "precinct," in which districts were defined and protected. This idea is in practice in many cities, including New York, which organizes its police by precincts to this day.

Through the Middle Ages, most laws were enforced by family or village groups. Keeping away unwanted people such as tramps and gypsies was a high priority. After the Norman invasion in 1066, English law was revised by the king to include areas called "hundreds," which supervised ten tithings and which were controlled by the constable. Ten hundreds were a "shire," which was headed up by the "shire-reeve," whose duty was to represent the crown.*

---

*In America, the shire-reeve morphed into the sheriff, the most visible cinematic representative of local law enforcement.

Police History: A History of Police and Law Enforcement notes that the Statute of Winchester, passed 1285, established the following laws:

- Every able-bodied man (must) possess a weapon
- Everyone in the countryside was accountable to help with the apprehension of criminals
- A watch and ward night patrol was established to augment daytime constables
- The parish constable system was formalized

During the American Colonial era, two systems of law enforcement were in play. The French system, going back to King Charlemagne, used gendarmes, who were agents of the crown. They could travel anywhere to mete out justice. This arrangement was centralized in nature, and is still used by many countries in Europe. The English relied on the volunteer and constable scheme, which was decentralized. The colonies leaned toward the latter. From the Revolution until the present time, a loose organization comprised of thousands of law enforcement departments protect, serve and keep order across the country.*

From colonial times until the nineteenth century, most big American cities like Boston and New York used volunteers who wandered the streets carrying rattles to signal each other. They weren't the most effective means of policing. Some criminals were apprehended and made to do police work as part of their punishment. Most of these watchmen were considered mentally deficient but up to that point only the United States Marshal Service had been established (in 1789). But its job was not to police cities or counties but rather to transport federal prisoners and to protect judges and courtrooms. Later, deputy marshals enforced federal laws in the Old West.

While Sir Robert Peel began England's first paid, professional police department in 1829, New York City started the first paid, professional police department in the States 16 years later. The slang for the police was "coppers," after the copper badge they wore on their uniforms. The department functioned 24/7/365 and the officers carried firearms. Other big cities followed suit. While the police departments were effective, they were also crooked, as city political machines like Tammany Hall used them to further their own greedy ends.

After 1900, police reforms, such as civil service and the development of police unions, became common developments. Citizens also found themselves on committees overseeing police functions, while women and minorities found jobs on police departments. Federal agencies such as the FBI and the Treasury Department, among others, sprang up to combat a number of crimes that local departments could not effectively deal with, particularly those involving crimes across state lines.† By the end of the century, American peace officers were the best-trained and most effective professionals in law enforcement. Most states had developed Peace Officer Standards and Training (POST) departments for their officers, which included certain background requirements and attendance at training academies. With the new millennium, Congress passed laws recognizing the right of local peace officers to carry their weapons concealed in any state of the union.

---

*This sword has two edges—both sharp. Most Americans prefer not to have a national police agency which could somehow undermine their freedom, like the Gestapo or KGB. However, without a centralized agency, criminals can and will elude justice because of confusion generated by the overwhelming number of police departments throughout the country.

†While these departments are national, they have very specific duties and do not enforce local laws.

The Early Days of Cinema

As law enforcement agencies professionalized standards and conduct at the beginning of the twentieth century, cinema developed along the same lines, moving from pictures flickering at a nickelodeon to full-fledged movies. Film was originally linked to vaudeville and theater, both popular forms of entertainment at the turn of the century. However, unlike cinema, those forms of amusement were live, their action unfolding in real time with a set number of actors upon a minimally propped staged. Film, a more complicated art form, relies on any number of commodities, from the actors to the gear being used to film them. Making a movie, then, involves a number of steps and the use of certain technologies and equipment.

Celluloid, or film stock, is the basis of any movie, since the action recorded by the camera, and the image projected by the projector, has been captured on film. Early film stocks were either light-sensitive paper or glass plates, neither of which would facilitate moving pictures. This quandary was solved when George Eastman developed flexible film in 1889.

One of the earliest gauges was 35mm, the large size needed because image quality would otherwise be poor. Perforated holes in the sides of the film stock allowed both a camera and a projector to thread the film through. As time passed, other gauges were developed: 8mm, which was often used in home movie cameras; 16mm, which became a staple for documentaries and low-budget films, and 70mm, which was used primarily in big-budget epics. Most films are shot in what is called the "Academy" format, which equates to about 1.33 feet wide to every foot high.

Among the greatest challenges facing inventors interested in capturing moving pictures was the development of a camera that could do just that. To accomplish this task, the camera would have to both take the pictures quickly—for silent films at a rate of 16 frames per second (fps), for sound films 24 fps—and do it in such a manner that each frame is advanced an equal amount between frames. Otherwise, the picture would be jerky and unsteady. Thomas Edison and his assistant William K. L. Dickson developed a working moving picture camera in 1889, the same year that Eastman marketed his flexible strip film; their first film was of a man who bowed, smiled and took off his hat.

Film is shot through a camera in an intermittent fashion, with a stop-start motion. At each stop the shutter opens to let light reach the film, then the shutter closes and a claw pulls the next frame down and the step is repeated. From the beginning of moving pictures into the late '20s, most cameras were hand-cranked, with an average of two turns per second. To slow down the action on screen, the camera operator would turn the crank faster; to speed up things up, it would be turned slower.

Cameras were mounted on tripods, which enabled the operator to pan the device horizontally or tilt it vertically. Dollies, cranes and other devices would be developed later to give much-needed mobility to the camera, which in the earliest days remained fixed in place. At a rate of 16 fps, more than 60 feet of film were required to capture one minute of action; 24 fps required more than 90 feet per minute.

The first projectors were really "magic lanterns," devices used in the late seventeenth century to cast pictures on a wall. A candle was mounted within the body of the lantern, to provide light; a sealed chimney allowed the heat to vent but kept out stray light. Slides consisted of long, rectangular strips of glass which contained a number of painted-on pictures. The slides were inserted upside down, so that the picture would appear right side up on the screen, and would be advanced to change the scene. While this procedure did not produce the effect of moving pictures, it did combine two important elements that would be essential in the development of cinema: a device that used light to project images onto a screen, and the use of the slides, which were divided in the manner of film frames.

Thomas Edison, who had been experimenting with moving picture cameras in the United States, patented the Kinetoscope, which featured a 15-second film which the viewer watched through a peephole. Later developed were the Mutascopes, machines that allowed the patron to see a longer film by peeping through a viewer at the top of the machine while turning a crank handle to make the pictures move. The limitation here was that these machines played to an audience of one.

Brothers Auguste and Louis Lumiere were Frenchmen who invented the Cinematograph, a camera that also doubled as a projector. To project their film, the two men used a powerful lamp which they stationed behind the camera as they cranked their film through. They showed the first "projected" movies in a Parisian cafe in December 1895 (scenes of a train running through a station and workers leaving their factory). As the story goes, the train's approach actually spooked many in the audience, who feared they would be run over!

Projectors would become bigger and more effective as time passed. They would be able to handle reels of up to a thousand feet; electric power would replace the imprecise movement of the hand-crank, just as it did on the camera. Arc lamps were incorporated into the machines, brighter light being needed to fill the larger screens. Modern projectors have a number of automatic functions, and can show films on an endless loop, thereby cutting the need for projectionists.

Edison initially resisted the notion of projected film, his thinking tied to the individual pay-per-view of the crank machines that he had developed and marketed. He viewed film as a fad, a passing fancy; while a visionary in other areas, was among the last to be convinced of the efficacy of projected film. His famous statement, "If we make this screen machine you are asking for, it will spoil everything. Let's not kill the goose that laid the golden egg," marked his first miscalculation with regard to cinema (Platt, p. 16). It would not be his last.

There is really no such thing as an absolute film language; semiotics, a branch of linguistic studies used to identify universal signs within film, has produced mixed results. Initial moving pictures were merely static shots of events that unfolded in front of a stationary camera. A parade. A coronation. A battleship coming into port. As film edged toward a narrative structure, the use of the camera and editing became a major asset in producing visual meaning. Eventually a number of filmic conventions became commonly accepted by the viewing public, and when employed during the shooting and editing of a film, resulted in the "realism" that marks most narrative features.

Where early films used one long, continuous shot, later filmmakers began to break up the scene into various shots, which would later be edited together. Shots were divided into *long*, which captures most or everything on a set or in a given area; *medium*, which might show a character from the waist up; and *closeup*, which focuses specifically on a particular item. By breaking up a continual scene (such as the aforementioned parade) into individual shots, the director not only heightens the viewer's interest but is able to control the film's content and impact.

One of the first, and still most common shots to evolve from the three basic shots was *three-quarter length framing*, which captures a character from the top of his or her legs on up. This shot imparts a comfortable, or normal feel to the viewer. *Closeups*, on the other hand, tend to isolate a character's reaction to something, adding a particular import to it. *Eyeline matches* produce a connection between a character and what that character is looking at. For example, a character looks toward something off-screen; a second shot shows what the character is looking at, thereby providing a sense of spatial continuity. Related to both the closeup and the eyeline match is the *point-of-view shot*, which allows the camera to take on the subjective viewpoint of a character.

Directors began to move the camera as well. In *The Great Train Robbery* (1903), among the first American films to feature a narrative storyline, Edwin S. Porter followed the fleeing outlaws as they made fast their getaway. Such movement, which included tilts and pans, enabled the viewer to see beyond the initial scene's framing, and like the *eyeline match*, facilitated the impression of space. Porter's film also offered simultaneous lines of action, something rare at the time; they depicted both the rescue of the telegraph operator by his family and the raising of a posse, all during the time the train robbery unfolds (Musser, p. 354). Such parallel points of action did not become standard until director D.W. Griffith made them a hallmark of his films.

The 180-degree rule was instrumental in creating the sense of realism that modern films induce. Simply put, the camera would not cross beyond an imaginary axis, or center line, drawn through a particular take or scene. Otherwise, characters and scenery would flipflop. Maintaining the camera position on one side of the line led to a sense of continuity, which, taken with the other methods, helped to produce the classic narrative form still dominant in film today.

Editing became more important as multiple camera set-ups replaced the one spatial camera when filming scenes. Shots would be spliced together using a flat bed editing board, though now, some 100 years after the first films, non-linear digital editing is the preferred method, even in low-budget films. In this mode, the film's footage is loaded into a computer and rearranged accordingly, the final result being a "seamless" flow of images that facilitate the appearance of realism.

Once these technological barriers were overcome, and aesthetic practices developed, the way for early narrative films was clear. From the very beginning, financial expenditure was always an intricate factor in any film production; the notion of art wasn't even considered. Films made on a shoestring budget were the norm and not the exception when they debuted in the early 1890s. Large amounts of money could be made on the sheer novelty of the process. As noted, these first films were rather crude, simple affairs: "actualities" really, merely scenes that the camera recorded.

As film passed from the peep machine stage advanced by Edison to the projection stage pioneered by the Lumieres, many fledgling producers, including Edison, battled over their own various versions of a movie projector. Edison's Vitascope* projected films in downtown nickelodeons (because the various shows cost one nickel), and the shows would consists of documentary-like scenes where the event merely unfolded before the lens. Popular with male audiences were boxing matches and hoochie dancers; women liked slice-of-life vignettes about home. Both sexes enjoyed the travelogues and "funnies," short clips of a practical joke or some comic event. The one thing all these film types had in common were their cost: little or nothing!

Films in these pioneering days of cinema were shot "for the moment"; that is, they

---

*Actually invented by Thomas Armat.

were made as cheaply as possible, used until the celluloid deteriorated, and then discarded. As often as not, the person or company that made the film would also exhibit it. Edison, Biograph and Vitagraph constituted the first studios; by 1908, they had formed the Motion Picture Patents Company, and along with other signatories, like the French company Pathe, formed a virtual trust that attempted a complete monopoly over the business of film, using the court system to bully any independents. Unfortunately for the Trust, their business strategy revolved around the selling of projecting equipment; films were merely by products to be exhibited on those projectors.

Since in this scheme a movie had no worth beyond its initial novelty, it made no sense to spend too much money on something. This began to change with the development of film exchanges, companies which catalogued and rented various films to exhibitors, and pressure from audiences and the independent filmmakers who wanted longer, narrative-oriented films. Movies were still being made on the cheap, but the exchanges presented an economic incentive, albeit a crude one, to make a better product, since, theoretically anyway, the more often a film was rented, the more money it earned.

Much more important was the change compelled by audiences, who desired expanded narrative in their films. Silent movies, from the shorts of the 1890s to the early Griffith period, generally featured some type of action; but typical reels (1000 feet or less) didn't hold enough film for the moviemakers to tell any type of cohesive story (Musser, p. 349). In another move taken with costs in mind, producers did not give screen credit to their actors and actresses, thereby insuring their dependence on the producer for work. The Trust companies opposed longer films, mistakenly believing that more money could be made selling shorts and projectors. Independents like Carl Laemmle, who began the "star system" when he hired Biograph Girl Florence Lawrence away from her studio and began to promote her name in his productions, and directors like Griffith boldly moved ahead and produced longer films. By 1912, the upstart independents had equaled the production of the Trust, and led the way to feature-length films.

European films also moved in that direction. Italy's *Cabiria* (1913) used grand sets and a large cast, greatly influencing Griffith and others. With Griffith's *Birth of a Nation* (1915), American cinema came into its own. Budgets climbed, as did profits for many of the fledgling studios. Griffith's follow-up film *Intolerance* (1916) cost $525,000, featuring a huge replica of Babylon, and literally a cast of thousands (Merritt, p. 21). It never made its money back, but the trail to bigger budgets had been blazed, and there was no turning around, though there were some low-budget detours. Two early police films, bordering on exploitation, were released in 1913. *Traffic in Souls*, a supposed exposé of forced prostitution, cost less than $6000 and made almost ten times that much; *The Inside of the White Slave Traffic*, also about prostitution, was banned by many theater owners for its unwholesome subject matter.

Law Enforcement and Cinema

Thousands of movies have been made about police officers during the last century, whether they were sheriffs, U.S. Marshals, Texas Rangers, feds, even beat cops walking the street. During the course of this study, we'll examine a number of movies from each category, as well as others, with an eye toward understanding them not only as cultural and historical documents, but where they fall in the film canon. The films chosen are not random —

each has something to say about society, either in the period they are set or the period they were filmed. Or they are fairly representative of the genre and present certain details about what it means to carry a badge and gun and walk that thin blue line. For example, *Star Packer* (1934) is a B film about an undercover federal agent infiltrating a gang of criminals. While this is a standard plot, what *isn't* is its connection to, and commentary about, the Great Depression, which had brought the nation's economy to a relative standstill. In *High Noon* (1952), Gary Cooper won his second Academy Award playing a town constable who stands up alone to a gang of criminals, while no one in the town will help. Considering the year it was filmed, was he also standing up to the House Un-American Activities Committee? In *Ride the High Country* (1962), Joel McCrea and Randolph Scott are ex-lawmen who have fallen on hard times. How does society treat such men who made their towns safe but now have outlived their usefulness? We will examine these films and others to determine what it's like to be a celluloid lawman.

Sources

Merritt, Greg. *Celluloid Mavericks.* New York: Thunder's Mouth Press, 2000.
Musser, Charles. *The Emergence of Cinema: The American Screen to 1907.* Los Angeles: University of California Press, 1990.
Platt, Richard. *Film.* New York: Alfred A. Knopf, 1992.
Real Police. *History of Police and Law Enforcement.* http://realpolice.net/police_history.html.
"US Marshal's Service." Microsoft Encarta. 1998.

II

EASY STREETS

They call me Mister Tibbs!*

Soon they'll breeding us like cattle! You've got to warn everyone and tell them! Soylent Green is made of people! You've got to tell them! Soylent Green is people!†

The police have always been pushed to the front lines of social change, whether it was the evolution from gunslingers on horseback to uniformed cops patrolling in Model Ts, or the advent of civil rights in the '60s and the slew of court cases which modified their way of doing things. As society fragments and older, more traditional ways of looking at things evolve or fall by the wayside, peace officers are expected to pick up the slack. An entire juvenile justice system was developed to handle children, only in many cases, the crimes which these children perpetrate are so heinous they must be tried as adults. Incorrigible or otherwise violent children are often placed in special custodial arrangements by the police, a job handled by parents in the past. In some jurisdictions, drug abuse or alcoholism is considered a disease, and police have to act as custodians, not enforcers, in getting the individual help. Even sick and mentally unstable people, once taken care of by their families, are now charged to law enforcement to find and commit to mental institutions. The following films highlight the often impossible social conditions in which law enforcement officers must work — and try to be effective.

Easy Street (1917)

In 1913, English vaudevillian Charles Chaplin was touring the United States as part of a theatrical review. One year later he made his motion picture debut in a Mack Sennett comedy short. By 1916 he was a screenwriter and a director, as well as an international star. In 1917, Chaplin turned his enormous talents toward social satire, writing, directing and starring in *Easy Street,* the first of many films that not only entertained audiences but slyly commented on the civic problems of the day.

The film co-starred Edna Purviance as a minister's daughter and Eric Campbell as the giant thug whom Chaplin, as the "Little Tramp" character, must overcome to bring order to the community. It is approximately 22 minutes in length, black and white, and was shot while Chaplin was with the Mutual Corporation.

**Detective Virgil Tibbs (Sidney Poitier) to Chief Bill Gillespie (Rod Steiger) in* In the Heat of the Night.
†*Detective Thorn (Charlton Heston) warning the population in* Soylent Green.

II. Easy Streets

In *Easy Street*, the Little Tramp falls in love with a minister's beautiful young daughter, whom he meets in church. After he leaves her, the Tramp reluctantly joins the police department and is assigned to "Easy Street," a rough-and-tumble neighborhood plagued by all manner of vice and viciousness. The Little Tramp is immediately confronted by a thug who terrorizes the area. The thug attempts to beat up the Tramp but the latter turns the tables on the thug and outsmarts him, using the thug's own strength against him. Unfortunately for the Tramp-turned-lawman, the thug escapes from police custody and begins wreaking havoc all about the Tramp's beat. The Tramp must confront the bully once again, and their ensuing confrontation takes place all along Easy Street. In the end, however, the Tramp once again prevails, restoring order and decency to the community.

Though *Easy Street* is a nominal comedy, the issues that Chaplin touches upon are generally the fare of more serious works. Police ineptitude, rampant violence, drug addiction, overpopulation, spousal abuse, crime and chaos were and still are nagging dilemmas affecting America's large cities. That Chaplin is able to address these problems in a humorous way is a testament to his ability as an artist and a visionary.

From the very outset, Chaplin establishes the Little Tramp as an outsider, albeit one with a heart of gold. The film opens with him asleep outside of a church, which functions as an institutional symbol of culture and order. Awakened by the congregation's singing, the Tramp enters and tries to fit in, only to succumb to old habits when he steals the collection box. However, he falls in love with the minister's daughter and returns the property.

Living on the margins of our society, the Tramp is not readily accepted. When he initially tries to join the police department, he is rebuffed, the officers and chiefs scoffing at his dress and demeanor. Only when the Tramp resorts to violence — slapping one of his tormentors — do they feel he is up to the job, thereby perpetuating brutality as both a means and an end.

The Tramp is given a badge and a stick and sent upon his way, with no other direction and no apparent training. Though he is now gainfully employed, his standing as an outsider has not changed, for his uniform now marks him as an authority figure, something certainly not accepted by the denizens of Easy Street, who are accustomed to the thug not only terrorizing them but just as routinely beating up the police, who are powerless to stop the chaos. The Tramp is given little chance to survive, yet, when he outwits the thug by sticking the brute's face into a gas lantern and rendering him unconscious, the Tramp becomes a hero to both his colleagues and those in the neighborhood.

Ironically, it is during this short interlude of social acceptance that the Tramp comes face to face with the hellish conditions which exist behind the tenement walls of Easy Street. As an impoverished fringe dweller, the Tramp got by the best he could, by hook or crook. However, as an authority figure, the Tramp must use those same skills to steal food to save a starving woman, and to outwit heroin addicts who attempt to molest the minister's daughter.

In one particularly funny yet telling scene, the Tramp is introduced to an impoverished family with a large number of children. Though such large families are often common among the immigrants from less developed countries that populate the sprawling cities, the Tramp's initial reaction to the situation is universal: Puzzlement at how people so poor could have so many children. Of course, since people from such places have a high child mortality rate and no social services available to them when they get old, a large family generally acts as a hedge against future hardship. The Tramp solves the problem — at least temporarily — by tossing grain to the children as if it were chicken feed, Chaplin's way of pointing out in a humorous way the difficulties associated with overpopulation.

Later in the story, the Tramp must again confront the giant thug, who at this point is slugging it out with his wife. A good portion of the couple's brawl takes place on and around their bed, a not incidental reference to the thin line between love and hate, while the kitchen stove, that object which helps sustain and nourish the family, is turned into a weapon as the violence escalates. Though Chaplin plays these scenes for laughs, with most of the fight having a rather cartoonish quality to it, the issue of domestic violence is anything but funny, a fact underscored by his ironic treatment of it.

Chaplin once commented that the policeman-type was the one person the whole wide world had it in for (moviediva.com). In the course of other Little Tramp films, this might be true, but it seems an incongruous statement with regard to *Easy Street*, since the Tramp *was* the police officer.* At any rate, the film ends on an upbeat, albeit unrealistic note. The community is united and peaceful, the dirty laundry and linen hanging from the tenement windows replaced by billowing light cloth and blankets. The church is now established at the front of Easy Street; the thug, his wife and the rest of the neighborhood fill the area as they head for Sunday services. Through his ability to match force with superior force, the Little Tramp is now a member of the community, an *insider* who has won the favor of the minister's daughter, whom he escorts to the church.

While such a happy ending may have pleased audiences, it merely serves to highlight the fact that there are no easy answers to such problems even now, almost a century later, though Chaplin's optimistically sweet conclusion belies a similar understanding and, perhaps, a certain futility about any permanent solutions.

In the Heat of the Night (1967)

In the 1950s, school desegregation became a reality, and there followed a real movement for civil rights equality for blacks and other minorities. In some places, particularly the South, politicians used the police to resist this demonstration, but by the end of the 1960s a number of civil rights laws had been passed. However, changing a law does not necessarily mean changing a mind. In the South, as in many other places around the country, having to treat blacks equally and without any discrimination was a hard sell, as Philadelphia police detective Virgil Tibbs found on his trip to Sparta, Mississippi, in *In the Heat of the Night*.

Detective Tibbs was in the South visiting family. On the night he was returning home, a wealthy businessman was killed, an important man to the community because he was going to develop some industry there. The police find Tibbs in a train station, a well-dressed black man with a lot of money, and immediately arrest him for the murder. Police chief Bill Gillespie checks Tibbs' story and releases him to leave town. The widow of the murdered man thinks differently, though, and wants Tibbs to investigate her husband's slaying—it's pretty obvious to her and the viewer that the Sparta police department is not the most professional in the world. Tibbs stays and solves the crime, but not before he learns a little more about the South than he wanted, and Gillespie learns a little more about police work than he ever figured to.

The appeal of the narrative is in the reversal of positions: a northern black man is put in charge of southern white men at a time when the notion of equal rights still rankled in places like Sparta. As Tibbs pushes the investigation, he breaks a number of taboos—including

---

*Most of Chaplin's life was controversial. He had to deal with a number of morals charges and eventually left the United States.

slapping a rich white man who slapped him first. Gillespie, not an intellectual but a clever southern boy, has to watch to make sure that Tibbs doesn't go after someone out of mere bias, like the white man who slapped him. This serves as another reminder to the chief and his department of what they have been doing for so long. Tibbs, a police officer in a large, metropolitan department in a racially diverse city, has never seen the likes of this kind of resistance based merely on his race. Gillespie has never met a black man who speaks perfect English and can run rings around his officers. Gillespie's main strength is his force in the community. When thugs working for the rich white man go after Tibbs, Gillespie arrives and establishes order. Even in Philadelphia, Tibbs does not command such respect and fear.

Had Tibbs been a doctor, or a lawyer, or even a trash collector with a genius IQ, his contributions

Chief Gillespie (Rod Steiger) in *In the Heat of the Night*.

to the community of Sparta would have been negligible, having still solved the crime. However, as a law enforcement officer, his association with the public is imperative, and what they see and experience has a lasting effect. Crooked or stupid cops, like some of Gillespie's men, give community members a bad feeling. A man like Tibbs leaves the opposite feeling. To say that the solving of one murder changes a town is a long way from true. To say that solving that murder opens a few minds and changes a few opinions, well, that's the start of understanding.

In the Heat of the Night was nominated for seven Academy Awards and won five, including Best Picture and Best Actor for Rod Steiger, who played Chief Gillespie. It beat out a number of fine movies in that banner year, including *Bonnie and Clyde* and *The Graduate*. Detective Tibbs returned to the screen in the 1970 release *They Call Me MISTER Tibbs!* (The title is a reference to Tibbs' conversation with Chief Gillespie, when the latter asked him what they called him in Philadelphia.) In the sequel, Tibbs has moved cross country to San Francisco, where he is investigating a girl's murder. A priest is suspected, and Tibbs goes to work to find the real killer. Sidney Poitier returned as detective Tibbs but Steiger was not part of the sequel, and the film suffered from the lack of social relevance that made the first film so important and fascinating to watch. In the last of the Virgil Tibbs trilogy, *The Organization* (1971), Tibbs goes after drug smugglers while trying to protect some citizens who get in the way. By now, Tibbs was just a cop doing a job like any other cop. His story ended just as "Dirty" Harry Callahan's was beginning.

Crash (2005)

Los Angeles, even more so than New York City, has become a human melting pot where things don't really melt — they just simmer, and below the surface they're ready to explode. That seems to be a prevalent theme in Crash, where people literally and figuratively "crash" into each other during the course of a few days in the City of Angels. A D.A. and his wife are carjacked by two black thugs. One of them blames the white man for everything bad in his life; the other seems to realize that the both of them are just lazy and don't want to work. A black detective and his Hispanic female partner are in a car accident, struck from behind by a Korean woman who speaks little English. A hard-working white LAPD sergeant and his young white partner jack up a rich black couple on a traffic violation, the sergeant feeling up the wife as he searches her. And on and on it goes, throughout the city, each group blaming or hating the other.

Don Cheadle is the detective, honest and without any ethical baggage. He's having an affair with his partner. While they're in bed, his mother calls; he tells her he's having sex with a white woman. When his partner protests that she's not white, Cheadle's reaction is, "You're not black so what does it matter?" His partner, incensed by his insensitivity, leaves. Their banter continues while she dresses, and she tells him she's not Mexican. His reply is more a joke than anything: He says they still park their cars all over the lawn.

Cheadle passes by a shooting and stops to talk to the detectives, who tell him that both the dead man and the shooter are undercover cops. The deceased is a black man; the shooter is white, and he's had other shootings, all ruled justified, involving black men. When Cheadle opens the trunk of the car, which does not belong to the dead cop, they find hundreds of thousands of dollars. The cop was working for a drug dealer transporting money, and the white officer's actions were justified. But the district attorney, who was carjacked by the two black men earlier, wants to scapegoat the white officer to pick up black support during the upcoming election. Cheadle and the D.A.'s inner circle are the only ones who know about the drug money. Cheadle refuses until an assistant D.A. tells him that Cheadle's younger brother — one of the carjackers — has a felony warrant. The D.A. will make it disappear in return for hanging the white officer.

Cheadle goes down a road he can't turn back from. He saves a brother who is more or less a punk and a thug, likable or not, at the expense of a fellow officer. But he doesn't do it because of race — he's promised his mother he'd look after his brother. But the D.A.'s actions are utterly reprehensible and almost unthinkable for those who don't understand big city politics. By holding up the white cop as a rogue bigot, the D.A. positions himself as the "good" white man out to protect the community — especially minorities. The D.A. insures he's not connected to the illegal deal with Cheadle by letting his assistant handle it while he's somewhere else. In fact, the D.A. is so sensitive to race issues in the county that when news breaks about him being carjacked, he downplays the fact that the assailants were black, much to his wife's chagrin. He even tries to find some event where he can appear to honor or decorate a black man to deflect that the criminals were black!

The most compelling story, and in many respects the most ambiguous, is that of the sergeant, played by Matt Dillon. His father, old and unable to work, can't sleep at night because of an enlarged prostate which keeps him in pain and on the toilet all night. Dillon calls his father's insurance company, but the woman, who sounds black to Dillon, is little help. Dillon reacts by taunting the woman. Still angry later on, he pulls over a rich black couple, and humiliates the husband verbally while humiliating the wife physically. Dillon stays up at night helping his father, then patrols the city during the day, seething.

But is he racist? He certainly crossed the line with the woman ... but why? Whatever the reasons, he should be disciplined immediately for such behavior, but the couple would rather argue with each other than call the station, even though LAPD now has one of the most responsive complaint systems of any police agency. Dillon eventually meets with the insurance woman he talked to on the phone, apologizes, and actually begs her to give his father a competent doctor. The woman refuses, taking the opportunity to get back at Dillon, even though Dillon tells the woman his father spent his whole life running a janitorial service, employing mostly blacks at good wages, until the city cancelled all his contracts so they could hire minority-owned firms. Dillon leaves, filled with more rage than ever. While on patrol, he runs across a car accident; the car is leaking gasoline and the woman trapped inside is the woman he groped.

Dillon's actions certainly don't jibe with those of someone who hates black people. Despite the fuel catching fire, and rescuers removing him from the car, he jumps back in

The "racist" sergeant (Matt Dillon) saves the life of Christine (Thandie Newton), a woman he had earlier humiliated in *Crash*.

and pulls the woman out as the car explodes. All they do is stare at one another as paramedics take her away. A brave man? Certainly. Embittered? Without a doubt. After his young partner talks to the watch commander to assign him a different partner, Dillon tells the kid that he's too new, that he'll understand one day. But understand what? That he sees the streets of Los Angeles aren't a fair or safe place, and that the values of white people like him seem lost, forgotten or, worse yet, rejected?

Dillon's young partner is the most naïve, yet at the same time the most hypocritical. Where the D.A. is using race to get ahead, and ruining a cop's life in the process, Cheadle is merely trying to please his elderly mother, though he's now just as dirty as the county's head prosecutor. Dillon may or may not be a racist, but one thing is for sure: He is a man seething with the tensions and anger he feels on the streets every day. And racist or no, when push comes to shove he does his job, beyond the call of duty. But what of this young man who doesn't approve of Dillon's conduct? He picks up a young black man hitchhiking; it's Cheadle's brother, the carjacker. The two men talk and trade jabs about the music on the car radio. The young cop begins thinking he's made a mistake picking up the man, and when Cheadle's brother reaches into his pocket to show him something, the officer shoots and kills him. He and Dillon have reversed positions: Where the sergeant's behavior on the job was questionable, off-duty he remains clean — he wouldn't even have picked up the hitchhiker. Conversely, the young man's conduct on the job is above board, but he acts with a suspicion born of bigotry, believing the hitchhiker has a gun.

Perception isn't reality, and what someone thinks doesn't make it so, not for Dillon, Cheadle or anyone else. Dillon's watch commander, a black lieutenant, cries he's been the victim of racism the entire time he's worked for the LAPD. But a white LAPD officer dealing with the department's strict Affirmative Action policies would come up with a different conclusion. A black officer watching the Rodney King verdicts come down from Simi Valley might feel the same way. There's no salvation for Cheadle. He must live up to the deal he made with the white devil despite the fact that his brother's now dead. And there are no medals for Dillon, no handshakes and pats on the back. The woman he's saved is taken away — and he'll get in his car and finish his shift. At night he'll stay up with his father who lingers in pain. Nothing really changes for any of the characters in a city where politicians and public employees use race and ethnicity as a weapon to advance their own causes.

Kinjite: Forbidden Subjects (1989)

While the police have the obligation of enforcing the law even in the midst of social change, what happens when the change affects the cop? In *Kinjite*, Charles Bronson, playing a police lieutenant working vice, finds the mores of the time seem to be passing him by. Across the Pacific, a business executive finds himself being transferred to California. As he and his family attempt to adjust to life in Los Angeles, Bronson deals with perverts and sex cases, and keeps tabs on a sleazy pimp who uses underage girls to turn a buck. When the Japanese man's oldest daughter, perhaps 12, is kidnapped by the pimp, molested by him and his men, then used as a prostitute, Bronson must find her. The fear of something like that happening to his own daughter drives him almost to obsession, especially after she is fondled on a bus.

The film's unpleasant subject matter appeared more salacious than it was because of Bronson's presence. Best-known for exploitative action flicks, Bronson threw something of a change up here — viewers found a sensitive, albeit sometimes violent cop not in touch with the sexual freedom among the young. Flashes of the old *Death Wish* character emerged in a few scenes, but the contrast between Bronson's cop and the Japanese family man provided the best glimpse into the sexual fixation troubling Bronson. The family man comes from a society where sexuality is not openly expressed. This repression often leads men to engage in dubious behavior, such as consuming underground, X-rated comics, or breaking the law by touching women on the crowded subway system. On the other hand, Bronson is saturated with sex, both from his work and society. He projects what he experiences onto his daughter, worrying constantly that she'll be somehow contaminated by it. In fact, she's a healthy, sensitive teenager who knows right from wrong. Where the Japanese man wants to be exposed to more sex, Bronson wants less. When the family man places his hand up Bronson's daughter's skirt, imitating the actions he saw on the subway, she screams and fights back, a much different reaction than the Japanese girl on the train. When the man's daughter is kidnapped and molested, he finds his own preoccupation with sex visited upon her. Bronson has to find a way to control his rage at all Japanese (for the crime against his daughter) in order to find the kidnapped girl. He never learns that the Japanese girl's father assaulted his daughter, but the man has been punished enough with the tragedy involving his daughter.

Bronson eventually catches the pimp and his henchmen, doing what Bronson does best. But the film's narrative raises unintentional questions: If Japan is too repressed, and America too relaxed, when it comes to sexual freedom and expression, where is the happy medium? Can the police effectively control such behavior when it is a matter of choice and association? Should they? Bronson would clearly say yes. Before coming to America, the family man might have said no. No one asked the daughters, who seemed to have the best perspectives of everyone involved.

Falling Down (1993)

Released a few years after *Kinjite*, a little over 25 years after *In the Heat of the Night*, and 75 years after *Easy Street*, director Joel Schumacher's *Falling Down* (1993) examined some of the same issues in the last two films, only in a much more violent and gritty way. D-FENS (defense) is the personalized license plate of an unemployed aerospace worker. Having worked hard to develop weapons to beat the Soviets, he finds himself out of a job now that the Cold War has cooled. Sitting in an endless traffic jam, with fumes rising up to the sky to match the man's simmering anger, D-FENS abandons his car and begins a quest that takes him across town, through various neighborhoods, and eventually into a violent showdown with Prendergast, the detective who has been tracking him.

Prendergast, played by Robert Duvall, is on his last day of work. He should be taking it easy, saying goodbye, cleaning out his desk. But, as the reports come in about a series of assaults throughout the city, the cop in Prendergast gets the better of him and he becomes involved. The ironic thing here is that the two main characters— D-FENS and Prendergast, as with the two main characters in *Easy Street*, the Tramp and the giant thug — suffer from the same angst and social ennui. D-FENS cannot find a job. Prendergast does not want to leave his. D-FENS feels anonymous in a society where everyone is supposed to melt in the same pot — but don't. Prendergast has a job, in part, because people don't come together, yet as each year passes, his

Detective Prendergast (Robert Duvall) takes aim at D-FENS (Michael Douglas), off-screen, in *Falling Down*.

ability to affect the course of the things he should affect diminishes. Roger Ebert puts it very well: "Prendergast is, in his own way, an example of the same syndrome afflicting the Douglas character (D-FENS). He feels impotent, unnecessary, and obsolete."

Both the Little Tramp and the giant thug are products of their environment — force is the only course of action they know or understand. In their world, it is the only way to get respect. The thug lashes out at the poverty he cannot change; the Tramp channels his aggression to control the thug. However, neither man can escape their social status, any more than D-FENS will ever be able get a job, or Prendergast will ever be able to affect the crime rate. The cop and the "criminal" are two sides to a coin: Both are white, middle-class, and are or have been under extreme pressure from work and family obligations. Like D-FENS, who is still laid off from his job as a defense worker, Prendergast is considered expendable by his superiors, and a has-been by his co-workers. Still, Prendergast holds it together, maintains his composure and his sanity, while D-FENS cannot.

D-FENS' first stop on his long walk home is a neighborhood grocery, like a 7–11 but family-owned — in this case by an Asian. He needs change to make a call. The store owner speaks broken English and won't provide D-FENS with change to use the pay phone. He has to buy something! D-FENS buys a Coke, but his change is not enough to make a phone call. The two argue, the store owner pulls a baseball bat and attacks D-FENS, who wrestles the bat away from him. When D-FENS begins to "roll back prices" by smashing up the store, a certain primal, even humorous sense of justice is delivered, which some critics called racist.

The bottom line is that the character of D-FENS, like the giant thug in *Easy Street*, is a man already seething from his own inner turmoil; the fact that he ran across a price gouger who set him off, then tried to bludgeon him with a club because D-FENS argues with him, precisely mirrors Prendergast's dilemma. D-FENS' actions are justified — he was the one attacked, or so common sense and well-placed decency tell him. But the times have changed some. What's right and what's legal often go in separate directions, and for Prendergast, sitting down, shutting up and waiting for his pension marks him as synonymous with the "not economically viable man" who protests in front of the bank. Prendergast has a job but no power; D-FENS has no job but is exercising more and more power throughout the day. But he will soon be anonymous and dead.

When the film was released, it caused a lot of consternation among critics and viewers alike. Some railed against it as a WASP–ish male fantasy. Others derided it as promoting stereotypes. Many people stayed away, probably for the real reason many of the critics and reviewers were pitching a bitch: Everyone in the big cities knows that urban life is a mess, so why pay to see it? For the political, intellectual and academic elite who protest such portrayals on screen, crying racism is a first resort — anything to deflect attention from their decades of failed social experiments.

Falling Down certainly takes a hard look at urban life — and what it says is not pretty, nor is it necessarily untrue. Like the title implies, the city is coming apart at its metaphorical seams, so whether it happens to be featuring a Korean grocer, who price-gouges people in his mini-mart; a cholo gang that shoots up a street full of innocent people just to get the guy they want — only to then miss; a burger joint which won't serve the customer what he wants; civil servants who will not work; or a neo–Nazi spewing hate, something is terribly, terribly wrong here. Though this film is decades removed from *Easy Street*, it reflects a similar perception of the police: it is once again the cops who are expected to be the stopgaps.

Soylent Green (1973)

In a future not so distant that we cannot see, but nonetheless everyone hopes is far, far away, America has become something of an overcrowded wasteland, and the East Coast a sprawling jungle of filth, corruption, poverty and hunger. While some may say that is how things are currently, the city where a detective named Thorn works boils a thousand times worse than anything ever imagined. Or so it is said to be. In 2022, New York has over 40 million people, most sleeping in the streets, alleyways, anywhere they can find shelter or a place to lie down. Fresh or natural food is rare. Fruit and meat are unheard of. Only rich people have decent water, or nice places to live (the high rises that cross the city). Apartments come with "furniture," women whom the new tenant can keep for his own pleasures. If the new tenant doesn't want the woman, she's out on the street. For young, beautiful women, the furniture option provides a temporary respite from the poverty of the outside world. However, with each passing year, the chance a newly arriving tenant will want her diminishes.

People are fed rations of Soylent Red or Soylent Yellow, a cracker foodstuff made of soy and lentil. When a new Soylent product, Green, is introduced to the public, it becomes quite popular, and riots break out whenever there are shortages. In this dystopia, the primary function of the police is to maintain control. Using large garbage trucks, they battle the rioters, then scoop them up. If someone important is murdered, then a detective may be assigned, but he's generally moonlighting from his riot-control functions.

When Thorn, played by Charlton Heston, investigates the killing of a high-placed executive of the Soylent Corporation, he's initially pleased at having access to the man's apartment. One of the only perks to being a cop is that they can take what they want from a crime scene (Silver Screen Reviews, n.p.). Thorn takes some liquor and towels, and becomes interested in the murdered man's furniture. Soon he is ordered off the investigation

Starving rioters attack law enforcement officers in *Soylent Green*. Have they ceased to be police?

by his supervisors, but he continues anyway, until he unravels a government conspiracy and finds out the real source of the food.

As a law enforcement officer, Thorn faces the same incapacity and frustrations as Prendergast, and the same need to rely on force as the Little Tramp. The film's opening sequence depicts the various environmental and technological changes which led to the disaster plaguing the Earth: smog; technology; cars multiplying out of control; factories and more factories with more and more smoke stacks (scifilm.org, n.p.). Thorn can't do anything about it, any more than Prendergast could do anything about the crime infecting his city. Each work in a society fragmented beyond anything they could remember as children. Both do the best job they can even as they realize the paycheck keeping them alive will be their only satisfaction. For Thorn, things are worse. Miss a few days from work and one can lose his or her job — it doesn't matter whether they're injured or not.

Thorn discovers the truth about Soylent Green, but, hurt and dying, as he yells out what the food is made of, who will listen? Or worse, yet, who cares? The society in which he labors has become so reliant on the government to distribute their Soylent rations that becoming cannibals is merely another step down the long ladder from civilization into complete madness. Thorn's "book," or research partner, played by Edward G. Robinson, refuses to descend completely. He solves the mystery first — then leaves Thorn the information he needs. Rather than live in a world where people eat other people, he chooses to end his life. Euthanasia is an acceptable, even preferred way for people to die. It lessens the strain on the planet. It leaves the alleys and streets short another useless person. And, ultimately, provides more Soylent Green.

Nemesis (1993)

The year is 2027. The place is Los Angeles. Is there a plot afoot to kill the President of the United States, or are these merely the machinations of some right-wing extremists who wish to use it as a pretext for violence against their enemies? Are those opposed to the government freedom fighters or terrorists? These are the questions facing LAPD operative Alex Rain in 1993's *Nemesis*.

Rain is a martial arts–trained cop on the trail of killer cyborgs. The film begins with him in a hotel room, accompanied by an amorous young woman. In the throes of passion, Rain blows off the top of her skull: "She" is a cyborg. As he flees the hotel, he is pursued by the cyborg's partners and, in the ensuing shootout, he is seriously wounded. He recovers, quits the force, but is "reactivated" when the LAPD finds that it requires his special skills, thereby setting in motion a chain of increasingly violent events which reveal a worldwide conspiracy stretching from Brazil to Java, one which threatens to enslave all mankind.

On the surface, Alex Rain is the key to *Nemesis*, serving as a filter through which we not only view a distopic world-gone-mad but its devastating effects on his own humanity. Though he is a living, breathing man, the brutality of his profession has created a hard and alienated being, as seemingly inhuman as the creatures he stalks. When Alex draws his weapon on the "woman" in the hotel room, she spitefully damns him for being a cop; after he terminates her, his retort is equally contemptuous, "Terrorist..." This distinction between established order and revolutionary chaos mirrors Alex's own personal fears: The more he kills, the more he becomes like those he eliminates.

Rain's trepidation over his diminishing human nature is well-founded; like the cyborg he shot, beneath whose imitation skin is visible a metal skull, Alex also contains non-organic parts. In fact, with almost each confrontation, Alex must be patched together anew (eyes ... forearms ... knee caps ...), to the point where the man resembles a machine, and the cop needs to wonder whether he must one day hunt himself.

This anxiety over what is and isn't human, what constitutes sentience and what is synthetic, is slightly reminiscent of another futuristic film from a decade prior, Ridley Scott's *Blade Runner*. However, while the main characters in both films track down androids (or cyborgs) even as they fall in love with artificial "women," only Alex Rain is unsure about his own mortality. In fact, where Deckard finds his sense of meaning and humanity through his relationship with the android Rachel, Alex is just the opposite, his uncertainty about whether he is still human ironically intensified by his all-too-human feelings for the cyborg Jarred, a fellow police operative who was once his partner.

Such is the incongruity in Alex's life: Though he can feel love for a being like Jarred, she cannot reciprocate. Quitting the force and leaving the country, he is forcibly returned when Jarred apparently defects to the cyborg "cause." Later, when he discovers that the police and government have been infiltrated by cyborgs intent on destroying all humans, Alex realizes he has been duped into killing off "good" cyborgs who are working with a human underground movement to save mankind. In effect, his metamorphosis is complete, for the lie he had lived has transformed him into that very creature which he despised the most, a "human cyborg."

When Alex is finally reunited with Jarred, who has unselfishly sacrificed herself for the human side by having her memory chip implanted into a hand-held CPU with a tiny video monitor, the two must fight off a slew of LAPD assassins. They rekindle their "relationship," but it is for naught. Unlike Deckard, who flees civilization to save Rachel, Alex must fight his way back to it in order to safely deliver Jarred to the Underground's command center, losing her forever in the process as the vital information contained in her memory is downloaded. Again the paradox: If cyborgs like Jarred can independently know right from wrong, can they not also develop and experience all the other emotions which make humans sentient? For Alex Rain there are no easy answers, but with a rebirth of his own humanness, he sets out once again to eliminate the cyborgs, only this time as a "terrorist" allied with man and machine alike.

Like its main character, *Nemesis* is a tale in filmic limbo, caught between the extremes of medium- to high-budget films and the parsimony of the made-for-video market. During Hollywood cinema's classic period in the '30s and '40s, B films were churned out on a regular basis to fulfill the requirements of the double bill. Filmed at smaller studios which operated on a thin profit margin and very little capital, most were guaranteed anywhere from $10–15,000 profit nationwide (Cook, p. 318).

Clearly *Nemesis* is well beyond that range, yet equally under the amount spent on comparable action or sci-fi films. Too expensive for merely the home video market and too small for theatrical release, *Nemesis* foundered at the box office and was trashed by critics like Leonard Maltin, who called it "Just another amalgam of ideas borrowed from better movies..." (Maltin, n.p.).

Maltin's dismissal of the film — which is admittedly not great art — is perhaps more an indictment of its *apparently* superficial plot than a commentary on what the film expresses subtextually. However, when one considers its veiled themes of social anomie and political instability coupled to a worldwide cabal, *Nemesis* merits much closer, more detailed scrutiny, for its two most intriguing aspects in this regard, the cyborg conspiracy to conquer man and the apparent division of the world along geo-economic borders, can be viewed as a manifestation of the same distrust, cynicism, doubt and fear felt by many Americans as the world approached a new century.

In this respect, Alex Rain is once again the pivotal figure. In essence a twentieth century man adrift in a twenty-first century world, he becomes the embodiment of all our fears, a repository of what it is to be human in an increasingly mechanistic environment. As a police officer, his futuristic struggle against the machines which endanger humanity mirrors our present resistance to a relentless advance of technology that threatens to completely overwhelm our cultural-political-religious social structure — the cyborg conspiracy, symbolic of the vanguard of the post-industrial revolution; computers; advanced telecommunications; globally integrated economies — all foreshadow the end of an era and a way of life to many people.

In a scene toward the end of the film, Alex's old boss Farnsworth — who was killed and replaced by the cyborg leader — momentarily captures Alex after a cruel and exacting pursuit across the Javanese rain forest. About to be terminated, Alex tells Farnsworth, "Killing all humans won't make you any more real." Interpreted literally, the comment means nothing significant, but figuratively it exemplifies this concomitant fear about, and urge to remain, the uniquely sentient beings we are. As America stood at the brink of a millennial abyss, Alex's anxiety about preserving his humanity is emblematic of our own dread of losing it. As the law enforcement officer, Alex's job is to hold the line, to reassure a frightened public, and to vanquish the threat to human survival.

That the conspiratorial themes present in *Nemesis* would surface in a science fiction narrative should not be surprising. Since a notable amount of the sci-fi genre revolves around such plots as alternative societies or technologies (Carroll, p.13–14), the possibilities for artifice and political machinations are infinite. Hence we see some of the very same conspiratorial elements in David Cronenberg's low-budget film *Videodrome* (1983) that we do in *Nemesis*, though the stories and premises appear radically different.

Alex, like Cronenberg's protagonist Max Renn, functions alternately as detective, villain and victim. On the trail of Jarred, who has supposedly stolen vital security plans, Alex takes on the investigator part, eventually ferreting out the cyborg conspiracy; Max, in search of the Videodrome, takes on a similar role. Alex and Max are both essentially "villains" at the outset, the former unwittingly killing "good" cyborgs while the latter deals in softcore pornography. Alex becomes the cyborg's victim as they chase him across the jungle while Max, interestingly enough, becomes like Alex — a killer — who in turn is a victim, killed by the conspirators he is "brainwashed" into serving.

The confusing turns of events in these narrative structures augur a postmodern incapacity to process historical-political eventualities. In dealing with the cyborg conspiracy that menaces mankind, Alex, and the viewer, come to that almost surrealistic point where neither is able to keep up with who is who. Cyborgs who are introduced as "terrorists" become "freedom fighters" while the authorities for whom Alex fought are revealed as the very thing he was supposed to be eliminating — synthetic life forms out to exterminate humanity. Humans engaged in sexual intercourse one moment, rip each other to bits in the next, only to find that one or the other isn't "human." Frederic Jameson, in his *The Geopolitical Aesthetic*, notes:

> It is at the point where we give up and are no longer able to remember which side the characters are on, and how they have been revealed to be hooked up with the other ones, that we have presumably grasped the deeper truth of the world system... [Jameson, p. 16].

Thusly, coping with an unending stream of misanthropic media revelations, from government complicity in foreign coups to hidden wars, from political corruption in Washington to all manner of vice and viciousness in the streets of their home towns, society seeks outlets for its apprehensions about life's increasingly perceptible irrationality, and finds art, in this case film, a natural aperture, and their local cops the one institution they can count on in the confusion. Such a postmodern interpretation is echoed by Corrigan, who asserts that the increasing cultural, racial and economic diversity of film audiences have resulted in narratives that mirror such social fragmentation:

> The anxieties and promises that accompany this disappearance of a clear and stable viewer clearly resemble those often associated with postmodernism and its reputed subversions of the traditional human subject. Just as critics and viewers have bemoaned the loss of "good" movies and wonder ... whom movies are being made for, observers of postmodernism commonly condemn contemporary culture's seeming dehumanizing vacuities and shifting, centerless visions... [Corrigan, p. 10].

The other subtextual gauge through which to explore *Nemesis* revolves around the film's portrayal of national borders, which have seemingly vanished as a result of a new geo-economic division of power between Northern and Southern sectors. While America and Japan have been united into one nation, "New America," along with the European Economic Bloc, the Third World nations, South America and the Southern Pacific Islands remain either independent or linked to an economic power called the New Rio Grid, which appears to be headed up by Brazil. Mexico, presently a popular vacation and retirement spot for Americans, has been partially absorbed into New America, though it is depicted as a technologically backward territory reminiscent of the nineteenth century West, a collection of small villages which serve as havens for men like Alex Rain, who uses the refuge to recover from his wounds and reconnect with nature.

The "Hammerheads" (those fighting in the human-cyborg underground) traverse both sectors of the divided globe, but must operate clandestinely in the Northern sectors. In the South they can function more openly, the cyborgs not yet able to fully penetrate the area and set up their network. Java, where Alex is dispatched to find Jarred, is a hotbed of revolutionary activity, the only authorities being Japanese gangs who play both sides against the middle, Hammerheads against the cyborgs, keeping the "peace" through extortion and intimidation.

Financially, the dollar has been replaced by the yen as the world's standard currency; Japan and America, while politically one nation, have a strained relationship as the former exerts its economic muscle. It's not overtly expressed, but the film intimates that the Japanese were either initially behind the cyborg conspiracy or responsible for the technology which created them.

Since narratives often work to resolve social contradictions symbolically (Turner, p. 133), they must also deal with existing political issues and take into account the questions and alarm they often raise. In confronting the cyborg conspiracy, then, the public's trust rests with the police. They are the ones fighting a "hidden war," not the military. *Nemesis* ends with Alex Rain turning his enormous fighting skill against the cyborgs. Though the odds are against him and the other Hammerheads, Alex is a formidable force, albeit a mortal one. We wish him success, though as we find out in the prologue of *Nemesis II*, "Alex Rain tried to stop the cyborgs. He failed..."

Rest in peace, Alex. You were all too human after all.

The endings of all the films leave a lot to think about. The Tramp and his street are at peace, but if the overpopulation, drugs and crime continue, the society he sees now will eventually turn into the streets where Prendergast works. Sexual freedom has broadened to the point that what was once considered wrong, or weird, is now common. Racism continues to be attacked in all forms, though more often than not the police officer finds himself the one discriminated against.

As D-FENS walks across his town, the groups he encounters continue to work as a wedge, something Prendergast has no answer for. To enforce the law does not mean change the system. When society implodes, as the water floods the boat, the police are often the last left on board bailing out. By the time a social system devolves into the environment Thorn must traverse, life is utterly without meaning, except to form a cracker to feed someone else. As riot police, and by extension government henchmen, law enforcement no longer serves a purpose except to protect the wealthy and harvest humans, something probably not on the initial job application.

Sources

Carroll, Noel. *The Philosophy of Horror*. New York: Rutledge, Chapman, and Hall, 1990.
Cook, David A. *A History of Narrative Film*. New York: W.W. Norton, 1990.
Corrigan, Timothy. *A Cinema Without Walls*. Piscataway, NJ: Rutgers University Press, 1991.
Easy Street. Moviediva.com. www.moviediva.com/MD_root/reviewpages/MDChaplinShorts.html.
Ebert, Roger. *Falling Down*. Roger Ebert's Video Companion. CD-Rom. 1994.
Jameson, Frederic. *The Geopolitical Aesthetic*. Bloomington, IN: Indiana University Press, 1992.
Lott, M. Ray. *The American Martial Arts Film*. Jefferson, NC: McFarland, 2004.
Maltin, Leonard. *Movie and Video Guide*. New York: Penguin, 1995.
Soylent. Green. Silver Screen Reviews. www.geocities.com/moviecritic.geo/reviews/s/soylentgreen.html.
Soylent Green. Tvguide.com. www.tvguide.com/Movies/database/ShowMovie.asp?MI=21373.
Turner, Graeme. *Film as Social Practice*. London: Routledge, 1994.
Warren, Jason. *Soylent Green*. Scifilm.org. www.scifilm.org/reviews/soylentgreen.html.

III

The New Deal Hero

This is a new one for me... Looks like I'm going to have to join a medicine show!*

By the time the 1930s rolled around, most of the large city police departments, federal agencies like the FBI, state troopers, highway patrol officers and county sheriffs were already firmly established and accepted as a part of American life. Westerns were a popular part of silent films, with the sheriff or marshal taking on the outlaws or protecting young women, but modern police narratives also became popular as the 1920s ended and sound was introduced into cinema. The sound element was rudimentary, and at first was exploited in musicals, but the aspect of hearing actors and actresses speaking enthralled film audiences everywhere. The studios eventually worked out the bugs with sound production, and the 1930s saw a steady move back to the artistic excellence that marked silent film in the late '20s.

At the time, Hollywood was nominally constituted by the big five studios: MGM; RKO; Paramount; Warner Bros.; 20th Century (later 20th Century-Fox); and the little three: Universal; Columbia; and United Artists. The distinctions were mainly drawn on financial strength and exhibition ability. The big five owned some of the theaters where their films played. The little three did not, and arranged distribution of theirs through the five. On its face, the industry appeared strong but, as the decade progressed, severe economic shifts would change moviemaking, and lay the groundwork for mass production of the "Bs."

The Great Depression and the Origins of "B" Movie

When the bottom fell out of the stock market in October 1929, the country went into an economic depression the likes of which it had never seen. By 1932, 12 million Americans were out of work and national income had been cut in half (Jordan, p. 363). Manufacturing and agriculture were particularly hard-hit sectors, the latter's condition made worse by a drought that literally turned much of the plains into a dust bowl, and which sent migrant farmers and sharecroppers sweeping across the west like locust, all searching for work. John Steinbeck's 1939 novel *The Grapes of Wrath*, documenting the plight of these migrants, won the Pulitzer Prize for Literature; John Ford's direction of the film version of the book won him an Academy Award as Best Director.

The film industry suffered too, though not so drastically at first. However, profits were

---

*John Wyatt (John Wayne) thanking his superiors for his next undercover mission in Paradise Canyon.

down the next couple of years, and complicating the situation was the fact that many of the studios were undergoing a financial crisis of their own: debt. When Warners started the sound revolution, other studios were forced to follow suit. To obtain the necessary capital to retrofit entire chains of theaters (the studios also owned many of them, primarily in large metropolitan areas) to accommodate sound, the film industry needed capital, and turned to Wall Street. Though motion picture production would seem an inherent gamble, the studios had found a way to mitigate their risks: generic stories and recognizable "stars." In his *American Cinema/American Culture*, John Belton observes,

> ... [M]otion picture producers face tremendous risks each time they make a film. These risks are increased by the very nature of the motion picture product... The star system and the genre system attempt to compensate for the dangers involved in this process [Belton, p. 115].

The banks found the picture show to be a worthwhile investment and the money poured in; however, financial control over the various studios was now based in the East. The Hollywood moguls found themselves in an uneasy truce of sorts: They controlled the content and output of their films, while Boards of Directors controlled the purse springs from New York. So long as the profits continued to roll in, the "money men" were content to let the "movie men" make their movies.

The coming of sound had cushioned some of the early effects of the Depression on the studios. Moviegoers would grudgingly apportion the price of a ticket out of their weekly budgets, meager as they might be, for the spectacle of singing, dancing and speaking. The initial novelty of these "talkies" provided a buffer of sorts, but within a couple of years, that buffer had worn thin. As the Depression deepened, movie attendance dropped (by 30 percent in 1932), and some studios went into receivership as a result of the debts owed to banks and large corporations during the conversion to sound (Turner, p. 17).

The moguls responded aggressively. At arguably the wealthiest studio, MGM, Louis B. Mayer cut the salaries of his players. Irving Thalberg, Mayer's brilliant partner and producer, objected, but the cuts stuck nonetheless. Darryl F. Zanuck at 20th Century Pictures balked at such measures, but something had to be done, and done quickly. Two avenues were explored: First, at the exhibition level, theaters began to offer weekday raffles and weekend giveaways. China and other housewares were presented so as to appeal to women. The reasoning was as simple as it was sublime: Bring in the wife and she will bring in her husband. However, this approach was short-lived. In 1933, the federal government passed a number of laws, and as part of the Motion Picture Code of Conduct, giveaways and games of chance were outlawed (for only 18 months it turns out) as "unfair competition" (Gomery, p. 282). With these lures unavailable, nearly all movie theaters turned to the second option and began to feature the "double bill," that is, the showing of two films for the price of one admission, which meant a change in production levels.

The major studios, already integrated, were so centralized as to be a model to the Soviets, though no one really gave it that much thought, at least right then, especially the capitalists running them. With their own prop, editing and wardrobe departments, commissary and even medical facilities, they were almost small cities unto themselves. The actors were under contract and paid weekly, as were other employees. Since everyone was collecting a check regardless of their output, the solution was to put them to work, to make more films. Hence the "B" movie was born, created to complement the "A" film. The goal: to make going to the show an experience well worth the money. The double feature would present a cartoon, some newsreel documentaries that showed things happening around the country and world, a serial episode, the "B" film and then the "A" film.

The arrangement had something for everyone. Kids loved the cartoons and serials; adults found the newsreels entertaining if not educational. Everyone liked the films. Harried parents could drop off their children and get the afternoon off. Most studios started actual "B" units while others bought films from what was derisively called "Poverty Row," made by that group of low-budget independents that sprang up to provide the "majors" and independent theaters with "B" films. Monogram, PRC and Republic were among the biggest producers, although the latter, riding the coattails of its biggest star John Wayne, was able to work its way up to the ranks of the big studios. Others, like Chesterfield, Invincible, Mayfair and Majestic, struggled in vain before disappearing into the black hole of film history.

Up-and-coming studio stars and starlets, newly under contract, broke in using these vehicles, while older, less popular or fading personalities could provide familiar faces as well. Chester Morris, Jack Holt, Preston Foster, George Zucco, Vera Hruba Ralston, Gale Storm, Toby Wing, Tom Neal and Louise Allbritton were some of the better known actors and actresses to grace the low-budget arena. The "B" films usually ran about an hour, maybe 65 minutes, and the Poverty Row studios even became associated with their product, just as the majors were. If MGM was known for its lavish musicals, Monogram was just as well-known for its "one-horse Westerns," so called because of the oft-repeated story that they would shoot one scene with the bad guy riding full out on his horse to escape the good guy; then film the good guy on the same horse heading in the same direction. It was up to the editor to work his magic and save the picture. There is no record of whether the horse was given a double helping of oats at feeding time.

New Deal Hero

Franklin D. Roosevelt succeeded President Herbert Hoover, and while he didn't have a panacea for getting the economy back on its feet, he knew something had to be done, and he knew the federal government had to do it, which is more than Hoover would acknowledge. Many of Roosevelt's programs were found to be unconstitutional; many just didn't work. But he kept on trying nonetheless, and many people found employment through federal job programs during the '30s. The Tennessee Valley Authority (TVA) opened the Tennessee River and eventually provided power — and employment, for many in the southeast. The Civilian Conservation Corp. (CCC) put many young men to work reforesting areas and building roads across the country. The Federal Deposit Insurance Corporation (FDIC) began inspecting banks and provided insurance for customers who deposited their money in covered banks. The president placed a lot of hope in the National Recovery Act, which expanded public works and regulated business to achieve fair competition.

Roosevelt's "New Deal" policies were sometimes reflected in films of the day, particularly the B films. Because B films were not designed to make a profit, just to supplement the A film, their content wasn't so tightly controlled by the studios. In early films, blame for the nation's economic problems was placed on bankers, lawyers and other shysters who mucked everything up so badly that it was impossible to get anything done. Once the public did away with such crooks, things would get back to normal. Only they didn't. As time passed, film narratives looked more to entertain than educate (though good ones could do both), so singing and dancing and carrying on proved quite popular with audiences looking to forget about their troubles, if even for just a little while.

Probably the best-known and most prolific of the B movie actors was John Wayne. Between 1930 and 1939 he made over 60 low-budget films, most of them Westerns, and many with him as the law. Other actors, such as William Boyd, who played in the long-running Hopalong Cassidy series, Gene Autry and Roy Rogers, the last two called "the king of the cowboys," also starred and sometimes produced their own low-budget films, but Boyd's movies were mostly popular with kids, and Autry and Rogers mixed their gunplay and fisticuffs with song. Wayne's films were generally meant to be taken seriously — though looking back through 70 years of hindsight, it's not always possible — and because he later became such a Hollywood icon, the films still have resonance with many viewers.

In *Star Packer* (1934), Wayne plays a quiet cowboy who rides into an isolated town which has already lost two sheriffs to a mysterious criminal called "The Shadow." Wayne robs the stage, but isn't seen by the drivers. Right afterward, the Shadow's men try to rob the stage — only the money is gone. Wayne becomes town sheriff after the third lawman is assassinated, right out on a public street, but no one can find where the bullet came from. Wayne returns the money to the stage office, infuriating the Shadow, who gives his men instructions through a safe in a wall to get rid of the new sheriff.

Wayne eventually discovers the Shadow's hideout, and finds it holds the worst outlaws in the country. He noses around, follows a few unsavory types and gets to the bottom of the Shadow's activities. When the secretive outlaw and his men ride toward town with a machine-gun packed away inside of a wagon, the sheriff deputizes the local cattlemen and they attack the gang, killing most of them, and saving the town from future violence.

Star Packer is interesting on a number of fronts. First is the concept of the government taking direct action to assist farmers and ranchers. The town has lost a number of sheriffs, and the notion of lawlessness is scaring everyone. The Depression became so severe, particularly in its early stages, that many people worried about anarchy. The citizens have appealed to the government for help — but none is forthcoming. The same could be said about the state governments which were so strapped, they had little or no cash left to help their residents. But Wayne's character is really an undercover federal marshal. The state and local authorities can't handle the problem with the Shadow, so *he* will.

Second is the symbolic nature of the Shadow. No one really knew what caused the economic tailspin. Some thought it was borrowed money used to purchase stock on margin, pushing prices into the sky. Others thought it was high tariffs stifling international trade. Some believed it was low wages and easy credit that overextended the population. The Shadow represented a certain invasive fear that no one could put their finger on. He destroyed banks and disrupted commerce. He took away the livelihoods of ranchers by stealing their stock. With no work or capital, even the land the people owned had no value. One of the first shots of the town, we see the Ranchers Union Hall, where the collective is meeting to plot strategy against the Shadow, who is destroying the organization. Roosevelt was a staunch supporter of unions; attacking the union meant attacking him. When Wayne puts the Shadow and his gang out of business, the values of the New Deal are upheld, as is the idea that government can be a force for economic good.

In *Rainbow Valley* (1935), Wayne moseys into town, a mysterious gunman no one knows anything about — except that he's as tough as they come. In the opening scene, he fights off a gang of highwaymen trying to intercept the mail, then takes a job as road builder, a rather dangerous position considering the fact that a gang of outlaws has killed the last few. The town is cut off from the rest of the county because of a washed-out road, and the marshal is over 60 miles away. Wayne foils the outlaws every step of the way, but the community loses faith in him when they learn he's an ex-convict. He joins the outlaws and tricks them into dynamiting the hills where the road is supposed to cut through, then beats up the leader and his henchmen, taking them in for their crimes.

As in *Star Packer*, Wayne is an undercover operative working for the government. The people of the valley are desperate and need help. Wayne is there to extend a hand to them, though they don't know it at first. They band together under his leadership, as Roosevelt asked the American people to do so many times in speeches and radio addresses. As a New Deal hero, Wayne is rugged and determined — what the town calls "a fighter." He doesn't talk, he works. When he puts the road crew together, he's down there with them, shovel in hand. He unifies under his leadership. He's also a modern law enforcer: He's college-educated yet street smart, having himself sent to prison so he could learn about the Rainbow Valley gang.

But there's also an unpleasant aspect to the New Deal hero. Sometimes, to get the job done, you do what it takes. If you're Roosevelt, it means having your programs declared unconstitutional by the high court; it also means threatening to pack the court if they don't

In *Rainbow Valley*, John Martin (John Wayne) finds out what's happening in the town by going to the post office. Note the picture above the clerk's head: Teddy Roosevelt, distant relative to FDR. Also pictured: George "Gabby" Hayes and Lucille Brown.

III. The New Deal Hero

John Martin (John Wayne) prepares to pummel one of the gang (unidentified actor) terrorizing the town in *Rainbow Valley* as LeRoy Mason, Lucille Brown and George "Gabby" Hayes look on.

start going along with your agenda. For Wayne, it's the exercise of wanton force. When he gets to town with the mail courier, he sees one of the bandits who tried to rob the man. The man denies it and they fight. Over and over Wayne pummels the man to the face, intercut with shots of the town's people admiring him for being a stand-up type of guy. At first it seems like typical Hollywood fisticuffs, but then it goes overboard, with Wayne hitting the man scores of times until it's a wonder the man is still alive.

Paradise Canyon (1935) takes place on a border town in Arizona. Counterfeiters are printing up fake twenties and passing the currency across the West. A federal agent (Wayne) is specially recruited by the Treasury Department to bust up the racket. The Treasury Chief thinks the culprit is a man they had caught ten years ago for doing the same thing. He received a lengthy prison sentence and then started a medicine show, traveling through the southwest under the name Dr. Carter. Or, it may be the man's partner, who disappeared after turning state's evidence against Dr. Carter. It's Wayne's job to find out which man is doing what.

The medicine show is traveling through New Mexico, heading toward the state line, the sheriff and his posse hot on their trail. Dr. Carter got drunk the night before on his "famous Indian remedy" and tore up a pharmacy, then left town without paying for the damages. Wayne, who had been trailing the show, catches them right before they cross into Arizona. Their truck gives out, so he pulls them across the line, saving them from the sheriff's attempt to put the show out of business.

Dr. Carter hires Wayne to be part of the act — he can't sing or dance, but he can ride and shoot. Wayne stops to rest his horse while the show motors on. It's suddenly attacked by gunmen. Wayne catches the gunmen and knocks all three off their horses. The gunmen work for "The Boss," Dr. Carter's old partner. He's the one doing the counterfeiting and he doesn't want Carter to see him in town, otherwise he could wreck the operation. Wayne spends the rest of the film protecting the show and getting the goods on the crooks.

Once again, Wayne works undercover to foil criminal activity, only in this instance the crime is, without doubt, economic — and grave. Counterfeiting can undermine an economy and reduce confidence in an administration's ability to govern. At the time the film was released, this was an overwhelming concern among business sectors and the public. Wayne solves the crime by actively involving himself in the investigation, not watching from afar like the Treasury Department had been doing. A national threat must be stopped by force: Wayne uses his fists, his guns, even help from Mexican police, to restore trust in the monetary system.

Each of the three films showcases different aspects of the Depression, and the avenues the New Deal Hero must take to save the day. *Star Packer* examines the fear caused by such an economic calamity: The Shadow is a hidden power, destructive and far-ranging. But once he is uncovered, he can be defeated. The citizens of *Rainbow Valley* have to band together to stave off tragedy. Roads and other infrastructure improvements take hard work, unity and a leadership willing to fight to get the job done. Economic threats from crime have to be dealt with immediately, and only federal authority is powerful enough to get the job done.

Lobby poster for *Paradise Canyon*. Wayne, on the left, takes a commanding position against those threatening the economy.

All three films were made by Lone Star, one of the low-budget companies supplying B material, within a year's span. Besides the political and economic implications of their stories, they also shared a number of other characteristics: Wayne's main adversary, or ally, has a daughter or niece who falls in love with him by the stories' end; the narratives take place in modern, or near-modern times, where cars share the road with horses; telephones and even slot machines can be found in saloons, but men still walk the streets carrying six-shooters; local law enforcement is impotent or not present.

As was the practice in classic Hollywood cinema, heterosexual romance was considered one of the rewards for the protagonists. The New Deal Hero was no exception. In fact, because of his vigor and energy, it would be requisite for young ladies to flock to him. Smart and fearless, lean and powerful, Wayne (and, by extension, other New Deal Heroes) rode tall in the saddle, projecting the brisk determination of a Roosevelt administration dealing with the worst national crisis since the Civil War.

Wayne himself, however, remains something of a paradox. He was only 27 when these films were shot, and not yet a major star, but the liberal leanings of the pictures certainly go against the stark conservatism of the later Wayne. But dichotomies like this existed the icon's entire life. The pride of the Marines, Army, Navy and Air Force. Jumping with airborne rangers on D-Day. Liberating concentration camps run by the Nazis, and organizing Filipino resistance to the Japanese. John Wayne was all this and more. He was also a man who undertook no military service. While his friends and acting acquaintances were all enlisting, such as Tyrone Power and Jimmy Stewart, Wayne stayed behind and won the war in Hollywood, becoming the number one box office attraction. Later, Wayne led the charge against Communism, believing these people were compromising the beliefs that made the country strong and free and certainly prosperous.

In many respects, history has proved him right, but the controversy surrounding the actor still remains a quarter of a century after his death. "The Duke," as he was known to his friends, always believed his good buddy Henry Fonda was soft on the "Reds." This is certainly arguable; what's *not* was that Fonda was certainly not soft on fascism, having put his career on hold to fight during World War II. Those close to Wayne often wondered why he didn't.

Sources

Belton, John. *American Cinema/American Culture*. New York: McGraw Hill, 1994.
Gomery, Douglas. *Shared Pleasures: A History of Movie Presentation in the United States*. Madison, WI: University of Wisconsin, 1992.
Litwak, Leon F., Winthrop D. Jordan et al. *The United States*. Englewood Cliffs, NJ: Prentice Hall, 1985.
Turner, Graeme. *Film as Social Practice*. New York: Routledge, 1994.

IV

COLD WARRIORS

The public doesn't give a damn about integrity. A town that won't defend itself deserves no help.*

At the end of World War II, a new kind of conflict developed between the United States and the Soviet Union, not one of outright war but rather one of threats, arms races, scores of multi-national alliances and, in some quarters of our nation, a borderline hysteria against the "Reds," or Communists, who were supposedly threatening our very way of life. On the battlefield, in places like Korea, American troops fought North Korean and Red Chinese soldiers, and for the next 50 years the two superpowers, as they came to be known, would engage in "Cold War," sparring across the globe using surrogate countries. Hollywood became one of those surrogate battlefields, pitting actor against actor, director against director, ruining the careers of many promising talents who had flirted with socialism during the Depression, or were merely left-wing in their politics. The Cold War landed in Hollywood's backyard when the House Committee on Un-American Activities (HUAC)† convened; its sworn duty was to "out" Communist sympathizers in the entertainment industry, and to unofficially make sure the studios blacklisted them.

Origins of HUAC

Between 1945 and 1950, American-Soviet relations hardened like stale bread and what resulted was a deadly chess game, with each country reacting to the other's moves: Stalin's intransigence regarding Eastern European freedom was matched by American unwillingness to provide the Soviets with economic assistance; Soviet intrigues in Turkey and Iran eventually wrought "The Truman Doctrine," a policy of aiding nations struggling against Communism, while applying immediate counterforce to block Soviet endeavors across the world which threatened our interests; the "Marshall Plan," in which the United States provided aid to Western democracies to get back on their feet economically was answered by Stalin's resurrection of the old Comintern, now called the Cominform, and the Berlin Blockade in 1948; America and its European Allies formed NATO in 1949.

When President Truman called for the United States to support free peoples resisting Communist subjugation, he did so with an eye toward freeing money from a Republican

---

**Martin Howe (Lon Chaney, Jr.) to Will Kane (Gary Cooper) in* High Noon.
†*HUAC is the common designation for the committee, even though technically wrong.*

Congress to aid Turkey and Greece, as well as establishing his credentials as an anti–Communist. However, he soon learned that being an anti–Communist abroad meant being an anti–Communist at home, too. Just as American-Soviet relations had entered a stage of act-react-act again with regard to each other's capabilities and intentions, so too did that between Congress and the president. Each entered a game of "one upsmanship," both moving to impress the American people with their firm stand against the Reds. Discovery of real spies and of spy rings fueled growing suspicion of Communism across the country, and Truman enacted a series of odious rules, such as loyalty investigations of all current and prospective federal civil servants, which made sympathetic association with any outlaw group grounds for dismissal or refusal to hire. The Loyalty Review Board, which administered the program, denied the accused the right to confront witnesses against them and accepted any information tendered as relevant for examination. Congress countered by reviving the House Committee on Un-American Activities.

HUAC's methods were as un–American as the unsavory elements it was ostensibly protecting us from. Ideas or beliefs considered bad for the country by committee members could be grounds for an investigation. Individuals holding such notions could be deemed Communists or "fellow travelers," while a refusal to testify before HUAC appeared as an admission of guilt. "Within the United States, the strains of the Cold War manifested themselves in a desperate search for internal security ... Never before had an individual's loyalty to country seemed more important. How to measure that loyalty was sufficiently clear — the intensity and consistency of a person's anti-communism" (Aaron, p. 418).

In 1947, Whitaker Chambers, an ex–Communist, testified before HUAC that Communists were operating in government circles, naming former State Department official Alger Hiss as one of them. Hiss denied the charges, contesting them before the committee. Hiss was convicted on rather flimsy evidence of perjury,* though ironically enough, we now know he was guilty. More importantly, however, was the strategy and methods of innuendo, aspersion-casting and presumed guilt which HUAC began to operate under, marking them closer to judges at the Salem witch trials than United States Congressmen.

Hollywood and HUAC

These events did not occur in a vacuum, and were not without an impact on other segments of American society, the movie industry being acutely affected by the fall-out. In looking at the entertainment business, HUAC attempted "to expose those elements that are insidiously trying to poison the minds of your children, distort the history of our country, and discredit Christianity" (Aaron, p. 420). The studios fell into — or courted, depending on how one looks at it — the "Red hysteria." Dozens of anti–Communist movies were made during this period, both to capitalize on the market as well as to display a love of country. The ease with which Hollywood could be persuaded (or intimidated) into cooperating is in some way a direct by-product of the studio system, which was in effect at the time.†

---

*The statute of limitations had passed for espionage.
†*The system was slowly disintegrating, however. The Supreme Court had ordered studios to divest themselves of their theater chains. Slowly, actors were released by the studios, which eventually became funding mechanisms for independents.*

Zanuck, Mayer, Warner and other studio heads tightly controlled actors, and often directors, through rigid contracts binding the individual to the studio. Fledgling actors and actresses would be signed to a contract, given a weekly salary, acting lessons if need be, and then slowly worked into movies. Depending on how they were received by the public, the actor or actress could be advanced or dropped. Studio moguls could thusly make or break the player under those circumstances, and only the biggest stars could avoid pressure by their studios to appear in a particular film when told to do so. Considering the power wielded by HUAC, it takes no great stretch of the imagination to understand the danger posed to entertainment figures who found themselves in the cross-hairs. Studios at first maintained that they would not blacklist, but an acrimonious writers' strike and the unwillingness of Eastern bankers to finance studio films if they did not cooperate with HUAC changed their thinking (Baseline Encyclopedia of Film, n.p.). An additional concern was the possibility of government interference in their business. The studios and HUAC became partners, if unwillingly, and employees were told they would be fired if they did not assist the Congressional committee if called. The blacklist, then, never admitted but uniformly applied by the studios, took care of the people whom HUAC found lacking in American values.

By the time the North Koreans crossed the 38th Parallel, even popular stars with liberal leanings, such as Henry Fonda and Humphrey Bogart, were quieted in the face of the Congressional steamroller. Some actors went to Europe to ride out the storm. Others, such as screenwriter Carl Foreman, director Herbert Biberman and producer Adrian Scott, were blacklisted. Some who were called to testify before HUAC and said what they had to in order to save their careers—director Edward Dmytryk and actor Sterling Hayden among them—continued to work in Hollywood, but were themselves tarnished by naming names.

High Noon (1952)

At the height of HUAC's power in the early '50s, three films showcasing three different views of HUAC and the Cold War hit theaters. One was extremely popular. One was extremely dull. One was extremely controversial. All involved peace officers, Communism and the Cold War. *High Noon* was among the most successful and critically acclaimed films of 1952. It starred American icon Gary Cooper in a Western, the most American of genres, and audiences flocked to the theaters; Cooper won an Academy Award as Best Actor. In all, the film was nominated for seven Academy Awards, winning four.

Cooper plays Will Kane, the lawman of a small town. At the film's opening, Kane marries outsider Amy and quits his post. As he is preparing to leave town, he's told that Frank Miller has been released from prison and is headed for town, along with his gang, to get even with Kane for putting him behind bars. The town fathers persuade Kane to leave, but a few miles down the road he changes his mind and returns to protect the town. Instead of finding himself wanted there, Kane is made to feel the opposite — unwelcome — the townsfolk believing it better to let the gunmen come to town, vent their anger without killing anyone, and then (the townspeople hope) depart. Kane finds himself abandoned by everyone, including his deputy, but resolves to do what's right and fight the gang. He prevails in a violent, running gun battle across town, then leaves with his bride, disgusted by the cowardice of the townspeople.

The film was scripted by Carl Foreman, and afterward he was blacklisted by the studios for refusing to cooperate with HUAC. The work cannot be so easily dismissed as just another Western, albeit a great one, especially considering its writer. Many critics hail the movie as a "metaphor for the threatened Hollywood blacklisted artists" (Dirks, n.p.). Kane, denied assistance by the townspeople, must face the outlaws without support. Actors, writers, directors and other industry professionals had to face HUAC by themselves, their studios having abandoned them. The lawman had two choices: He could turn tail and run, which would be wrong and cowardly, but would placate the town, or he could stay and fight and face the chance of being killed. Similarly, with those called before HUAC: They could placate the committee, make the statements which would destroy others, or they could face the Congressmen, speak their peace, and risk jail and the blacklist.

Frank Miller is a brutal killer. He has a reputation and many in the town are scared. Kane himself is afraid, and the fear is highlighted by a number of closeup shots. Just before the gunfight with the gang, he lays his head on his desk in despair. Those in Hollywood felt the same sense of fear and hopelessness. HUAC had everyone in the industry looking to their past. Had they attended some Socialist meeting while in college? Did they associate with someone who did? Would their name come up? Kane's life was similar. He wasn't considered a Christian. His former lover was a woman with (seemingly) loose morals. His past comes back to victimize him. When he appealed to the populace, to the social institutions of law and religion, he

Marshal Will Kane (Gary Cooper) prepares to fight off the Miller gang in *High Noon* over the objections of his girl (Grace Kelly). Should Kane have left when the town asked him to?

was rebuffed. Leave, go, they tell him, the threat will eventually pass. When those concerned about HUAC looked to the courts and religious organizations, these institutions were silent, or even hostile. HUAC's examinations of its witnesses' lifestyles were often enough to find them "un–American."

Just how many Americans initially understood the allegorical implications of the movie is uncertain. The producers were certainly covered. In casting Cooper (a beloved actor as well as the archetypal American) and Grace Kelly (America's newest sweetheart), and by cloaking their statement in the garb of a Western, they assured that no one, not even HUAC, would feel confident in attacking them. Attacking *High Noon* would be like attacking America! After dispatching the gunmen, Kane flings his badge to the dirt. For those opposing HUAC, Kane's action mirrored their own concern about the law and where it was going in this country.

Big Jim McLain (1952)

If *High Noon* was a model of subtlety, *Big Jim McLain* hits the viewer over the head with a sledgehammer. No symbolism or allegory was needed here. John Wayne played the title character, a special agent working for HUAC. He flies to Hawaii with his partner Mal (James Arness), where they team up with real-life police chief Dan Lieu to investigate and bust up an international Communist conspiracy aimed at the United States. Wayne follows a number of trails and eventually finds the group. Only he's bound by the law, while the Communists are not. When Mal is killed, Wayne kicks into high gear, bringing in the entire bunch; however, Wayne can only watch in frustration as the ringleaders "take the fifth" during HUAC's questioning.

Ironically enough, *Big Jim McLain* practices exactly the evils it rails against. It's subjective, addresses problems in black and white (no shades of gray) and keeps politics simple, i.e., right and wrong. The "wrong" are Communists and their fellow travelers, and in the film they are portrayed as stupid lugs or scheming eggheads who also happen to be Communist spies (Pfeifer, p. 163). In the story, Wayne, as the special agent, is everything he wasn't in actual life. As a war veteran, he represents the "patriot," someone who fought to protect the country from the fascists. As a law enforcement officer, he is established as a "guardian," looking out for the public and keeping them safe from the Soviet menace. As a red-blooded American man, he's two-fisted and desired by a number of women. The Communists are the opposite: stupid; conniving; hypocritical; ready to break down the walls of democracy any way they can. Without men like Big Jim McLain to enforce the law, the things Americans hold dear (freedom, religion, capitalism) will be stamped out.

High Noon and *Big Jim McLain* point up the general views which two groups in Hollywood held with regard to the domestic impact of the Cold War: the dangers of the Communist influence on the film industry (and country) versus the constitutional freedom granted to all Americans. Into the former category fell Wayne, Adolphe Menjou and Cecil B. DeMille, all members of the Motion Picture Alliance for the Preservation of American Ideals. The organization was founded to combat the spread of Communist propaganda through films; Wayne eventually became its president. The latter group was comprised of people like Albert Maltz, Dalton Trumbo and John Huston, who saw their liberal leanings distorted as left-wing sympathies. Civil rights were being trampled on while the freedoms guaranteed by the Bill of Rights were by passed in the nation's search for the ever-elusive Communists.

McLain (John Wayne) takes time out from chasing the Red menace for a little romance with Nancy Vallon (Nancy Olson) in *Big Jim McLain*.

Salt of the Earth (1953)

Salt of the Earth was actually produced by a company of blacklisted film artists. Unable to gain work in the entertainment industry, they began looking for good stories. A strike by Local 890 of the Mine, Mill and Smelter Workers Union against a zinc company in New Mexico caught their attention. The entire union had been kicked out of the CIO for possible Communist influence in 1950 (Lavender, p. 1–2). When the film was completed, the projectionists' union refused to run it, so it was hardly played in the U.S. It was shown widely in Europe, however, and won some awards at various film festivals. Herbert J. Biberman directed the film. It was his first work in six years, and afterward it took another 16 before he could work again.*

The story followed the miners and the attempts of the mine owners to break them. Like *Big Jim McLain*, which made sure not a single point was lost on the viewer, the producers, director and screenwriter made sure they threw everything they could to get across their message as well, including the kitchen sink. The miners want to be treated the same as their white counterparts, and they are certainly being discriminated against, to the point where they will be arrested if they walk the picket line. So their wives strike in their place.

---

*Biberman was one of the Hollywood Ten, the name given to ten screenwriters and directors who refused to cooperate with HUAC and were eventually jailed for short periods.

This causes something of a problem for many of the men, who feel it is not right for women to stand up for them. As the stand-off continues, the women find their own sense of worth beyond being wives and mothers, and the men have to respect them as equals. Because of its treatment of women, elevating them above usual window dressing status, and making them real partners in the quest for justice, the film still has critical relevance 50 years after being made, though its leftist message now seems hardly controversial.

Biberman used many real miners in the film, with Will Geer, who played the sheriff, the only recognizable American actor. Geer was also blacklisted at the time, but his portrayal of the sheriff, who does everything he can to stop the strikers, was inversely similar to Wayne's portrayal in *Big Jim McLain*. The sheriff was racist, thuggish and corrupt, while Geer's ideals regarding freedom and the Constitution showed him to be anything but. Wayne and Geer's lawmen are also similar in their one-dimensional take on things: The Communists are bad; the miners, who mouth socialist platitudes, are bad. Only Wayne believed it while Geer mocked it, playing the character to the hilt and making the viewer realize that nothing is worse than a corrupt peace officer.

The lawmen involved here represent three different jurisdictions and three different ways of handling their jobs. McLain is a federal agent who goes anywhere the case takes him. The sheriff is a county officer, elected, and to an extent worried about public opinion. His peace officer status is recognized across the state, but his job is to enforce the law in his county. Kane is a local lawman and again, like the sheriff, he is a peace officer within the state, but he stays primarily in his town. McLain works with local authorities to break the Red conspiracy. In fighting against the Communists, the feds must take the lead and shepherd their local brothers in the battle against Soviet world domination. The sheriff wants to shut down the strike, in part because he hates who they are, and in part because voters in the area think the strikers are Socialists. But he's outsmarted by the strikers' wives—how will it look to the public if he is too brutal on the women, Communist or not? The Kane character fights alone—no help coming from any other lawmen—and, in fact, Kane's allegorical fight against HUAC is really a fight against the feds.

Other films during the decade embraced either side of the fight. In *Johnny Guitar* (1954), Joan Crawford plays the saloon owner who has to face off against Mercedes McCambridge, the leader of decent townsfolk who want Crawford run out of town. Crawford, like Kane, fights back. Elia Kazan and Budd Schulberg, who cooperated with HUAC, answered their critics with *On the Waterfront* (1954), the story of an ex-prizefighter (Marlon Brando) turned dock worker who has to stand up to the mob and testify before a committee investigating their murderous control of the wharfs. After testifying, he returns to the dock, faces up to the mob leader and, in a brutal fight, beats him in front of his co-workers. The message was plain: Sometimes naming names has to be done.

The Red scare eventually died down as the Cold War heated up. The Cold War cops remained, however. Wayne's portrayal of Big Jim McLain was the prototype law enforcement officer, a harbinger of what was to come. J. Edgar Hoover and his FBI continued to monitor Communists until his death in the '70s, and to this day the Bureau is the lead agency in dealing with domestic issues, including groups out to undermine the country. Will Geer's sheriff remains a cinema stereotype of corrupt rural peace officers and can be found in many films and television movies. Gary Cooper's Kane is more conflicting—he fought a fight that others in the town did not want him to fight. Allegorically he battled HUAC. In the fight viewed on screen, he is a scared man who only prevails with his wife's help. In his battle against HUAC, however, he stood alone and successful. But *High Noon* just didn't fade away. Its political message might have been lost on most viewers at the time, but the idea of a cowardly town and a sheriff asking for help didn't sit easy with a few actors, and one very powerful director, so another film would answer it at the end of the decade. A film which would be just as popular.

Sources

Dirks, Tim. *High Noon.* Filmsite.org. www.filmsite.org/high.html.
Hollywood Ten. *Baseline Encyclopedia of Film.* Baseline, CD-Rom, 1995.
Lavender, Catherine. *Salt of the Earth.* cuny.edu 1998 www.library.csi.cuny.edu/dept/history/lavender/salt.html.
Litwack, Leon F., Winthrop D. Jordan, et al. *The United States.* Englewood Cliffs, NJ: Prentice-Hall, 1985.
Pfeifer, Lee. *The John Wayne Scrapbook.* New York: Citadel Press, 1989.

V

SCI-FI COPS

If you would like to be a contestant on The Running Man, *send a self-addressed stamped envelope to I.C.S. Talent Hunt, care of your local affiliate, and then go out and do something really despicable.**

I never broke the law. I am the law!†

During the 1950s, Soviet aggression and rising Communist power across the globe manifested uncertainties in American society. Film, as both an impressive medium and an impressionable industry, sublimated some of these concerns by merging horror and science fiction to produce a distinct hybrid film, one that was readily exploited by independent, low-budget producers like American International Pictures (AIP), who were in a hurry to take advantage of an expanding market. As with youth problem films, the budgets in these movies were low — rock bottom in some instances. For example, director Edgar G. Ulmer took less than two weeks to finish both *Beyond the Time Barrier* and *The Amazing Transparent Man*, filming them one after the other in Texas in 1959. If this was low, then what to think about Phil Tucker's *Robot Monster* (1953), which told the awesome tale of Ro-Man, an alien invader who appears to be an ape with a helmet on his head. Having destroyed everyone but a handful of people with his "Calcinator Death Ray," which is activated when he flaps his arms, he promptly carries off an unconscious though buxom female survivor; the remaining survivors have to figure out how to get her back.

One form of assault looming ominously during the period was identity deprivation. In one way or another, the loss of what made a human "human" was the topic of a number of these films. *Invaders from Mars* (1953), one of the best, features a small boy who suspects something is terribly wrong with his parents. There is. They have been taken over by Martians. Much of the film's suspense comes from the boy's increasing awareness that something is out of whack, and his growing fear that he may be next. Allied Artists' *Invasion of the Body Snatchers* (1956), often considered the model of Cold War manifestations, concerns alien pods which clone people as unfeeling citizens. AIP's *It Conquered the World* (1956) and *Night of the Blood Beast* (1958) fall into the same category: aliens either taking over the bodies of people or using their bodies to hatch. Like the Communists, who had subjected feeling to reason, and God to science, these invaders posed grave dangers to the American way of life, dangers which were usually quelled by the end of the film's running time — that is, until the following week, when a new threat would emerge on screen.

**Commercial television announcement on the television show* The Running Man.
†*Judge Dredd (Sylvester Stallone) venting to anyone who will listen in* Judge Dredd.

42

The science fiction and horror genres play on fear, and they usually flourish during times of high social stress; its form is perfect for absorbing such societal anxieties into its iconography. Past examples include Expressionism during the Weimar Republic years of in-between-wars Germany, and the Universal horror films during the Depression era. The latter cycle often showed their monsters in a sympathetic light — Frankenstein's Monster and even the Wolf Man were "outsiders" who, through no fault of their own, were thrust into their predicament vis-à-vis society. This corresponded to a Depression-ravaged nation wherein one out of every four men had no job. They, too, were outsiders, economic victims of something over which they had no control.

Conversely, when the decade of the '50s rolled around, and Communism had replaced the Depression as the country's major obstacle, engendered by the Korean War and the strident tones of the Soviet Union as a force to be reckoned with, science fiction films followed with monsters as invaders, cold, unfeeling, uncaring creatures out to conquer humanity. Revelations of Communist espionage, culminating with the execution of the Rosenbergs, Soviet deployment of nuclear weapons as well as their lead in the space race, all contributed to a "Red scare," where Americans, for perhaps the first time with real justification, felt vulnerable, and the "menace" from space or atomic testing reflected these anxieties. Robin Cross notes,

> It was this climate of hysteria — generated by fear of invasion, atomic war, or the accidental or deliberate use of nuclear power — which produced a series of classic Bs whose very lack of production values, outlandish plots, incoherent acting and frequently laughable special effects point a demented finger at the deep unease lying beneath the bland surface of Middle America [Cross, p. 112].

However, unlike in the '30s, this time there would be no sympathy for the monsters — they had to be destroyed, just as the sky had to be watched! And destroyed they were. In *Tarantula* (1955), a giant arachnid appears in the desert. Fortunately, the Air Force is around with a little napalm, expertly targeted by pilot Clint Eastwood in an early role. That's not to say spiders had a monopoly on terror. Other insects had their time in the spotlight as well. In *The Black Scorpion* (1957), Mexico gets its chance to be ravaged by a mutant scorpion. In *The Deadly Mantis* (1957), a football field–length bug goes on a rampage in a few big cities. The granddaddy of all these insect films featured two cops, one a fed, the other a state trooper, who join together with a scientist to track and destroy nests of behemoth monsters created by our own hand.

Them! (1954)

Deep in the isolated portions of the New Mexico desert, giant ants have evolved genetically into killers of anything or anyone in their way in *Them!* It's a truly suspenseful film, bolstered by an excellent sound motif that accompanied the appearance of the creatures. Its influence carried over into future films, such as Jim Cameron's *Aliens* (1987).

James Whitmore plays Police Sgt. Ben Peterson, a highway patrolman who is investigating the disappearance of a family. Their trailer is in a shambles, and sugar appears to be something that prompted the attack. But who would kill or kidnap for sugar? And if the thing was an animal, which would be large enough to cause such damage? Dr. Medford, a renowned expert on insects and their behavior, investigates, along with his daughter Patricia (also a scientist). They find that common ants have mutated due to bomb testing in the

A giant ant looks for a snack in *Them!*

area. Radiation has spawned monstrous ants able to easily pick up a human or a car. If the nest isn't quickly found and destroyed, the giant ants will spread unchecked, eventually destroying everything on Earth.

   Atomic testing during the decade was not unpopular with the American public, but at the same time it was not uncontroversial. No one really knew what the effects of radiation would bring 20, 30 years down the road. Most would say they weren't in favor of blowing

Traces of a giant ant are recovered in Them!

up all those bombs in the desert, but because the "Reds" were testing, so must we. Like many films of the era, *Them!* sends mixed messages. As a strict warning against radiation poisoning of our planet, the narrative could not be clearer. As a caution against the futility of an arms race, a significant number of viewers probably came to the same conclusion. However, though the correlation between the Communists and the ants seems rather obvious now, how many drew such an implication then? The ants live communally, in a nest, underground, hidden from prying eyes. The Soviets and the Chinese promoted collectives, and kept their societies closed to Western observation. The ants, like the Communists, are ruled from the top down. The ants work for the queen. Those suffering under Stalin and Mao do the same. The ants kill efficiently and without emotion. Their entire existence is to serve the queen and spread to more and more locations. The Communists view killing as they do any other activity — its purpose is to spread and promote their ideology. Right and wrong are subjugated to the needs of the state.

Federal agent Robert Graham, played by James Arness, joins Sgt. Peterson, assembling a task force and beginning the hunt for the ants' nest. Once finding it, Graham and Peterson use flame throwers to destroy the place, killing every ant inside. Unfortunately, some new queens have escaped — three, Dr. Medford estimates. If their nests are not found, human existence will be on borrowed time. Two are found immediately — one lands on an American naval ship. But one is still out there. Because of the flight paths of the other queens, Dr. Medford thinks Southern California might be a good starting point to search for the last one.

Graham and Peterson comb the City of Angels, working with the LAPD. After some children come up missing, the cops believe the ants have nested in the flood control channels around the LA river basin. The authorities go on television and warn the population. As the city is put under martial law, the military moves in and closes the various openings into the channel tunnels. Sgt. Peterson and Agent Graham lead Army units in to burn out the queen, again using flame throwers. The nest is destroyed, but with no small price to pay.

Sgt. Peterson and Agent Graham make a good team. Peterson is gruff, knows his way around, and will fire any gun he can get his hands on, be it a .38 or machine-gun. Graham is impressive, a large man who dresses in a suit and seems to use his head more than his fists (though judging from his size, he certainly could use them without a problem). Graham and Dr. Medford's daughter hit it off—falling in love is fine, but Peterson is more interested in killing the ants. The two men demonstrate the need for cooperation, not competition, between law enforcement agencies. They work together, and the menace is defeated, although at no small price. Not only are many of Peterson's friends killed, but Peterson forfeits his life to save the children.

Not coincidentally, *Them!* presents a society ill-prepared for the onslaught which threatens to overwhelm it, and must be saved by the armed forces. Many people felt the same way during the Eisenhower years, though the country's state of military readiness was probably better than at any time in its history. Because the danger is originally discovered by a local police officer, the state mobilizes its forces but cannot meet the challenge. Federal agents then join up and help in the hunt for the ants. When the civilian authorities are faced with being overrun by the creatures, the armed forces step in and pick up the slack. Even the film's name is ambiguous. "Them" refers to the ants, but it can also refer to anything or anybody unnamed, particularly something lurking and waiting in the darkness. While America and the world are saved by the film's end, it's not because of some secret weapon but rather the dedication and courage of two cops, one of whom makes the ultimate sacrifice that comes from wearing the badge.

Outland (1981)

On Jupiter's moon Io, a mining camp is making record progress. The conglomerate is happy about its productivity, and many workers are rewarded with bonuses for their hard work. The conglomerate's chief executive at Io, Sheppard, has a free-wheeling attitude about what goes on there. His men work hard and play hard. In other words, "boys will be boys." O'Niel, the new federal district marshal, arrives to take charge of law enforcement operations, and immediately runs into trouble with some of the workers who are exhibiting bizarre, almost paranoid behavior. One opens his suit in space and blows up; the other attacks a company prostitute. O'Niel investigates, asking the mine's doctor to find the cause. Both the doctor and O'Niel suspect some kind of drug, and the doctor finds it. Sheppard tells O'Niel to back off. When he doesn't, Sheppard sends for three hit men to silence the marshal.

If this sounds like *High Noon*, well, the critics thought so too. But that isn't a drawback any more than it is necessarily an advantage. A film must stand on its own merits, just as O'Niel must. The corruption within the mine camp runs deep. O'Niel has plenty of deputies, all well-armed, equipped with the latest equipment, as well as state-of-the-art surveillance devices. What he doesn't have is an honest man or woman among them. Sheppard has spread his money around. If nothing else, he's generous. His name is his job—he "shepherds" his

O'Niel (Sean Connery) tries to determine why some of the company's employees are becoming psychotic in *Outland*.

O'Niel (Sean Connery) faces the company's killers in *Outland*.

flock in the camp. Just as with Will Kane, O'Niel finds that no one really wants him interfering in the mine's operations. When the hit men arrive, it's O'Niel who has to face them all by his lonesome, with the doctor providing a little bit of help.

The major difference between Kane's Hadleyville and O'Niel's Io is the variation between cowardice and apathy. Few people really care what Sheppard's doing, and the ones who *do* don't care enough to do anything about it. The pay's pretty good; no one complains all that much about the living conditions; and there's plenty of entertainment, from go-go dancers to company prostitutes. The reality of O'Niel's fight is much less noble yet much more serious than anything Kane did. The drug that Sheppard is allowing in the camp is illegal. It can cause paranoia and violence, but not always. In enforcing a law that most don't agree with in a colony millions of miles away from earth, the marshal is clearly establishing federal authority over local rights.* O'Niel is brave and upholds his duties to the badge, but one has to wonder ... was the fight really worth it?

Silent Rage (1982)

In a small Texas town, a killer goes berserk, bludgeoning a family. Sheriff Dan Stevens, played by karate legend Chuck Norris, goes into the house after the man, who is both monstrous and a monstrosity. Stevens overcomes the man using his martial arts prowess, but later has to kill him as he tries to escape from custody. Three doctors, who have been developing a reanimation formula, take possession of the killer's body and use the experimental procedure on him. The killer revives, worse than ever. The doctors try to keep him contained, but eventually he gets loose and murders all three men. Stevens has to step up to meet the challenge. How does one stop a rampaging killer who can't be killed?

In stories of this nature, the limits of human knowledge are skewered over a pit of flaming ego. Men (or women for that matter) cannot play God. In attempting to create life, extend it, or prevent death by using forbidden or unscrupulous scientific means, human aspirations are sinful and border on madness. Once the doctor has breached these ethical barriers, no arguments can dissuade him, and nothing can stop him — except the creature itself. The doctors in *Silent Rage* find out the hard way. Though their purpose is noble, the product is not. The moral here, and in other like films and novels, is that some things should be left alone, and when they're not, the results are far from what was intended.

Herein the doctors and the creature are somewhat alike. Both work in an atmosphere of secrecy. The doctors cannot reveal any information about their experiments; the monster cannot reveal his presence. Both are the best at what they do. The doctors and the killer are all are extremely bright. Sheriff Stevens is also pretty smart, but he works in and for the public. As the sheriff he's elected by the people, and to the extent he can without jeopardizing an investigation, he reveals whatever information is pertinent. One similarity shared by all three parties (the doctors, the creature, and the sheriff) is a certain dedication which borders on fixation. The doctors want to increase scientific knowledge and help patients; the monster is a pathological killer; the sheriff has sacrificed relationships to do his job the best way possible. Like John Wayne in *Rio Bravo*, Stevens runs his town tightly, has a rather odd deputy, and refuses any help, preferring to do in the monster all by himself (Lott, p.76–77).

---

*Similar activities are occurring in federal courts, which have been interpreting (some would say interfering with) state laws legalizing the use of marijuana for medical purposes.

In the final confrontation, Sheriff Stevens and the monster go toe to toe. Stevens, the normal man, has to find a way to defeat a killer so pumped up on the reanimation drug that he literally cannot die. This portion of the narrative foreshadows the showdown between boxer Rocky Balboa and the Soviet fighter Ivan Drago some three years later in Sylvester Stallone's *Rocky IV* (1985). Balboa trains in a rural atmosphere, with nature, and is dwarfed by his opponent, who uses modern training facilities and syringe after syringe filled with steroids. Rocky triumphs, as does Sheriff Stevens, who kicks the beast into a well which (presumably) he cannot escape, at least until the sequel, which to this point hasn't come.

The Running Man (1987)

Arnold Schwarzenegger plays Ben Richards, a police officer framed for a mass murder in an America much different than the one presently constituted. Or is it? When Richards objects to officers firing into a demonstration, they do so anyway, and he is railroaded into prison. He escapes, and meets up with Amber, a woman whom he uses as a hostage when he tries to board a plane out of the States. The police catch him and sentence him to participate in a national game show where he has to survive a number of dangerous trials, pitted against killers like "Fireball" and "Subzero." But Richards, who's now known as "The Butcher of Bakersfield," is saddled with a companion: Amber, the woman he held hostage.

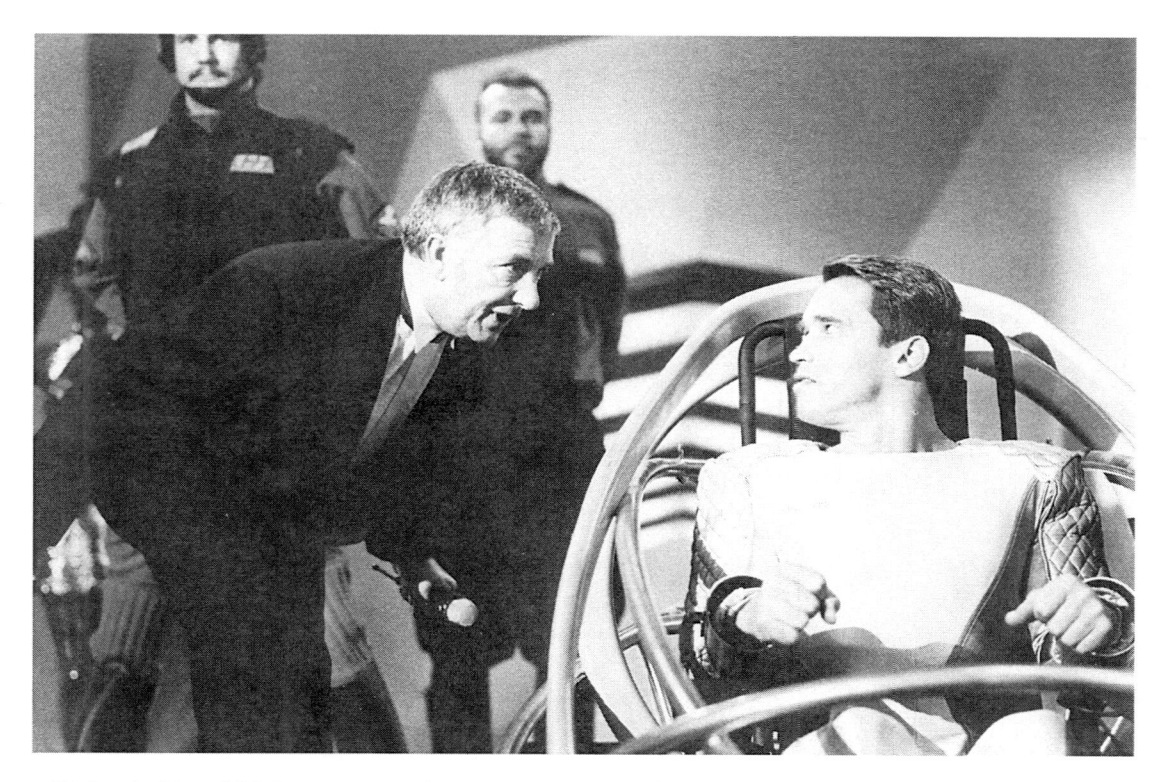

Richards (Arnold Schwarzenegger) prepares to enter *The Running Man*. Richard Dawson (*left*) is Killian, the game show host.

The authorities want her silenced because she had accessed files which prove that Richards is not guilty of the massacre.

One by one, Richards takes on the killers and prevails. But the game show, which is rated number one in the country, continues to throw worse killers into the mix, trying to take Richards down. Killian, the game show host, is played by Richard Dawson, who, in real life, was one of the most popular game show hosts around. He exudes a sense of oily evil hidden beneath a $1000 suit. However, as viewers around the country begin supporting Richards, odds and bets change as he mows down the thugs coming for him. Killian becomes desperate. He digs deep into his reserve of killers but none are capable of defeating Richards. In fact, some of his men quit — Killian has lost respect for the rules of the game and so they want no part of it.

Rebels hoping to hack into the government's satellite signal team up with Richards, who continues to move through the maze without problems. Killian then orders his staff to make a false tape which depicts Richards being killed by one of his men. It is the same type of fraud that the government used to frame Richards for the massacre. Killian wants to play it for his audience to stop them from going over to Richards' side. However, when the smoke clears, Richards has defeated the Running Man game and helped the rebels break into the government's signal. He returns to find Killian and takes a suitable revenge.

Though Ben "The Butcher of Bakersfield" Richards didn't earn his name or even commit the crime in question within the text of this film, we have no idea whether he'd ever committed any other atrocities. The government he works for is totalitarian. By working as a cop, he supports the state apparatus. After escaping from prison, he uses a woman as

Richards (Arnold Schwarzenegger) gets the better of Subzero (Toru Tanaka), one of many miscreants he has to face in *The Running Man.*

cover, not caring what will happen to her if they get caught. Even during his engagement in *The Running Man*, Richards' sole task is to survive. He's not interested in politics. But the game *is* politics for government. It serves as bread and circus to the oppressed masses, much the way the Romans filled the Coliseum to placate their restless population, or the Soviets kept vodka cheap and available to theirs.

Besides staying alive, then, Richards' motives are ambiguous. With every victory over the game's assassins, his popularity rises with the viewers. But does he really care about them? Has he renounced the repression he was part of? By joining with the rebels, he may have helped them get on government airwaves, but what can they actually accomplish in the long run? If Richards takes over the insurgents, aggression is the only thing anyone can be sure of. The new boss looks a lot like the old boss, only much more violent.

Total Recall (1990)

Arnold Schwarzenegger returned a few years later as a special agent run amok during an undercover assignment on Mars. He plays Quaid, a construction worker with a happy life on Earth, a beautiful wife and a nice home. The complete American dream — only something is bothering Quaid, something about Mars, where the government has authorized colonies. Unfortunately, an insurrection is rising in both mood and force on the Red Planet. While no clues are given as to how things are governed on earth, the Mars colonies are under an oppressive, fascist administration. Every day, news reports describe the fighting between mutant workers, scarred from radiation, and government troops, who give no quarter.

Quaid has never been there, but he can't stop dreaming that he has. On his way home from work he goes to a virtual travel agency, one which will "implant" memories of a trip to Mars without him even going there. When the doctors open up Quaid's mind, however, they see it has been tampered with. Quaid begins insisting he *is* an agent; the doctor is able to knock him out and the staff gets rid of him. At this point he becomes a hunted man, and finds out from his "wife" that she's not his wife — she's another agent's wife and her job is to monitor him. Also keeping tabs on him are many of his co-workers on the construction site where he labors.

Quaid escapes and makes it to Mars, where he attempts to unravel his forgotten life as a federal agent. The government is expecting him, though. It seems that Quaid had infiltrated the mutant rebels in the past. Then he had his memory "wiped" so he could disappear for awhile, to convince the mutants he was for real and not working for the government any more. When the time was right, he would go back to Mars, infiltrate the mutants again, and the government would follow — destroying them.

Total Recall, like *Blade Runner* before it, was based on a Philip K. Dick story. Reality was an important theme in Dick's fiction and it is the key to understanding this film. Is Quaid *actually* experiencing what is happening on screen or is it merely part of the memory implanted by the virtual travel agency? At a certain point the lines of reality become blurred, like the white lines on a lonely highway for a sleepy trucker. As a federal agent working for the corrupt colonies' government, he's more or less an extension of that sleaze and brutality, much like Ben Richards was in *The Running Man*. When Quaid continues to fight for the mutant cause against the government, we learn that as an agent he was ruthless and thoroughly despicable. Now he's committed to a good cause and good people — his own virtue is seen in his actions, standing up for the downtrodden, which the Mars

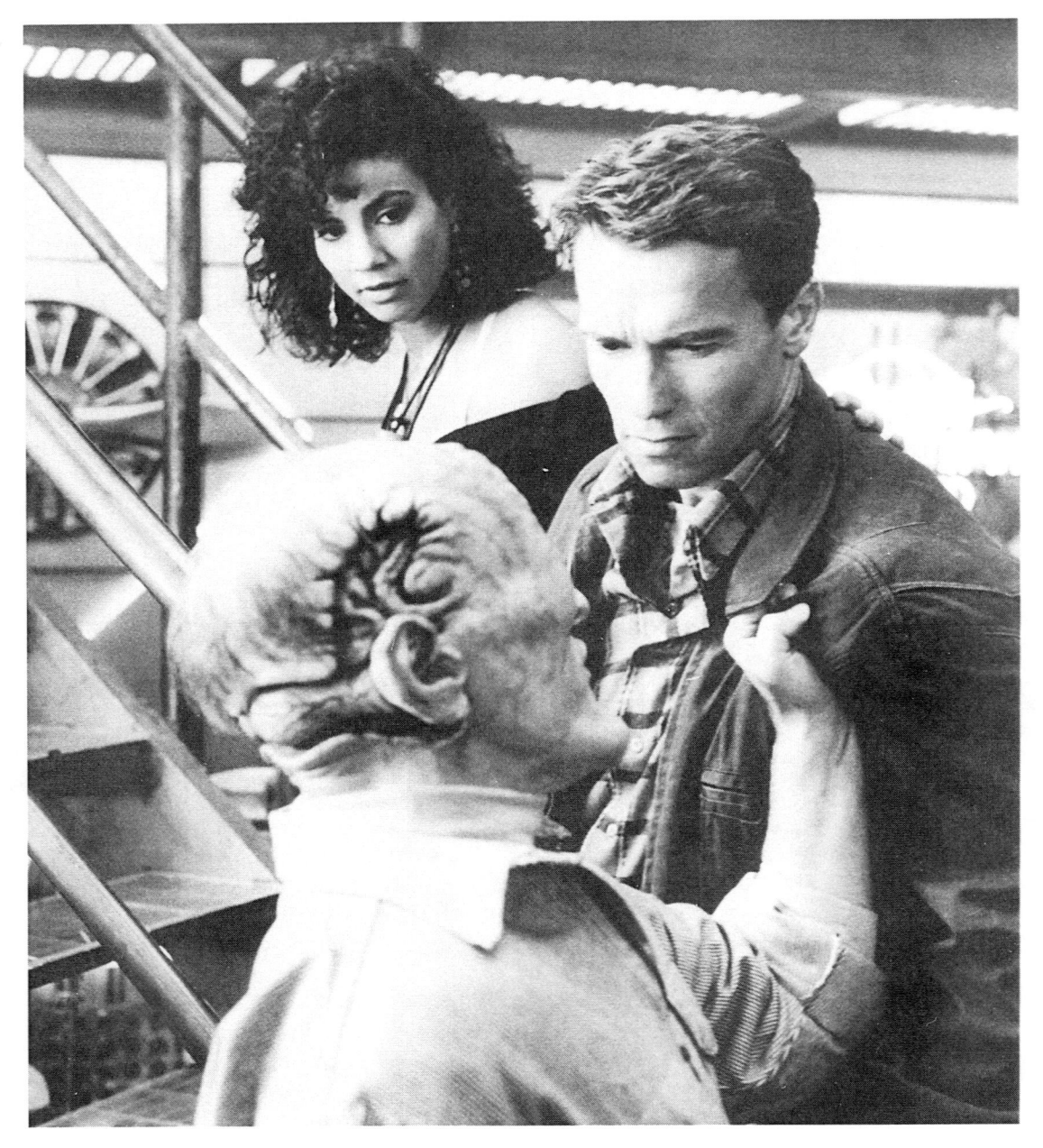

Prime specimens versus mutant: Quaid (Arnold Schwarzenegger) and Melina (Rachel Ticotin) gape at a man one eye short of a full face (Dean Norris) in *Total Recall*.

government wants to eliminate. However, if the entire mission is a virtual memory, Quaid's lost nothing, and the government has a proven weapon to use to "clean" the memories of enemies or dissidents whenever it wants.

Because the reality factor played a big part in the narrative, other messages were lost in the extreme violence and special effects. The mutants rebelled because they had been exposed to radiation by a government which sought only to make a profit. The rebellion

Quaid (Arnold Schwarzenegger) engages in a gunfight on a crowded escalator. Good police tactics?

is more or less a fight for survival, as the administration wants to eradicate any trace of these "things" to cover up their own culpability. Some of the people were born missing limbs. Some women have three breasts. The mutant leader has grown out of the side of another person, and grotesquely comes to life to impart wisdom and advice. The effect of uncontrolled exposure to toxic wastes on the bodies of people takes a back seat to jokes and sordid looks at creatures barely human. In one scene, when Quaid makes contact with the mutant rebels, a one-eyed man tells Quaid he has nerve showing his face around there. Quaid replies that the one-eyed man should talk! Even if the viewer made it past this, the misogyny would very well do many in. "Women are punched, slapped, insulted, and, at one point, ordered up on a menu" (Cinebooks, n.p.).

Just as Ben Richards did, Quaid overcomes the government, and the rebels triumph. The original Martian inhabitants had left behind some type of generators which shoot oxygen into the environment. When Quaid sets them off, the government's power is broken, though this is more "understood" than explained. The "new" Quaid, with his mind wiped, is a much better man than the old Quaid, whose reputation preceded him everywhere. But what happens to the people on Mars if he decides to have his old mind restored?

Demolition Man (1993)

John Spartan is a no-nonsense cop who pursues criminals without mercy or quarter. Simon Phoenix is a criminal who hunts and terrorizes his victims with the same intensity and aggressiveness as Spartan. The two are opposite sides to the proverbial coin. When Spartan has Phoenix cornered in a large building in a suburban ghetto, he makes his move to capture the man — or preferably kill him. Unfortunately for Spartan, the entire building goes up in an explosion just slightly smaller than that of Hiroshima. While Phoenix is certainly guilty of many crimes, the politicians find it expedient to sacrifice Spartan as well. Both men are put into a cryogenic sleep until they can be rehabilitated. Phoenix is awakened for a parole hearing and promptly escapes. Secretly working for the city's controller, the doctor, Phoenix begins hunting rebels who live below the city. The rebels oppose the doctor's control and want things to return to the way they were in the past, where every move wasn't controlled for the sake of safety and harmony.

The authorities decide their only option is to reawaken Spartan — he's the one man who's ever brought Phoenix to justice. Spartan finds himself suddenly thrust into the middle of the twenty-first century. Overwhelmed, he is teamed with a female partner who is anything but aggressive. In fact, the entire society is passive. If Spartan is going to capture or destroy Phoenix, he'll have to do so without any help. After a number of confrontations with Phoenix and some thoroughly bewildering experiences, Spartan kills his nemesis, but with the doctor having been killed by Phoenix, the society is no longer being controlled for "their own good." It's time for the people to be free — if they can remember what that is.

Demolition Man, like many other sci-fi films, raises salient issues it doesn't always address. The city is a version of Skinner's Walden II, a glimpse of behavioral psychology taken to extremes. No one is violent; when Phoenix is challenged by police officers, he easily dispatches them. More or less, the police are merely ornaments. They look good but have no real function, unless enforcing rules against cursing counts. Activities considered negative or harmful have been banned through behavioral modification. While Spartan was in deep freeze, he was taught positive or constructive actions, like knitting. The city's controller makes sure that Phoenix is trained in martial skills, like fighting. But who exactly decides what conduct is bad and what isn't? The rebels believe they've been oppressed and want some latitude. Phoenix looks at the city and sees a field of sheep where humans should be. With their primal instincts essentially gutted, these people can no more defend themselves against him than a dog can without teeth. Sex has even become a long-range affair — the participants do it from computers.

Sgt. Spartan's decision is a tough one. He can go after Phoenix, take him and his gang down, and return the city to its normal state of moderation and controlled behavior. Or, he can fight with the rebels, bring down Phoenix and the controller, and give the city its freedom. Spartan chooses the latter option, but in doing so he's opened the proverbial Pandora's Box. Eventually, the police will need to be "police." Society will sink to a level where social safeguards become necessary. Crime and all the attendant vices will return. And at that point, Sgt. Spartan will really earn his stripes.

Timecop (1994)

Max Walker is a timecop, a federal police officer whose sole job is to stop people from going back in time and changing things. Walker's a torn man, however. His wife was killed before his eyes ten years before, and even though he could go back and alter things, his sworn duty is to prevent any kinds of change from ever occurring. A senator who wants to fatten his campaign coffers is sending his own men back to the past to make him rich. It's up to Walker to catch him. Eventually he does, but the possible permutations of time travel

A cop of the future (Jean-Claude Van Damme) fights an assailant in *Timecop*.

certainly outweigh the simple story. In going back to the past, what manner of things should be changed for the good of society? Is it possible to adjust one thing without affecting another? Who should make the decisions about what should be changed?

Walker doesn't bother himself with the heavy details. He goes back, catches the offender, and brings him or her in to face the time court. The only element of note here is the type of cop needed to perform this task. More so than any other law enforcement job or assignment, an officer assigned to this detail must be incorruptible. To that extent, Walker is the perfect man. His dedication to the job has trumped even the need to save his family. Walker's confrontation with the senator leads back to his family, and as a by-product of him doing his job, they are saved. *Timecop* avoided serious issues and remained a basic good guy–bad guy formula. Despite the big budget, it was leagues behind *Terminator* (1984), which looked at the effect of time travel in a serious manner.

Timecop 2, a.k.a. *Timecop: The Berlin Affair* (2003), was a much lower budgeted feature — made for video, with none of the characters from the first one. The narrative was jarring at points, as the timecops work to prevent the assassination of Hitler. On the surface, killing the madman seems a pretty good idea. The tyrant was responsible for more deaths than probably any man in history. How could anyone *not* want him removed? But this goes back to the questions posed earlier. When one or more changes are made then, what happens now? Do people disappear in the streets? One of the timecops, who is working to change history, goes back to eliminate the relatives of the timecops opposing him so as to eradicate their existence. Things become quite confusing. Do wars suddenly appear, as in this film, when the timecops come back and find battles raging around their headquarters?

"B" films, or those going directly to video, are often more willing to take chances than

"A" films released in theaters. Much of this reasoning has to do with broadening audience appeal. Jean-Claude Van Damme, who plays Walker in the first Timecop film, uses his martial arts skills to fight the criminals, but much less than he had in other films, possibly to attract more viewers. The second film made no bones about being a science fiction *and* martial arts film. It's clear that the science fiction aspects are used to showcase some very good fight sequences. The timecops, though minus Van Damme, use their formidable skills against each other in a series of well-choreographed sequences, and for good cause. Where *Timecop* tiptoed around serious issues, its sequel dived in. Whether or not time travel is ever possible, it's certainly a profound idea, and without incorruptible cops willing to save the past from present manipulation, what *could* happen boggles the mind.

Judge Dredd (1995)

Sylvester Stallone, who played John Spartan in *Demolition Man*, returns as another sci-fi cop in *Judge Dredd*. It's the future, and the society where Dredd lives is a wasteland. Cities are surrounded by huge, desolate areas where hardly anyone can survive. Violence is endemic. The only law is that of the Judges, heavily armed cops who enforce the rules and often apply justice on the spot — no need for any trials. Dredd is one of the most respected officers, and one of the most violent. When he yells out, "I am the law," no one doubts it. Dredd is framed for murder by a cabal hoping to take over the Judges. He should be executed, but his mentor, an older Judge and the head of a council, argues for imprisonment.

Judge Dredd (Sylvester Stallone) in action. Can a democratic society have a police officer who is also a judge?

In return, the mentor steps down and journeys into the wasteland, where he, like other Judges who have lived to a certain point, go to spend their remaining years. Judge Dredd escapes from prison, makes it back to the city and finds the people responsible for the conspiracy — his own brother, who he didn't know existed.

The idea of police officers with the power of Judges is a right-wing fantasy bordering on fascist. Dredd and Spartan are the same in their response to crime and criminals, only Spartan has some guidelines to which he must pay lip service; Dredd has none. Both, however, get their man. At that point, the similarities end. Spartan is awakened to find a city so peaceful it is almost unreal. Dredd's society is so violent and unlivable it is almost surreal. The only thing the Judges have going for them is the fact that all the criminals are guilty. Cases of possible innocence are not seen — everyone Judge Dredd contacts is guilty of *something*. So, those he passes "judgment" on in the field get what's coming to them. The idea of Dredd (or any Judge) making a mistake is unheard of. In a world of black and white, where the police are always right, justice can come swiftly. In a world consisting of shades of gray, the judge has his job, the cop has his. Should they ever become one, the taxpayer might save money, but certain freedoms would be the first casualty and a mighty high tradeoff.

Marabunta (1998)

A small village is threatened by deadly South American soldier ants, the kind that stay underground for years and years, only to emerge, eating anything and everything in sight. A famous scientist is on holiday at the village but, by the time he, the schoolteacher and the sheriff realize what's killing and stripping people of all their skin, it's too late. The ants are spreading across the forest. Nothing can stand in their way, so the best the villagers can do is flee on the main road out of town and out of the valley — otherwise they'll be dinner. Of course, stragglers are everywhere. The sheriff and his deputies do their best to get them out, only pretty soon the ants begin eating them, too. Now it's a race to get out of the valley, and things don't look good for the trio.

Marabunta has some superficial similarities to *Them!*, mostly in the structural setup of the heroes. The sheriff and his deputy represent the law enforcement quotient, while the scientist and the schoolteacher figure out the intricacies of what makes the ants tick. Once they've been identified, guessing where they'll emerge is the next problem. But that's not the group's only problem — the sheriff's deputy is a complete idiot, leaving the sheriff to handle things pretty much on his own. The scientist traces the ants to a ship from South America which ran aground years before. When a major company began tinkering with the environment, it warmed it enough for the ants to survive, even thrive.

Just as *Them!* was a warning about both environmental poisoning and the dangers of not being prepared for any emergency, particularly from certain countries, this film splits the difference. Playing with the ecosystem leads to disaster and the big corporations which do it are responsible for the Frankensteins they create. However, there's no sense of pressing disaster befalling the world. The valley is remote, and where the giant ants in *Them!* were in a desert environment, where they could thrive naturally, the soldier ants are in Alaska. For the sheriff and his partners, blasting closed the one opening to the valley can cut the ants off, keep them contained, and come winter, the cold should kill them. Unfortunately, the heroes never discuss what to do with the ecosystem offenders. Even if they contain the ants this time, there's a chance that others, still underground, may emerge again if the conditions warming the ground aren't reversed.

End of Days (1999)

The millennium is ending. Satan stalks the earth. And the Catholic Church has to find a way to stop him. Fortunately for them, Jericho Cane is after him, too. And with the priests doing all the praying, and Cane doing all the shooting, they just may have a chance. But not much. *End of Days* has some state-of-the-art special effects, but in the end, it's an ex-cop who remembers what it is to be the law that makes the film work.

Satan turns up in NYC as a high-powered businessman. According to Biblical prophecy, the Devil must return to Earth at the end of a thousand years and father a child, who will then be the anti–Christ. The young woman with whom he will couple has been protected and sheltered her whole life by a coven of the Devil's best followers. She has no idea that any of these people are connected with Satan or her purpose in fulfilling the "end of days" prophecy as recounted in Revelations. Cane, a burned-out cop turned security guard, learns that his employer and his minions are stalking the young lady. Soon he and the girl are chased all across the city, and the Devil's disciples are everywhere, from cops to priests. No one can be trusted. Not even the Church. Cane stops the Devil and saves the girl, but not in the way most would think.

A cop's job is never done. Cane (Arnold Schwarzenegger) confronts the Devil in *End of Days*.

As the twenty-first century approached, societies

everywhere seemed a bit paranoid about the coming new millennium, and many film narratives were infused with doom and gloom and a feeling of dread and anxiety. Here, even the characters and institutions show a skewed sense of identity: Cane was a cop but became a bodyguard. Satan is the king of evil, but masquerades as a businessman. The Catholic Church sends out emissaries to find the girl and protect her; yet rogue priests also join the hunt, spreading out, hoping to kill her before the Devil can mate and produce an abomination. The girl unites all of them, but each has a different notion of what to do with her.

Cane lost his wife and child. He spends most of his time drinking too much and not taking care of himself, though you couldn't tell by looking at his body. Life has little meaning, and God is a cosmic joke to him. Protecting the girl comes to Cane more by instinct than any other reason. He couldn't care less if the world ends — his ended with the death of his family. Despite all of Cane's weaponry, he cannot keep Satan from the girl. The evil one actually finds them in a church. He easily fights off his adversaries and prepares to consummate the relationship with her right there. Cane finally realizes something he should have figured out a long time ago: Why is there a Devil if there is no God? Understanding he is powerless, he asks the Lord for help, and finds that the means to effectively battle evil and overcome Satan is spiritual, not worldly.

Eight Legged Freaks (2002)

Almost a half-century later, the country is again menaced by giant rampaging bugs—this time spiders. In what has become almost its own genre, "dramedy," a serious film is infused with a good deal of humor, some of it bloody, or gross, which makes the film almost half-comedy, half-drama and, in this instance, all sci-fi.

Prosperity is a dying town in a remote valley where the area's livelihood — a gold mine — is played out. A big corporation wants to buy the mine and the shafts that run under property owners' homes so it can bury toxic waste. The corporation, which has been transporting barrels of the toxic waste through the valley, loses a barrel, which rolls into a local pond. A local man who runs a spider farm finds the arachnids growing without limit. After they kill him, they escape and begin to terrorize the town.

Facing up to the giant spiders are the town sheriff, her clumsy deputy and Chris the mine owner. They warn the people to evacuate to the only place where a possible defense can be mounted — the town mall. Most laugh, thinking it's a joke. But when the phone lines go down, the highway out of the valley is cut off, and no radio or cell phone transmissions can get over the mountains, the people realize something is seriously wrong. When the spiders finally make their final push into town and head down Main Street, destroying everything in sight, the survivors head for the mall, but by then more than half the town is already dead.

The sheriff is able to hold the mall until a giant tarantula busts open the steel doors. Once the spiders get inside, the people fight a running battle to a large utility room, where they take refuge. The room leads to the mine, which is located beneath the mall. As the spiders pound away at the door, the last few survivors head into the mine, trying to find a way back to the outside. The people are picked off by spiders in the mine as well, but when those left get to the outside, they light the leaking methane gas on fire and burn the spiders — as well as the mall.

If the subtext to *Them!* was political, then *Eight Legged Freaks* presents a big-business warning wrapped up in a lot of blood and guts. The "corporation," nameless, spreads everywhere, like the spiders. Their toxic waste is what causes the original problem, yet they are nowhere around to accept responsibility. In fact, they could care less about what effects the stuff they want to bury in Prosperity will have on the town or its people. Unlike the monster ants of 50 years before, most of the spiders don't eat the people they hunt; rather, they kill them in the most horrendous way possible. The tarantula is their big gun, like a multinational corporation or giant business. It knocks down barriers along with competition, like a Wal-Mart moving into a neighborhood and closing down the small mom-and-pop and union grocery stores.

The twist here is that the sheriff and deputy are just as brave as the two cops in *Them!*— it's just that the sheriff is so beautiful she could be a model, while the deputy could be a fat Barney Fife. When a spider breaks into the sheriff's house, Chris tries to kill it with some scissors. The woman grabs a riot gun and blows the creature in half. Immediately sensing the danger to the town, she calls her deputy and tells him to bring every gun available from the station. She starts arming the survivors, and as the spiders surround the mall, she remains outside, blasting away until the last person is safely inside. When the creatures bust into the mall, she holds her ground, and then orders the people back to the utility room. Her deputy chooses to remain. Using his 9mm, he kills as many spiders as he can until the gun is empty—but the people have made it safely behind closed doors. Surviving this, he and the town's deejay brave moving through the streets, even though the spiders are everywhere, to find a radio to get some help.

During the trek through the mine, Chris, like *Them!*'s Sgt. Peterson, puts his life on the line and stays behind, searching for any remaining survivors that the orb-weaving spider might not have sucked dry. He tells the sheriff to light the methane coming from the tunnel as soon as she gets outside—whether he's out or not. Chris finds his aunt and they ride a dirt bike through the tunnels, spiders scrambling behind them, until they fly out, fire all around them—but safe. As the film ends, Chris has resisted the corporation's push to take over the town, and reopened the mine. He has found a new vein of gold, and Prosperity now lives up to its name. However, the corporation is still out there, like the ants in *Them!*, watching, lurking, and waiting to strike again.

I, Robot (2004)

When machines created to assist humans in their everyday life pose the risk of running amok, the world's economy, not to mention its population, are threatened beyond imagination. Will Smith stars as Del Spooner, a big-city cop of the future assigned to investigate whether a robot has harmed a human. The victim, Dr. Alfred Lanning, is the creator and mastermind behind the mass production of automatons. His prize robot Sonny, created somewhat differently than others of its type, is the murder suspect, but therein is the rub: Robots are programmed never to harm humans. If Sonny malfunctioned, then it is possible that *any* robot can do the same thing. Since millions of the metal helpers work throughout the country, if not the world, the impact would be devastating.

Like *Blade Runner*, the production of robots is controlled by one massive corporation, in this case, the U.S. Robotics Corporation. Unlike *Blade Runner*, the robots do not look human, and rather than being banned from Earth, they are everywhere. So Smith's job is the opposite of Deckard's: Rather than kill Sonny, he investigates the crime as if a human

Detective Spooner (Will Smith) searches for a renegade machine in *I, Robot*. When a mechanical being understands the nature of "I," has it gained sentience?

committed it. Smith unravels the mystery, and finds that the new version of robots have been allowed to hurt humans in order to "save the species from destroying itself." The robots are deprogrammed and shelved after a battle with humans that rages across the city.

In conducting his investigation, Smith is handicapped by a blind spot the size of the Grand Canyon — he harbors an intense dislike, or prejudice, for all robots. Those behind the robot conspiracy use this to their advantage, and only after Smith acknowledges his own bigotry is he able to solve the mystery. But by that time, it is almost too late. Sonny turns out to be Smith's best friend, not his worst enemy, and Smith realizes that some of his hate is self-directed. He was involved in an accident where his car and another one plunged into the river. A robot rescuer dived to the wreckage, but it calculated that Smith had a better chance of surviving than a child trapped in the other car, and despite Smith's repeated orders for the robot to rescue the child, it pulled out Smith. Not only did he survive, one of his arms was replaced with a robotic limb. Smith is wrestling with guilt over the dead child, *and* a component of him is robot: He is what he hates.

The film's title is certainly provocative. When a robot can consciously identify itself as "I," no longer is it a robot. Whether sentience as we know it can be attributed to the machine is arguable, but it now has a sense of self. Sonny actually dreams, which was built into his program by Dr. Lanning. However, the program doesn't control or even suggest what "he" dreams. Is this life? Philosophers and ethicists can debate the issue and come to their own conclusions. Smith knows that whatever it is, he can't let himself be shortsighted when it comes to any robots—ever again.

The officers and agents in all of these films had a job to do. Most did them extremely well, despite either the futility of their task or the utter impossibility of prevailing. In a number of stories, rebels and insurrection movements threatened the country and the officer had to make a choice about where his duties lie. The novelty about watching insurgents is that it is an unknown factor here. Except for the Civil War, the nation has not been scarred by such fighting. But, if the country slides into a totalitarian state, then the police become forces for oppression and not the guarantors of liberty as in a free society. If toxic waste builds to the point where mutations, both human and insect, proliferate, where do the police stand? The most provocative thing about science fiction is that eventually, the science *will* catch up to the fiction. The question then becomes, will we be ready?

Sources

Cross, Robin. *The Big Book of B Movies*. New York: St. Martin's Press, 1981.
James, Ken. *End of Days*. "Christian Spotlight." 1999. www.christiananswers.net/spotlight/movies/pre2000/endofdays.html.
Lott, M. Ray. *The American Martial Arts Film*. Jefferson, NC: McFarland, 2004.
Nusair, David. *Timecop 2*. "Reel Film Reviews." 2003 *www.reelfilm.com*.
Total Recall. Cinebooks. CD-Rom. 1996.

VI

THE PROFESSIONAL

— I should have taken you this morning.

— You should have tried.*

Howard Hawks was one of the most respected and prolific directors in Hollywood cinema. Working for over seven decades in the film industry, he was in his mid–70s when he helmed his last movie, *Rio Lobo* (1970). In his work, Hawks developed a certain affinity for heroes who were professional, men of honor who had a job to do—and did it. While directing films in every genre, "his personal vision transforms those genres," and rarely did he ever use cinematic tricks or call attention to the camerawork (*The Cinema Book*, p. 179). He let actors "act," and got some of the best performances out of some of the most famous actors, including Cary Grant, Gary Cooper and John Wayne.

The last two, Cooper and Wayne, were good friends, but their respective 1952 films *High Noon* and *Big Jim McLain*, and the lawmen they played in them, were poles apart with regard to the political climate in Hollywood at the time, particularly the investigation being conducted by HUAC. When Cooper won the Best Actor Academy Award for his portrayal as Will Kane, Wayne was happy for him. But Wayne was upset with the subject matter of *High Noon*, believing that no American would turn his back on the sheriff and allow criminals to run the town. Fortunately for Wayne, Hawks despised *High Noon* as well. *Rio Bravo* (1959) was their answer, a serious story with light-hearted moments, a film in which what isn't said is just as important as what is, a film which celebrates the *professional* lawman.

Rio Bravo

Wayne plays Sheriff John T. Chance, a man stuck between the proverbial rock and a hard place. Joe Burdett has killed an unarmed man in front of dozens of witnesses—but he's the younger brother of the most powerful rancher in the district. His older brother Nathan begins hiring killers and gunmen, waiting for an opportunity to get the drop on Chance and spring Joe. Chance's deputies are Dude, a drunk trying to break the habit, and Stumpy, a crippled old man whose ranch Burdette stole. Along the way they pick up Colorado, a top gun hand, and fight off Burdett's men. When Dude is captured by Burdette, Chance and his friends are forced into a showdown against overwhelming odds—odds that only a professional lawman would tackle.

**Sheriff Hendricks (Mike Henry) to Colonel McNally (John Wayne) in* Rio Lobo.

Hawks sets up the same dilemma seen in *High Noon*. When Chance jails Joe Burdette, Burdette's father's gunmen surround the town and monitor traffic on the roads, making sure that Chance can't transport Burdett to the U.S. Marshal's office. Like Will Kane, Chance is surrounded. Unlike Will Kane, he does not go hat in hand begging for the town's citizenry to help him. Like Kane, Chance is a tall man. Unlike Kane, his face radiates assurance, not

Chance (John Wayne) exudes confidence despite the fact he's outnumbered and outgunned in *Rio Bravo*. The "professional" is always well-armed.

desperation. Both Kane and Chance, Cooper and Wayne, were almost the same age when the movies were shot. Hawks frames Wayne against a number of objects, like the beams holding up the porch roof, the hotel, the jail door, highlighting poses where Chance appears calm and reflective, yet ready to move at a second's notice with confidence and assurance (Ford, p. 347). Kane moves with lethargy, unsure of himself, his body drained by a hopeless quest. For him, the triumph comes in beating back his fear and doing what he knows must be done, despite the likelihood of his own death. Sheriff John T. Chance wouldn't even recognize Kane as a peace officer — everyone feels afraid but a lawman can't show it. He knows it's imperative that Burdette's men see him as unflappable. His situation is tenuous at best, but showing fear would be like tipping his cards in a poker game, something Chance would never do.

In Kane's town, grown men will not venture out of the church to help him. Chance has to refuse assistance. When his friend Pat drives a wagon train into the town, he offers all of his men as potential deputies, and the sheriff refuses. The men are amateurs, well-meaning, but family men — he needs hard men like himself, men who can take the pressure. Even as he rebuffs the town's assistance, he finds a few worthy civilians who rise to the challenge anyway. Feathers, a gambler-turned-dance hall girl, falls in love with Chance and does everything she can to help him, including sleeping with a shotgun in front of his hotel room. The more Chance discourages her, the harder she works to protect him. Carlos, the owner of the hotel-saloon, is a tiny man, perhaps 4'11", but he stands up to Chance, impressing the sheriff. At the final shoot-out, Carlos joins Chance, carrying a shotgun almost as large as he is.

Once Dude begins feeling the effects of his going sober, not only must he battle the sickness and pain from that, but keep vigilant on the road into the town where he watches for Burdette's men. One of the men who volunteers to be Kane's deputy is a town drunk — Kane declines, then gives him money to get another drink. Chance doesn't undervalue Dude because he's a drunk; Dude used to be his deputy. He walks a tight line, keeping Dude motivated for the impending showdown with Burdette, but also breaking him of the need for hard liquor. Kane, who seems more afraid than brave, turns away possible assistance. Anyone can fire a shotgun — if the drunk has the grit of Stumpy, he's more of a professional than Kane, and certainly less afraid.

As Kane walked the streets looking for help to do his job, many of his so-called friends hid, or rode out. Is the image of Will Kane so pathetic and Frank Miller so strong and evil that no one in town will stand up? Compare that with Chance. As he and Dude walk the streets on a night patrol, Chance fronts some of Burdette's gunmen, and they slink away, somewhere between roaches and snails. When one of them takes a pot shot at the two men, Dude fires as the man escapes, winging him on a dead run. Not only are Chance and Dude unafraid, but rather, they are raring for a fight. The two lawmen again bust into Burdette's saloon, this time Dude taking charge. Burdette's men laugh at him, but Dude finds the assassin and kills him. Burdette's men are put on notice that the sheriff is not a man to be taken lightly — his deputy either, when sober — and as the sheriff walks the streets, the townspeople nod and greet him. He is respected, not pitied like Kane. We know that Kane cleaned up his town years before, but he had a group of hard deputies working with him. Perhaps Kane doesn't have a reputation because he let the others do the work. If this is the case, the town is wise in getting rid of him. Though Kane prevails in his struggle with the gang, it's only by luck and not by any superior qualities on his part. His wife shoots one of the men in the back, then distracts Miller so Kane can get the drop on him. Chance does everything he can to keep Feathers from being anywhere near the action.

In the final showdown, everything is above board. Chance and his deputies match shot for shot, though terribly outnumbered. Stumpy, who was left by Chance at the jail because he can't move well, comes anyway, as does Carlos. With Dude and Colorado's superior shooting skills, Burdette's men are pinned up. When some break to flank Chance, Stumpy cuts them down with his double barrel. Chance's ability with a Winchester turns the tide — he fires at dynamite which Stumpy throws at Burdette's men, killing and wounding many of them. As Chance and his deputies take the Burdette men to jail, the badges are still on their shirts. No need for a professional to throw it away when he wears it voluntarily and with pride.

Even the opening sequences underscore the difference between Chance and Kane. At the start of *High Noon*, Kane is married, then shuffled out of town at the news that the Miller gang will soon arrive, seeking revenge. In *Rio Bravo*, with only the sound of a tinny piano and background saloon noise, the character of Chance is etched in stone, along with Dude's to a lesser extent, and the battle between good and evil established in the shot of a smoking gun. Dude, begging for drinks, meets Joe Burdette, who tosses him a coin for whiskey. Only he tosses the coin into a spittoon! Dude, with all eyes upon him, reaches down to get the coin. Chance suddenly appears. A point-of-view shot from Dude shows

In ***Rio Bravo***, Colorado (Ricky Nelson) warns Chance (John Wayne) and Dude (Dean Martin) that trouble is coming. Contrast the Professional's demeanor with that of Marshal Kane in ***High Noon***.

Chance standing tall, framed as the hero he is, disgusted by Dude's behavior. Chance kicks the spittoon out of the way and turns to Joe, but Dude, enraged and humiliated, hits Chance over the head with a stick. Joe and his men beat Dude to a pulp, until a concerned citizen stops him. Joe shoots the unarmed man, then wanders into another saloon, this one owned by the Burdette family.

Somehow, the bloody and dazed Chance stumbles into the saloon where all of Burdette's men are. But he arrests Joe nonetheless, assisted by Dude. In a few scenes, with little dialogue, the viewer sees that Chance is a man of action, and that the badge he wears is not only a symbol of law, but of the kind of man needed to enforce that law. Not every man can carry it. When Dude finally quits, Chance takes his badge; when Dude has a change of heart, he puts it on again, but no words to swear him in need be spoken. Same with Colorado. When he helps Chance gun down some of Burdette's men, Chance isn't concerned with the exact words needed to swear him in, just that he'll do his duty to enforce the laws. Stumpy, guarding Joe in the jail, holds his double barrel on young Burdette. He doesn't appear to be the typical deputy (he can barely walk), but he has the hardness Chance needs. In the world of Hawks and Wayne, Will Kane need not apply for any position carrying a badge and gun.

El Dorado

Hawks and Wayne reunited in the mid–60s for *El Dorado* (1967), at a time when the country once again needed the professional. Across the country, various organizations were demonstrating, from civil rights groups to anti-war protestors. Police response was sometimes vicious, particularly in Southern cities, where officers used water cannons and dogs to quell disturbances. Later in the decade, full-scale riots broke out in cities like Detroit and Los Angeles, and municipal law enforcement agencies were often overwhelmed. If the nation needed a breather, a look-back at simpler times with even simpler solutions, then *El Dorado* was their ticket. Wayne played Cole Thornton, a gunfighter known throughout the territory. He's hired by a large rancher to take care of a "problem." Upon arriving in town, he learns the problem is his best friend, Sheriff J.P. Harrah. It seems rancher Bart Jason has hired an army of gunfighters to rid the area of another rancher named MacDonald, and Harrah is standing in the way.

Thornton talks with J.P. and then rides out to Jason's ranch to turn down the job. On the way back to town, he's shot at by one of MacDonald's young sons and Thornton returns fire, killing him. Thornton is later ambushed by one of MacDonald's daughters, who puts a bullet in his back, which is too close to the gunfighter's spine for the town doctor to operate on. Until the bullet is removed, he will have to deal with temporary bouts of paralysis. When Thornton is able, he leaves town, still feeling the guilt of having killed MacDonald's young boy. On the way to Mexico, Thornton finds out that infamous gunman Nelse McLeod and his gang are on their way to kill J.P. Harrah. Thornton saves a young gambler named Mississippi from some of McLeod's men, and the two ride to warn Harrah. Only Harrah has turned into a drunk, so it's up to Thornton to put on a badge and pull J.P. together, otherwise Jason will start a deadly range war with the MacDonalds.

As in *Rio Bravo*, the lawmen must face a number of obstacles to keep the peace and prevent the bloodshed coming. Like Dude, J.P. has a problem with the bottle, and he has to get sober quickly. Going into the saloon for some whiskey, he's humiliated in front of McLeod and his men. Later he returns to the saloon and arrests Jason; he's tested by some of Jason's men but his skills return to him, at least for that moment. Thornton and J.P. chase some assassins into a church and shoot it out. They also have to keep McLeod's men from rescuing Jason, who's locked up in the jail. Finally Thornton has to face McLeod, even though he is partially paralyzed by the bullet that MacDonald's daughter put in his spine.

Thornton is the linchpin which keeps the peace. When MacDonald hears that the gunman is backing Harrah against Jason, he stops his men from attacking Jason's. He agrees to allow the law a chance to succeed, something it hadn't been doing when Harrah was drunk all the time. McLeod, on the other hand, has to keep his men back because he knows how dangerous Cole Thornton is; if he tries to rush the jail, not only will Jason be killed, but so will be many of his men. Thornton has to walk a thin line himself. If he lets J.P., who is simmering from his humiliation, go too far, people will be brutalized. If he isn't forceful enough, Jason and MacDonald will start fighting, and the town will be torn apart.

During the '60s, police were often faced with these same choices, and finding the middle ground was often difficult. Thornton knows instinctively, though, what choices to make

Thornton (John Wayne) backs up the rather drunken sheriff (Robert Mitchum) in *El Dorado*.

and why, but unlike in real life, where the causes for a problem can be many, difficult to isolate, and more difficult to implement solutions for, Thornton returns the town to its normal state merely by jailing Bart Jason.

As the professional, Thornton does his talking with his gun, judiciously of course, but nonetheless violently. Once he sees the problem, like Chance did before him, Thornton solves it directly, with force, but only on the quandary at hand, thereby maintaining order and law, respectively. Taken to its logical extension, professional lawmen like Chance or Thornton could solve the problems of riots by eliminating radicals and agitators, and end the problem of police overreaction and brutality by taking charge of the agency and dictating the proper force himself.

Rio Lobo

Hawks and Wayne teamed up one last time for *Rio Lobo*, though by this time the professional lawman has turned into a violent, almost obsessed symbol of federal authority. Wayne is Cord McNally, late of the Union Army, where he was a colonel heading up special operations involving gold shipments and such. McNally's last gold shipment before the war ends is hijacked by Confederates, who kill a number of men the colonel is close to. McNally is also captured by the Confederates, but he turns the tables and escapes. McNally knows someone in his outfit is an informer, being paid by the South, but the Confederates whom McNally's men capture will not divulge any information during the duration of the war. When the war ends, McNally finds the men in a prison camp and they tell the colonel what they know. The colonel gives the men an address where they can reach him in the event that they ever come across the man again. A while later, McNally receives word that the men have seen the traitor and he rides to Texas to capture him. What he finds is a range war and a town being controlled by a large rancher. To get to the traitor, McNally and his Confederate friends will have to go through a crooked sheriff and his gunmen.

Unlike Hawks' other two films, which involved the professional lawmen holding the jail and its prisoners, the scheme is reversed here, with Wayne and his allies in the open, fighting the men who control the jail. McNally is an unusual officer to say the least. While running his command efficiently and with great respect from his men, he's also a gunman. When the war ends, he hires on with the government, tracking down men like the traitor. When riding into a town, McNally asks an old acquaintance — the sheriff — if he's seen the Confederate who was supposed to meet him there. The sheriff immediately tells McNally that the kid isn't good enough to take him (McNally). Obviously, McNally's reputation precedes him wherever he goes.

When McNally and his Confederate partners go up against the sheriff and the rancher (who is the traitor the colonel is seeking), local townspeople rally to his cause. However, in this instance they are all ex-soldiers — professionals like McNally — so he leads them against the sheriff and prevails, killing him and the traitor. The need for the professional's return is twofold. With the election of Richard Nixon as president, the country swung to the right, and though the Vietnam War continued, as did the fight for equality (both racial and gender), a patriarchal counterweight was necessary to temper too far a leap in too short a time. McNally, in straightening out the wrongdoing in the town, also becomes a father figure to women in the story, especially Shasta, who curls up with McNally when nights get cold, assured of McNally's honorable character. Equal rights are fine so long as who is ultimately in charge is not forgotten. The notion of the traitor is also significant. While the American military wasted away in the jungles of Southeast Asia, young people at home, as well as left-wing academics, intellectuals and others, continued to do whatever they could to end the war. The hijacking of McNally's gold shipment is an example of what happens when soldiers are betrayed by their own. It was up to a professional to rectify this.

Further readings on the film can be somewhat ambiguous, however. Though McNally is an honorable man, he is also a killer, far removed from his officer status during the war. When he finds the traitor, who is the rancher running the corruption in the town but who was one of his sergeants during the war, he beats the man almost to death, then turns him over to a half-crazed accomplice who points a sawed-off shotgun at the sergeant's head and keeps it there most of the film. McNally's character can be viewed as establishing the honesty and supremacy of federal regulation over local jurisdictions.

This would certainly coincide with Wayne's own hawkish views. However, in a schism that still plagues conservatives who trumpet strong laws, they also support "states rights," and the two cannot be readily reconciled. As the undercover federal agent, Wayne goes back to his *Star Packer* roots. McNally uses conservative values such as force in the right cause to rectify the local law enforcement problem, but is assisted by the local population. In effect, he lends leadership to the townspeople who in turn restore honesty and integrity to the system.

The evolution of the professional lawman, from *Rio Bravo* to *Rio Lobo*, followed a prescribed arc: In the first film, Sheriff Chance established that law enforcement was the job of the expert, paid to protect the populace, not the other way around. When Cole Thornton rode into town, he buttressed the local sheriff and restored confidence in the law. In the wake of demonstrations, riots and lawlessness, the professional was the man the people turned to, like a baseball relief pitcher in the bullpen He knew what to

Colonel McNally (John Wayne) trades in his Union uniform for free-flowing Western gear in *Rio Lobo*.

do, how to do it, and would not hesitate. Colonel McNally is a warning to traitors and those forcing equality too fast, too furious. The professional played by Wayne in all three films holds everything together. He is assisted by a partner with similar abilities but with problems, such as alcoholism. There's a funny-crazy sidekick, like Stumpy or Bull, and a young dandy who rises to the occasion when the chips are down. The professional recognizes how to motivate men, to appreciate the abilities others overlook, and guide younger men down the right path. Chance, in showing Kane how a real lawman does things, is virile, romancing Feathers, who is half his age. When Thornton rides to help his friend, the sheriff, a young friend of Thornton's, Maudie, tries to kindle a romance. But the gunmen's romance days are over. He has a job to do. McNally shepherds and protects the women he comes across, all the while restoring law to the town.

In doing his job, then, the professional law enforcement officer manifests conservative principles while championing local rights. From the man who wears his badge and handles the job he's contracted to do without help, to the man who steps into the breach and restores order, to the man who has to take total control until the locals are ready, the professional is the ideal peace officer: unafraid, committed to getting the job done, and doing what is necessary, even if "necessary" means operating just windward of the law.

Sources

Cook, Pam. *Authorship and Cinema. The Cinema Book*, ed. Pam Cook. London: BFI, 1985.
Ford, Greg. *Mostly on Rio Lobo. Movies and Methods: Volume I*, ed. Bill Nichols. Berkeley, CA: UCB Press, 1976.

VII

WANTED: DEAD OR ALIVE

There's some things a man can't ride around...*

— *Well! The belted earl has spoken. All I see are hired thieves.*

— *These boys are promising young men. Acquiring an education.*

— *Well, I've had you pegged as the type that likes ... educating young men.*†

The spectrum of law enforcement covers a wide range, from the flatfoot walking the beat to the border patrol officer four-wheeling the desert hills of the Southwest. But, while some occupations fall outside the recognized parameters of the peace officer, they still involve many of the same duties. Civilians acting as auxiliary peace officers were a common occurrence in the nineteenth century. Anyone owning a gun and a horse could be held by the sheriff for a posse. In *Unforgiven* (1992), the sheriff deputizes a significant number of the townspeople to go after Clint Eastwood's character, with the county outfitting the expedition and paying expenses.

Bounty hunting was dangerous work, but it often relieved municipal, county and federal authorities of having to send out much-needed peace officers to track down wanted criminals. These men were prevalent during the nineteenth century, mostly in the West, going after any rewards posted, even rescuing captives being held by Indians. Bounty hunting originated in England, where someone was designated to stand in the accused's place as a custodian. This was a good news-bad news proposition. No money was needed to stay out of jail for those awaiting charges; however, if that person did not show up, the custodian could receive the man's penalty (Watson, n.p.).

British Parliament passed the Habeas Corpus Act, which established bail as we know it — a monetary bond to insure a prisoner appears in court. The Eighth Amendment to the Constitution forbids extreme bail amounts, and a United States Supreme Court decision in *Taylor v. Taintor* provided bounty hunters authority to act as the agent of a bail bondsman and to pursue bail jumpers into other states, if necessary. Now every state has laws regulating bounty hunting, and while the days of the Old West are long over, the popularity of the bounty hunter has taken a sudden turn for the better, in part because of Arts and Entertainment Television's weekly series *Dog*, which follows Duane "Dog" Chapman as he

---

**Sam Boone (Pernell Roberts) to Carrie Lane (Karen Steele) in* Ride Lonesome.

†*Lawrence Murphy (Jack Palance) to William Tunstall (Terence Stamp) regarding Tunstall's rather undisciplined group of cowhands.*

hunts jumpers in various parts of the country.* HBO is currently developing a 2006 reality series which will follow a family of bounty hunters in New York City.

The Past

Cinema's opinion of bounty hunters has not always been so favorable, instead presenting a mixed bag of conflicting images and narratives. In some way this is a reflection of the profession itself. The bounty hunter straddles a thin line, assisting law enforcement when they are honest, being no better than the criminal they pursue when not. *The Hired Gun* (1957) is a good example. The first film produced by Rory Calhoun's company after the actor was dropped by Universal, it stars Calhoun as Gil McCord, a jaded gunman with a reputation of doing anything for a price. He is hired by a wealthy rancher to bring back the rancher's daughter-in-law, who has been convicted of murdering her husband — the rancher's son. The woman claims she is innocent, that the rancher's other son was the murderer, but she is sentenced to hang, an unusual punishment for a woman, even in Texas.

The woman is broken from jail and takes sanctuary in the New Mexico Territory, where the governor will not extradite because he believes the Texas trial was rigged. McCord is deputized as a peace officer and sent to retrieve her. Unfortunately, the badge means nothing outside of Texas, so he becomes a bounty hunter once he crosses into New Mexico. Having found the woman and made off with her, McCord has to deal with a small posse sent after him, and a band of Apaches who want the woman. We see just how good McCord is with his Colt when he dispatches one group and then the other.

When McCord crosses the Texas line, he puts his badge on again. From gunslinger to peace officer, to bounty hunter to peace officer again, all in a matter of a few days and a few hundred miles. The gunman eventually figures out the truth and kills the man responsible — but, interestingly enough, *not* when he is a bounty man but when he is a peace officer. In this case, the job makes the man, not vice versa.

Charles Bronson began starring mostly in low budget films during the late '50s, while still playing supporting roles in higher budgeted productions. *Showdown at Boot Hill* (1958), directed by low-budget maven Gene Fowler, Jr., follows Bronson as a bounty hunter who arrives in a small town looking to collect his money. Instead he finds nothing but animosity from the people who don't appreciate that he killed one of their own. The emphasis here is on character, not necessarily action. Bronson falls in love with a local girl who has her own troubles. Passing the time, Bronson takes her to a dance, but the partygoers stop dancing! The girl doesn't understand why Bronson does what he does — when he tells her, it seems bizarre but it also offers a psychological insight: Bronson was teased as a kid for being short. As he got older, he found he was good with a gun, and when he hunted a man it didn't matter if he was tall enough in the eyes of others. (In the films of Alan Ladd, Steve McQueen, James Cagney, even Sylvester Stallone, all of whom might be considered height-deficient, such things were smoothed right over.) At the film's end, Bronson heads to Boot Hill, where he confronts the townspeople, but he doesn't use his gun. He gets clobbered, but it's clear he doesn't need a gun to feel like a big man anymore. His girl is waiting for

---

Chapman skyrocketed to public attention when he captured a convicted rapist who was an heir to a large cosmetic fortune, in Mexico. Ironically, Mexico, with one of the highest crime and murder rates in the world, does not allow bounty hunting and arrested Chapman. Chapman posted bail, and then skipped the country! Truth is sometimes stranger than fiction.

him, and he realizes that hunting and killing men, even bad men, isn't always a necessity. Sometimes life in a small town can be just as rewarding as the big city, so long as you have people who care about you.

In the best light, then, bounty hunting is a tricky proposition. Take *Ride Lonesome* (1959), a Ranown production, directed by Budd Boetticher, produced by Harry Joe Brown and scripted by Burt Kennedy. The story is intensely psychological, taut, with no fat and lots of action, and only 72 minutes long. Randolph Scott is Brigade, a terse and torn man working the New Mexico Territory as a bounty hunter. Brigade captures Billy, a young murderer with a price on his head, and heads back to town with him. Brigade knows that Billy's outlaw brother Frank will try to stop him, yet he keeps to open country and takes his time.

Brigade meets up with two other bounty hunters, Boone and Whit, and a woman the three have rescued from rampaging Indians at a desert outpost. An uneasy alliance forms between the men, made palpable by their mutual respect. Nothing is said. Boone talks around things, about how a man should be. Brigade says little, but he's the kind of man Boone refers to. Billy is what Boone *was*. Brigade is what he'd *like* to be. The woman stands in between, a newcomer to the west. She witnesses brutality, experiences horror, but travels with men who share a common bond, a code of honor, and will protect her even if it kills them. The rub comes from the men's intentions. They all want Billy, so the tension builds three ways: Brigade and Billy; Brigade and the other two men; Brigade and Frank.

Brigade hangs Billy from a high tree, forcing Frank to charge. Brigade kills him, then

Brigade (Randolph Scott) captures his prey in *Ride Lonesome*. This bounty hunter's actions are legal — but are they moral?

gives Billy to the other bounty hunters, having no further use for him. Frank was who he wanted from the beginning; Billy was just a lure to get him. Two sides of a man are visible in Brigade. As town sheriff years back, he followed the law and sent Frank to prison. When Frank got out, he took his revenge on Brigade's wife, hanging her from that very same tree. No longer the law, Brigade exacts his own justice, bordering on madness. His mission complete, Brigade burns the tree, freeing himself from the burden he has carried so long. While the woman and the other two bounty hunters head for town, Brigade remains alone and isolated, unable to rejoin the community he rode away from.

In *Comanche Station* (1960), Randolph Scott repeats his performance in *Ride Lonesome*, only this time he plays Cody, a former military man who bargains with the Comanches for the release of a white woman, only to later have to face off with whites who *also* want her. In both films, Scott plays a bounty man, and in both films he is joined on his trip back to civilization by unwanted traveling companions. Though Indians track Scott in both movies, at the end it is his own kind he must square things with. Ben Brigade and Jefferson Cody are men with wounds no one can see — their wives have been ripped away from them. Brigade can even things with outlaw Frank by hanging him from the same tree where Frank hung his wife. But Cody's wife was taken hostage by Indians, and for years he's roamed the desert looking for her, rescuing any woman he hears the Comanche are holding. Without any closure, he wanders the wastelands looking for a reckoning which he knows will not come.

Cody (Randolph Scott) takes cover behind a water trough during an Indian attack in *Comanche Station*.

When Cody and the woman reach Comanche Station, a stage and rest stop, the Indians attack. Lane and his two traveling companions, Frank and Dobie, are being chased. With Cody's gun blazing, the Comanches are beaten back. But the source of the raid is disputed; Cody, who knows Lane as an Indian killer, believes he provoked them. As it stands, Lane and his partners have been looking for the woman Cody rescued. With a $5000 reward at stake, Lane lets it be known that he wants her. However, Cody's main flaw, like that of Brigade, is a rigid stubbornness. Brigade didn't want the outlaw he had; he used him to draw out the man's brother, Frank. He could have easily promised his catch to Boone, but he waited to the last minute to turn the man over to him. Cody does not want the reward for the woman he rescued. He could give Lane the credit and let him get the money — he doesn't — and has to kill Lane, even though Lane saved his life earlier.

Lane and Boone are similar and different, like fraternal twins. Both men have a code of honor. They want the bounty hunter's catch, Boone to get amnesty and Lane for cash, but they won't shoot him in the back to do it. They save Scott's characters when they easily could have let him die and then taken what they wanted. They know that Brigade and Cody are men most can't handle straight on — but Boone gathers his courage to face him, while Lane figures on picking him off from a long distance. The difference between Boone and Lane is the difference between Brigade and Cody: Boone wants to start life over again, clean; Lane is twisted by the reward money. Brigade, too, wants to start again, and killing Frank will free him to do so. Cody's wound is much deeper. He doesn't care about money, but the pain of never knowing about his wife — is she alive or dead? What did the Indians do to her? Is she a squaw?— twists him like Lane. He warns Lane not to draw, but Lane tells him he has to have the money. Neither man knows compromise, and in shooting Lane down, Cody merely kills a reflection of himself.

The last portion of the trip, Cody and the woman make by themselves. Lane's partners have been cut down by the Indians or by Lane himself. But something Lane told the two by the campfire almost comes to fruition. A bounty hunter like Cody had rescued a woman from the Comanche. On the way back to town, the two fell in love and they ran off together. The woman's husband never had to pay his reward, nor did he ever find out what happened to his wife. For the rest of his life he'd be like Cody, wondering and torn up inside. It is clear that the woman and Cody have fallen in love, though no words are spoken. And it's just as evident that the woman can mend what ails Cody inside. As they arrive at the farm, the woman's husband and son rush out to greet her. The man is blind. She hugs her husband, but her tears are for Cody as he rides away. As with his missing wife, Cody finds some things are just not meant to be.

The following year (1961), John Ford shot *Two Rode Together*, which covered much the same ground as *Comanche Station*. A group of white settlers has camped at a fort at the edge of Comanche territory, calling for the Army to rescue their loved ones from the Indians. James Stewart plays Marshal Guthrie McCabe, a cynical lawman hired to bargain for any white captives the Comanche may have. Like Cody, McCabe is known by the Comanche, is trusted to a point, and he has successfully done business with them before. But otherwise, McCabe is everything Cody, and even Brigade, is not: friendly, mercenary, prone to talk, and willing to twist his ethics to make a buck. He is accompanied on his trip by Richard Widmark, an Army officer who is supposed to make sure that the marshal does what he's been hired to do. The Indians only have two captives, a lovely Mexican woman who hasn't been with the Comanche long enough to forget her culture completely, and a boy who is completely native.

VII. Wanted: Dead or Alive

Cody (Randolph Scott) accompanies the Comanches to their camp in *Comanche Station*.

The boy is a handful of trouble, and McCabe knows it's better to leave him with the Comanche, but he takes him along because one of the fort's civilians has offered to pay him a lot of money to bring back a white boy to satisfy his wife, who lost her son to a Comanche raid years before. In the end, no one benefits from the trade but the Indians: McCabe gives them rifles, which he was not supposed to do, and the boy kills one of the settlers. The whites, who revile the Indians as savages, show just who the savages are by stringing the kid up. The Mexican woman, who descends from an aristocratic family, is treated with scorn and ridicule at a dance by the Army wives, who want to know, in a roundabout way without directly asking, what it's like to be married to a beastly Indian.

The film, despite its talented director, all-star cast and huge budget, was vastly inferior to the lower budgeted, stark Scott production. In part this was due to different objectives. Ford's later films, particularly *The Searchers* and his last Western, *Cheyenne Autumn* (1964), cast an eye on racism and bigotry toward Indians, certainly a large and difficult canvas to paint completely. Conversely, Cody and the woman he rescues talk about how she will be viewed, but not directly. Rather, they let the prejudice fester in the air, coloring everything that happens. The actors were problematic as well. Richard Widmark, who was supposed to be a *young* officer, was closing in on 50 at the time, and his part in the story at times rambled, sometimes comically. Scott's Cody was of undeterminable age — his face was lined as worn leather, and though at 62 he was older than both Widmark and Stewart, he seemed more vigorous, like a large bobcat ready to spring. Even the films' running times were hugely different. *Two Rode Together* clocked in at 109 minutes, *Comanche Station* a tense 74 minutes, spare and taut like Scott's rail-lean body.

Marshal McCabe rides off on the stage with the Mexican woman. He'll take her to California, where presumably things are much better. Widmark proposes to Shirley Jones, 20 years younger than he, and she accepts. Cody disappears into the desert where he first appeared, alone and searching like only a bounty man can.

After a stint on television's *Rawhide*, Clint Eastwood rocketed to stardom in Sergio Leone's spaghetti Western trilogy, *A Fistful of Dollars* (1964), *For a Few Dollars More* (1966) and *The Good, The Bad, and the Ugly* (1966). The first film, a remake of *Yojimbo*, introduced Eastwood as "The Man with No Name." In *For a Few Dollars More*, the Man with No Name teams up with the colonel, played by Lee Van Cleef, to get the bounties on a number of psychotic bandits terrorizing the Southwest. Unlike *Ride Lonesome*, which featured conflicted heroes trying to escape their past, Eastwood and Van Cleef are twisted heroes with no past at all. The colonel's motivation is hinted at: The leader of the outlaws raped and murdered his sister. But Eastwood's is purely mercenary — money and plenty of it. The colonel has developed something of a reputation, but is he even a real colonel? Eastwood doesn't even have a name. Neither man is conventional; killing, after all, is second nature to them, and bystanders getting between them and their prey take their chances.

Colonel Mortimer (Lee Van Cleef), right, and The Man with No Name (Clint Eastwood) face off with a gang of killers in *For a Few Dollars More.*

The Good, The Bad, and the Ugly pushed the idea of the anti-hero to the extreme. Eastwood returns as the man with no name, this time as a bounty hunter with a unique scam: He turns in his prisoners, then rescues them by shooting the rope off of their neck when they're about to be hung. When Eastwood and another man learn some clues as to the whereabouts of a hidden treasure, they set in motion a series of events, one more bloody than the next, until a final three-way shootout settles things once and for all.

Some of this story was told in a 1951 Monogram B film entitled *Wanted: Dead or Alive*. A group of outlaws bust convicts and other outlaws out of jail, only to kill them for the reward money. In this case, a trio of brave marshals has to bring the men to justice; two of them go undercover to infiltrate the gang. Whether or not Sergio Leone knew of this quickie Western, the premise was similar. But the blood quotient under Leone was sky high.

At this stage, Eastwood had finally transitioned into his own Western persona, that of the existential cowboy, a rugged man, independent, highly capable and willing to kill. The agnosticism of Eastwood's characters is usually set off against the conventional moral values of the time — he is not the best man, but he is better than the small-minded hypocrites enforcing society's morality. He keeps his word where others won't, but the level of violence he employs is just short of a small war.

In this film, the Man with No Name is considered "good." His character is probably not what Merriam-Webster had in mind for that word, however. He scams towns out of reward money, frees wanted murderers, and kills or wounds any number of people in his pursuit of easy money. In any other film, the Man with No Name might be compared to Doc Holliday, a villain with some redeeming qualities. However, in a landscape gutted by war, filled with a thousand brutal and senseless deaths of soldiers who have forgotten what it is they are even fighting for, the Man with No Name seems an angel.

Van Cleef portrays the "bad" bounty hunter. The main distinction between his character and Eastwood's is that the latter doesn't always kill. Van Cleef murders anyone he encounters while seeking the treasure. He is slick and efficient, rarely prolonging the death unless agony serves a purpose. He has the third piece of the puzzle to where the treasure is. As the men band together to find the riches, Van Cleef never pretends to be anything other than what he is. Obviously he will turn on the others when the time comes, but not until.

The worst is saved for last: the ugly, played by Eli Wallach. Wallach's character Tuco is a criminal bounty hunter employing great cruelty and cynicism as he murders his way across the Southwest. Unlike the Man with No Name, who recognizes some loyalty, this man is driven by a pathological need to inflict pain and savagery. He tortures Eastwood by making him walk through the desert, drinking and eating in front of him, and otherwise kicking him. In a hotel room he rigs a rope up to the ceiling, surprises the Man with No Name, then hooks him up in the noose. Only a well-placed Union cannonball saves Eastwood's life.

At the end of the film, Eastwood keeps his word. In a gunfight he kills the bad and allows the ugly to live. The wisdom of this further complicates the nature of the story. A rapist, multiple murderer, thief, robber (and anything else one can imagine), the ugly is now free to continue his rampage. Only millions of dollars richer.

Eastwood's trend of bad bounty men in an even worse society continued. In *Hang 'Em High* (1969) he's a lone rancher who buys some cattle from a murderous gang of thieves. The pursuing posse finds Eastwood with the cattle and lynches him. Fortunately, Eastwood is cut down by a U.S. Marshal, played by Ben Johnson, and he is recruited to become a marshal himself. Only Eastwood's marshal is not a lawman, like the Ben Johnson character, but a bounty hunter with a badge, and he proceeds to track down the various men who wronged him. When Johnson, the honest marshal, is killed, Eastwood's actions appear justified. Doing things right and legal only leads to a quick death.

Joe Kidd (1972) finds Eastwood as a bounty hunter hired to track down Chalma, a Mexican fighting for the interests of his "race." While Kidd is a highly skilled gunman, he prefers doing nothing, or getting drunk. The plot is dragged down by its "power to the people" aspects, as Chalma terrorizes townspeople to get the local land records restored to the poor from whom they were taken. Politics in Westerns have always been a delicate proposition, and Eastwood appears uneasy as he tries to balance the proper amounts of bloodshed with Angela Davis ideology. Only John Saxon's horrible Mexican accent takes the focus off Clint.

Twenty years later, Eastwood completed the cycle. In *Unforgiven* he stars as Will Munny, a notorious outlaw and killer of children who has disappeared into the reality of the West: a dirt-poor pig farm on the northern plains, where he raises two motherless children. When two cowboys cut up a prostitute in a Wyoming town, the whores offer a bounty, and Eastwood and two associates go after it. Unfortunately for Munny, he can't shoot anymore, so he has to bring a shotgun with him. After years and years as a farmer, rust has set in.

The story's complexity resides in its outward simplicity. The sheriff of the town wants things peaceful and no one getting hurt; to accomplish this he resorts to a brutality which shocks the townspeople. A famous lawman himself, he knows if he doesn't stop this bounty

The title character in *Joe Kidd* (Clint Eastwood) smashes an attacker with a rifle butt.

thing cold, the whole town will be running over with killers. When infamous gunman English Bob arrives, the sheriff beats him like a dog in the street, almost to the point of death. This is the message he wants the bounty hunters to hear and see: Stay out of the town.

English Bob is released and leaves. Munny and his associates arrive. The sheriff finds him in a saloon, and beats him to a pulp as well. Eastwood recovers, but one of his partners no longer has the stomach for killing. Eastwood forces him to go along and they kill one of the cowboys. They kill the other one in an outhouse. Both cowboys are murdered in a cowardly fashion, without a chance. One of Munny's associates—his best friend—is captured as he flees back to the plains. The sheriff whips him to death trying to find Munny. Munny downs a bottle of whiskey and, in a Dionysian rage, guns down the sheriff and most of his posse. He rides out of town, a legend, never to be heard from again.

The character of Will Munny is both despicable and likable at the same time. Eastwood uses this, and his own status as cinema hero, to play against standards, completely confusing the audience as to where its sympathies should lie. While no one is "good," Will Munny is the worst of the characters. The sheriff is the best, arguably, a heavy-handed man who uses force often but with the intent of keeping his town peaceful. Having worked the cow towns of Kansas, he doesn't want assassins and gunmen bringing in chaos and bloodshed. When Munny's friend is killed by the sheriff, the showdown occurs between the one and the many—only this time the one is a cold-blooded killer and the many are the law. Audiences erupted as the bounty hunter mowed down the peace officers, establishing a sense of moral ambiguity rarely seen or felt in film. The Eastwood character had come full circle from the '60s, synthesized into the larger-than-life character of Will Munny in the '90s.

Lee Van Cleef continued to play bounty hunters as well. In *The Big Gundown* (1968),

Bounty hunter Will Munny (Clint Eastwood) prepares to avenge his friend in ***Unforgiven***.

he plays Corbett, a gunmen hired to track a rapist-murderer into Mexico. The case seems cut and dry, and Corbett's orders are to kill the man. When he begins thinking for himself, he runs into trouble, first with Mexican police who jail him, and then later with his employer, who hires a whole squad of Mexican bounty hunters. With the Mexican police crooked, and the Mexican bounty hunters brutally beating peons to find the rapist, Corbett becomes the only semblance of good in a terrain of evil, and the only party interested in justice. He clears the man he's been hunting, but then must face off with his employer and his employer's German gunman. Corbett prevails and heads back to the States, but with no reward and a bullet in his shoulder. For the bounty hunter, being honest doesn't always correlate to making money.

In *Chisum* (1970) we find a simple plot with underlying complexities. John Wayne plays the title character, a cattle rancher at odds with a land baron attempting to take over the county. The story, loosely based on New Mexico's Lincoln County wars (in which Billy the Kid figured so prominently), was written by Andrew Fennady and shot in Durango Mexico. Wayne's adversary, Forrest Tucker, initiates a killing spree, then hides one of his men in the hills. Enter Nodine, played by Christopher George, a grim, jaded bounty hunter with few social skills and no sense of humor. Nodine brings Tucker's man back to town over a saddle to collect the reward. Impressed, Tucker immediately makes the man sheriff but now Nodine continues his ruthless and sometimes psychotic behavior with a shiny badge to make it legal.

Chisum puts Pat Garrett, also a sometimes bounty hunter, on his payroll. The two sides are now lined up against one another, set in black and white, like pieces on a chessboard. Chisum runs his cattle honestly, sells them at a fair price. Tucker rustles the cattle from the other ranches, then bribes the Army to get contracts at jacked-up prices. Chisum allows small ranchers to water their stock on his land. Tucker tries to steal all the water rights in the county. Garrett, a crack shot with a Sharps, stands with the law. Nodine pretends to be the law yet is anything but. Garrett is a man of his word. Nodine is a ruthless killer. His word is usually followed by a shot to the back.

What results is a tug of war between right and wrong with Billy the Kid in the middle. Billy used to ride with many of Nodine's posse of rustlers and outlaws. They promise easy money and all the killing that Billy can stomach. Garrett befriends Billy and maintains the viability of staying true to the law and one's friends. Unfortunately for Billy, he splits the difference, doing right by his friends but breaking the law in the process. With a huge bounty on his head for murder, Billy flees, but Pat does not pursue. Nodine, on the other hand, pursues with a vengeance, beating information out of Mexican peasants who know where Billy is hiding. Even when Garrett gets the drop on Billy he does not kill him. As the two sides square off, Pat joins with Billy to fight off Tucker and Nodine and the two remain friends.*

While the bounty hunter's image is ultimately shown to be an honorable profession through Garrett's courage and loyalty, *Chisum*'s content has subtle ironies which subvert its text. The film, shot in 1969, with Vietnam raging thousands of miles away yet on the living room TV every night, portrays a brutal cattle war fought mainly over power and control. The politicians involved are duplicitous and weak, and the military ineffectual. Nodine tortures civilians for information, and the Indians who once lived in that country

---

*Garrett eventually killed Billy when he became a lawman in the New Mexico Territory. The facts surrounding the shooting remain unclear.

Chisum (John Wayne) shows his niece Sally Chisum (Pamela McMyler) the town in *Chisum*.

but are now penned up on a reservation, will be starved in the coming winter because of the corrupt beef contracts signed by the Army.

Critics of the war in Southeast Asia pointed to similar circumstances involving our own country with that of the Vietnamese. And anyone seeing the Saigon police chief executing the Viet Cong prisoner during the height of fighting at Tet could easily draw parallels with Nodine's savage killing of a storekeeper trying to surrender in front of hundreds of people. For many, right or wrong, America was viewed as the biggest bounty hunter of them all.

Young Guns (1988) boasted a ridiculous story of the same Lincoln County War, this time focusing on Billy the Kid and his partners. The film was more or less a chance to put together a number of hot young actors, nicknamed "The Brat Pack," in a movie guaranteed to make money off teens and young adults. It did. Billy and his friends work for a cattle rancher who provides juvenile delinquents a place to reform. When the cattleman is murdered, the war is set off, and Billy and his friends are deputized as "regulators," an auxiliary police force with the power to hunt down their bosses' killers. In essence they are bounty hunters carrying badges, much the way Nodine did. They can be just as terrible, as shown in the roadhouse shootings, and soon they find that they themselves being hunted by Buckshot Roberts and John Kinney, notorious bounty hunters and killers, though not necessarily in that order.

As the two groups of bounty hunters maneuver for a kill, the regulators forget their commitment to justice as Kinney and those he is aligned with rebuff all calls for decency. The film twists inward: The law is bad, bounty hunters are bad. In effect they are the same thing. The rich and powerful dominate society, and the military bolsters these people. Only extreme violence committed by rogue psychopaths can protect society from this oppression. The only question not answered is, who protects society from degenerates like Billy? *Young Guns II* (1990) provided no answers, just more killings by the same psychopaths.

El Diablo (1990) was similar to *Unforgiven* in its revisionism, only this film came across as a parody. The story concerns a tenderfoot Boston teacher who lives his life through the Kid Durango dime novels he reads. When a bandit gang robs the town's bank and kidnaps the teacher's prize student, the teacher goes looking for Kid Durango to help him get her back. What he gets is a black bounty hunter, played by Louis Gossett, Jr., who routinely shoots the people he's after in the back and steals whatever he needs. The violence quotient reaches extreme levels, including Gossett shooting a number of other bounty hunters in the back. In one running gag, the tenderfoot shoots horse after horse after horse, and in the final gunfight kills the bandit leader with a number of shots into his back.

Both of these films have the specter of the dime novelist lurking in the background. As it turns out, Gossett is the model for Kid Durango, only his exploits have to be cleaned up. Back-shooting and robbery are not the stuff the West is made of. The idealized hero is compared to the "real" bounty hunter and we see the Western image is false. The dime novel writer attempts to uphold the code of the West, and initiates a showdown with the bandit leader, only to be shot down before even reaching for his gun. Aside from the broad humor, the message is clear: The West was a hard land filled with despicable people, few heroes, and honor comes second to survival.

Rio Diablo (1993) starred Kenny Rogers as a very greedy bounty hunter. The story is rather trite: A bandit gang raises hell in town, and interrupts a wedding, kidnapping the bride — almost the same as *Diablo*. Rogers isn't interested in taking the bridegroom along as he hunts the game, same as Gossett and the tenderfoot. The conclusions are similar, except for some unexpected brutality in the final scene of *Rio Diablo*. Interestingly, the level of greed among bounty hunters, expected to be shocking as they fight over the possessions of the people they kill, comes off comical.

Modern Manhunters

The portrayals of cinema bounty hunters during the last third of the twentieth century evolved much the way those of the West did, only in a different direction. As the Westerner went from a tough but honest breed to back-shooting and thieving, the modern bounty hunter's began with hard times and tough cases, to a more cosmopolitan man — and woman.

The Glove (1978) starred John Saxon as Kellough, a down-and-out bounty hunter hustling the streets for whatever jobs he can pick up. He gets an interesting assignment: Stop a huge black convict who is using a deadly glove to kill people who have wronged him. Since the amount being offered is not substantial considering the dangerous nature of the job, it's more a reflection of Kellough's poverty than his bravery. While Saxon is surrounded by a veteran supporting cast who keep things light, the troubling questions raised by the story remain. When a bounty hunter tracks a man for money, even though the hunted man is morally right if legally wrong, what does that make the bounty hunter? At what point does the bounty hunter exchange places with the man he's after and himself become a lawbreaker?

For a peace officer serving a warrant and bringing someone in, the question of innocent or guilt does not apply. This is for the judge and jury, as the cliché goes. But for a bounty hunter, discretion is the watchword and he is not required to bring anyone in. Like Corbett in *The Big Gundown* or McCord in *The Hired Gun*, a good conscience comes from doing what's right, not legal. Kellough could have let it go, but he steers away from the right by trying to stay legal, and in doing so eventually wins the final fight. But at what expense to himself?

The Hunter (1980) was Steve McQueen's last film, and was ironic because his first success came in a television show about a bounty hunter. The film wasn't a hit, and McQueen looked ill in many of the scenes; he was already suffering from the cancer which would take his life later that year. Playing a real-life bounty hunter named Ralph "Papa" Thorsen, McQueen hunted lowlifes and dirtbags, hardly heroic. In some instances he didn't even use a gun — he used a bean bag gun. Like in *The Glove*, the bounty hunter's job is unpleasant and not exactly lucrative. Many of Papa's cases are bottom of the barrel, or so routine that the payoff cannot justify the amount of time and money he has spent investigating.

Contrasted with Papa's bounty hunting are scenes of him at his pad. He is clearly a man out of his time — he cannot drive very skillfully, and prefers old toys and the like to the new things society has to offer. His home life is a happy one, if not a bit out of whack. Friends, ex-cons, people he doesn't even know play poker at his place until all hours of the night. His girlfriend is pregnant and he isn't very interested in being a father. Critics of the film contended that this disorganized but contented home life seems disconnected from Papa's bounty-hunting lifestyle, and in some ways minimizes the sense of danger and threat Papa faces when he's out tracking someone (Heilman, n.p.). Conversely, for a bounty hunter like Papa, this could be more real than not, however, because these men live by pursuing their prey — they won't eat if they don't catch. Keeping the rigors of the job from invading the home seems smart, not cute.

The "dead or alive" concept of bounty hunting, of tracking fugitives for a reward, has passed, though the "alive" part still remains. The '70s were tough times economically for many, and for true-to-life bounty hunters, most of the work came down to skip-tracing on people jumping bail, not finding wanted murderers as in the Old West. However, like the characters in soap operas who always have money and never seem to work, Hollywood began moving away from the reality of bounty hunting to a more chic image, starting with *Wanted: Dead or Alive* (1987).

Rutger Hauer plays Nick Randall, the great grandson of Josh Randall of the late '50s-early '60s television series *Wanted: Dead or Alive*. Josh was played by Steve McQueen, with a level of cool probably only surpassed by Elvis on stage. McQueen carried a sawed-off Winchester as his handgun, which was fascinating for most folks, if not ridiculous for gun enthusiasts who knew the weapon was not the most effectively used in that manner. This was a time when many TV cowboys carried special, larger weapons, which could mean any number of things. Perhaps the show wanted a different look, something to set it apart. Perhaps the star looked good carrying the thing. Or perhaps it was an unconscious desire of Americans to project an image of bigger and better weapons in a time of Soviet threat. Whatever the case, Josh hunted his bounty, more or less legally but in a way that showed everyone — including the Soviets — that he would get his man.

The connection between Nick and Josh is mentioned but then more or less forgotten. As the conservative temperament of the '80s under President Reagan continued to manifest itself in film, Nick has become something of a raconteur, able to shoot fast like his predecessor but also able to enjoy the fruits of his labor, in this case a nice yacht

Papa Thorsen (Steve McQueen) plays with his train in ***The Hunter***.

where he lives with his girlfriend. And so people know he's got it good, he keeps a fortified building full of weapons, a shooting range, even a workout center. But Nick has a secret: He was a CIA agent and they need him to track an Arab terrorist, now in the country blowing up things.

The bounty hunter has become hi-tech and wealthy, but when his country needs him he's there. Roger Ebert notes that these type films follow a certain pattern, where the hero is an ex-member of law enforcement or a government agency living a quiet life — until a powerful criminal strikes and the hero is the only one who can deal with him. The shift from tracking common criminals to terrorist types follows certain conservative tenets of the era: Sometimes the law is ineffective, or inefficient, and a hero must circumvent it to save it. Otherwise we will be destroyed by evil forces which don't follow our rules.

Midnight Run (1988) followed some of the same patterns noted by Ebert, plus adding some other film characteristics. Robert De Niro is Walsh, an ex-cop turned to bounty hunting after parting from the Chicago Police Department. He takes a job tracking a Mafia accountant who has embezzled millions of dollars from an Atlantic City mobster. As in many of the modern films regarding bounty hunters, the men quickly find their quarry, putting the police to shame. Walsh is no different. He hooks up the embezzler (Charles Grodin) and spends the rest of the movie trying to get him to Los Angeles to collect his cool $100,000. The film combines a number of genres, such as the buddy-film, the road film and character comedy.

Like Nick in *Wanted: Dead or Alive*, Walsh's background makes him an ideal candidate for this type of work. Similarly he's honest and willing to buck the Mafia to do what's right. Where Walsh bucks the cosmopolitan trend is in the cash department — Nick doesn't hurt for money, while Walsh has to borrow money from his ex-wife just to get back to Los Angeles. However, Walsh is collecting unheard of bounties, so it wouldn't be too long before he became a man with plenty of cash in his pocket.

Eastwood returned as a bounty hunter in 1989's *Pink Cadillac*. The movie was supposed to be funny and breezy, but the plot involved a white supremacist organization going after the woman Eastwood is trying to bring in. The pink Cadillac in the title has a quarter of a million dollars hidden inside, which is what the bad guys want. But Eastwood and the woman fall in love, so a showdown is coming. Such seriousness clashed with the various disguises Eastwood employs during the course of his job. Like so many other films which straddle the line between comedy and drama, the two cancel one another out, leaving something of an aftertaste for anyone trying to describe what they saw.

Pink Cadillac's low-budget counterpart was the aptly entitled *The Bounty Hunter* (1989). Robert Ginty, a B-movie Eastwood, co-wrote and directed the film, and starred as a bounty hunter who heads to a small Southern town to investigate the death of a close friend, an Indian who refused to sell his land to the oil company which wants to drill in the area. Ginty is immediately jacked up by the sheriff, who wants him to leave town. The bounty hunter has other ideas; he stays to protect his buddy's family, and eventually gets the goods on the sheriff, who was killing Indians who wouldn't sell out.

Relations between the Native Americans and the whites in the town are bad and growing worse by the day. The whites blame the Indians for being selfish — the oil company will bring much-needed jobs to a community hard-pressed for any work at all. The Indians believe it's another attack on their property and won't sell. Judging from what the Native Americans have accomplished, they don't need the jobs. Ginty and his friend's sister tour the reservation. The Indians work in a co-op and have everything they need: Medical center; crops; a legal defense fund which protects them; and a "Freedom School," *a la Billy Jack* (1971), where the children can learn about their culture.

Rather than take a balanced look at the conflict, Ginty merely employs violence and more violence to find his friend's killer. Both the whites and the Indians are placed in opposite corners, and just to make sure where the sympathy lies, stereotypes are pulled out faster and more often than Ginty's guns. The whites are fat and uncouth, and prone to violent, stupid and/or racist statements. In almost every restaurant or building, a Confederate flag adorns the wall. They carry shotguns and rifles everywhere, and what would the day be without drinking as much booze as possible?

The Native Americans fare no better. They will not sell their land, even if the sheriff kills them. They never provoke trouble, don't drink alcohol, and don't carry around firearms. Whenever the white man pushes them, they suffer proudly, waiting for someone like Ginty to rescue them. If it wasn't for the fact that Ginty wants to avenge his buddy, there would be no violence. However, if the tribe just turned the entire matter over to their distinguished legal team, there'd be no violence either. After Ginty brings down the sheriff, the Indians gather around the police station to show support. The camera pans up to the American flag—the rednecks might be living in the past but Native Americans aren't.

By 1993, television star Lorenzo Lamas had transitioned into direct-to-video action films, most with a martial arts flavor to them. *Bounty Trackers* was one of his more successful films, boasting a good story and above-average martial arts sequences, including a scene of nonstop action in a dojo where he goes to obtain information. Lamas plays Damone, a successful Boston bounty hunter in the Nick Randall mode. Handsome, intelligent, and not without means, Damone visits his brother in Los Angeles, only to find him under police protection for money laundering. A hit team kills the cops and his brother, so Damone begins tracking the killers—and killing the killers. The final showdown between the hulking Mathias Hues—leader of the hit team — and Lamas is well worth the wait.

Lamas' portrayal of a bounty hunter synthesized many of the qualities seen in other films. Tough, like Kellough, personable and friendly like Papa, breezy and debonair like Nick, but hard when necessary and always resourceful, like Walsh, the bounty hunter at the end of the century no longer has any qualms about tracking his prey. Issues of right and wrong subside into the larger issue of bringing the guilty to justice—and in many cases these lawbreakers are not ordinary criminals but terrorists or thugs with a political agenda.

Michael Dudikoff, whose big break into film came through the low-budget but quite popular *American Ninja* series* produced by Cannon during the '80s and early '90s, moved away from the *faux* martial arts when the production company went belly-up. However, his image wasn't broadened much, and he never made it into any big productions, even as supporting characters, though he remains a staple in cable and direct-to-video movies.

In *Moving Target* (1997), Dudikoff played Sonny, a bounty hunter who has to think more than fight. He walks a fine line between Russian gangsters looking to kill him after he's tricked into finding one of their men on an assignment. Sonny is followed, and the man he's tracking is killed after he leads assassins to him. The fight brewing between Russian gangsters from Russia and those living in the United States is then pushed to the edge, with each side wanting to know who killed their men and why.

Dudikoff sat out #3, returned for #4, then opted out for the last.

"Breaking point" would probably be a better title for the film, as each faction is pushed to desperate measures by Sonny's action. His wife Casey wants him to quit. She's pregnant and doesn't want him to be killed like his bounty hunter–father was years before. She lays down an ultimatum and he accepts it, only he keeps up his man-tracking without her knowing. Sonny's best friend's Jake and "Rac," both of whom are cops, agree with Casey, so keeping up the lie is becoming more difficult for him with each passing day.

The Russians have a war coming, and the only way to stop it is by finding out who killed the man in Sonny's custody. The head of the American Russian family gives him a few days to find the killer; the man's son keeps trying to stop Sonny, usually by having his partners beat him up. Add to this the police pressure on Rac to bring Sonny in for the killing of the man in his custody. When Sonny's wife leaves him, and Rac is killed helping him, the bounty hunter's life hits rock bottom.

Moving Target is a throwback to *The Hunter* in the sense that the life Sonny leads is not only unpleasant, it's not very lucrative. Even when Sonny finds his prey, sometimes he has to pay for information, and if the man gets away, he's out the cash and bail. The opening sequence shows what Sonny has to work with — and it makes the normal person wonder, "Why?" He's given the wrong address and a dominatrix opens the door. He has to pay her to get the bail jumper next door to open his door — then has to fight the guy, only to have two guys he busted years before coming after him.

He fights these guys across the rooftop in between dodging the shots they fire at him. Finally he wins out and takes all three men in to the police station in the back of a raggedy truck on its last legs. His wife Casey teaches computer classes and drives a new Jeep Cherokee. Somewhere, somehow, Sonny's priorities are messed up. Everyone around him is doing fine, but he seems content to stay mired in work that's dangerous and not worth the financial effort.

And then of course, there's the pain and hurt involved. Everyone connected to Sonny's case is shot, killed, beaten, lied to and pretty much jerked around. And for what? The man Sonny was tracking was scum; the persons Sonny worked for were scum; and the people who killed Sonny's assignment were scum. Sonny was fooled into taking the job by scum — an old couple posing as the man's grieving parents; Sonny fooled Casey by lying about what he was doing, and exposed his friends to violence by not telling them what was really going on with his case. Sonny eventually proves who killed the gangster and clears himself of all charges, but by this time there's no upside to his profession. The only way to go is down.

In the same year, Dudikoff starred in *Bounty Hunters*, which provides a somewhat different look at the profession than did *Moving Target*. Jersey Bellini is a man-tracker with state-of-the-art equipment. Unlike Sonny, who drives a truck he appears to have bought from a junkyard, Jersey has a huge black van, filled with every type of weapon imaginable, from pump-riot shotguns to machine-guns to every model of semi-auto pistols.

In the opening scene, Jersey goes after an arsonist who has skipped bail and is living as a survivalist in the woods. Jersey immediately spots a trip wire that the fugitive has lain for any unwanted company, but sets off another device which warns of his presence. During their shootout, the arsonist uses a homemade flamethrower. Jersey runs away, only to come back in his van and ram the man's trailer. As the man reaches for a gun, Jersey calmly tells him that he can reload or he can reconsider.

The bounty hunter is shown here to be well-trained, well-equipped and hard to beat. However, in the next sequence, at the police station, where Jersey is bringing his suspect, two handcuffed prisoners attack the police, and Jersey and his soon-to-be partner BB, a female bounty hunter, fight them off. But in beating two handcuffed men, the pair look amateurish and unprofessional. This distinction of specialists versus jokers carries on throughout the narrative, as BB and Jersey have to team up to take down a Mafioso who has kidnapped a young boy who is friends with Jersey, holding him hostage in return for a prostitute the two had rescued from him.

They find the prostitute in the trunk of a stolen car hidden in a chop shop as they track a fugitive thief. After fighting off an entire army of goons and mechanics, Jersey gets the thief into his van, along with BB, and head for the police station. Along the way they stop to talk about some personal problems they're having working with one another, and the criminal waltzes right out the van doors. One minute determined pros, the next clowns who don't have the sense to close the doors where they have a prisoner waiting to be taken to jail.

Jersey and BB return to the chop shop figuring the thief will go there to get back the car he stole. Instead they find the prostitute, who saw the Mafioso kill a man. They take her away so the killers can't get her — good move. Then decide to protect her themselves until they can figure out what to do with her — questionable move. The prostitute goes back with BB to her house, while Jersey goes to his, and contents himself with building little traps to keep out burglars — bad move. The killers immediately find the car thief, something Jersey and BB couldn't do, and he tells them about Jersey being after him. They attack both of them, though the prostitute makes her escape — good for her but really bad for the boy who hangs out at Jersey's.

Of course, Jersey and BB win the day, but any reasonable viewer has to ask, "How?" Alternating between Starsky & Hutch and Laurel & Hardy, they find their men — or women — but they can't hang onto them. Of course, much of this is built into the old narrative: the teaming of a male and female who feel an attraction but can't admit it because something's happened in the past between them. She's punctilious — he's laid-back. She tracks her assignments carefully — he relies on gut instinct.

The schism here extends to Jersey's personal life. Thousands of dollars of equipment in his van, a nice house, but a bill collector calling him about owing some money? Tons of guns but sometimes he enters warehouses filled with criminals carrying nothing but a can of tear gas? The difference between Jersey and Sonny is the difference between hindsight and foresight. Both Jersey and Sonny like the job, but Jersey only looks ahead to his next job. Sonny knows his world is closing in — his wife is going to leave him and his best friends are being pressured into arresting him. Jersey looks back at what he's done and only wants to get even bigger assignments; the fact that's he's been lit on fire, beat up, almost shot repeatedly, and has endangered the life of a little boy, fades with the prospect of his next job. Sonny goes through the same experience and realizes the end has to come, sooner rather than later, if he's going to keep his family.

In *Bounty Hunters 2: Hardball*, Dudikoff returns as Jersey, as does BB, only the positions have reversed. Jersey's madly in love with BB and they're living together — yet she's the one having second thoughts about the relationship. In the opening sequence, their differences are played up once again: Bass, the fugitive they're after, is worth 20 grand. But he's the getaway driver of a jewelry heist about to go down. BB wants to break up the robbery, Jersey wants to take Bass and be on their way. BB busts the robbers and Jersey gets Bass. They get their money but BB believes Jersey to be unreliable, so she leaves him.

Once again they're working separately, only they run afoul of the gang that controls the jewel thieves, who now want Jersey dead. The gang hires a hitman to kill Jersey; he blows up his house, but Jersey walks away, angry and broke. He goes after the gang and BB throws in with him. It takes the two a while to get to who's doing what and where, but when they finally pinpoint the gang's whereabouts, and more explosions follow until everyone is taken care of. Well, almost everyone.

Bounty Hunters 2 is so similar to *Bounty Hunters* as to be little more than a mere reworking of a few minor points in the narrative. In both films Jersey runs afoul of Mafioso types upset with him for interfering in their business. They try to kill him. They fail. Jersey and BB put aside whatever differences they are having at the time to team up and foil the criminals. At the end, after winning the fight, the two partners are reunited. Something is usually blown up or burning before the end credits. A romantic may say it's Jersey and BB's passion expressed symbolically. A cynic might demur; perhaps it's the logic behind the film. In any case, the same actors, director, writers and production company returned to the well, only once to often.

The theme of the expert versus amateur "bounty hunter" continues into this film, only no pro emerges this time. In the opening sequence, Jersey reminds BB they are not police officers—the bank robbery is not their concern. Taking Bass is their job; once they call in and report the crime, they should not interfere. BB actually breaks into an armed robbery—*in progress*! Of course, even though four robbers have guns, they put their guns down when BB tells them to. Jersey then drives by his partner as she's getting detained by the police with Bass in the back of the getaway truck and waves.

Later, the hitman who blew up Jersey's house plants a bomb under his black van. The bounty hunter hooks him up and locks him inside. They go for a drive—Jersey knowing the bomb is ticking. He tells the hitman to give him the information he needs about the Mafioso; the man does and then Jersey jumps out of the van and lets it blow up, killing his prisoner. Not that murdering a murderer means all that much but what about the money the fugitive was worth? A few scenes before Jersey was broke, and now he's killed a good bounty and wrecked the only piece of property he had left.

At the film's climax, Jersey is being held in a warehouse, where he is beaten to within an inch of his life by the Mafiosos. But being the types of men they are, they double-cross each other, giving Jersey a chance to escape. After much killing and mayhem (and of course explosions), Jersey gets out with the help of BB. The only gangster left, the most vile and sadistic, attacks Jersey, yet after beating him up, Jersey just leaves him and walks off with BB! Arm and arm they're a team again, but the worst killer of all is right behind them — as well as whatever reward he's worth. When BB tells him she finds it hard to believe that Jersey was once a Navy SEAL, she's not the only one.

In *Moving Target*, Sonny was a man at the end of a way of life; it might have taken a while for him to break away completely but he had to, if he was to keep his family. In *Bounty Hunters*, Jersey was a man who loved the job and didn't give a lot of thought to the future. He liked working alone and arming his house with all kinds of gadgets to stop people from breaking in. In *Bounty Hunters 2*, the gadgets were still armed, only they didn't stop the hitman from planting bombs everywhere around the home and then blowing it up. The only significant changes are Jersey's feelings for BB and the fact that, by this point, neither bounty hunter has any common sense.

That all three films were completed in the same year is a little ironic. As the real-life experiences of bounty hunters are being documented on cable television in popular reality-type shows, these films attempted to do the same. But by showcasing the bounty hunters as having romantic, unrealistic, mega-action-oriented lives, the stories actually debunked them, making their existence appear shallow, unprofitable and a dead end. One character realized it. One had no clue.

Future Bounty Hunters

Science fiction films have often boasted bounty hunters, either as lead or secondary characters. In George Lucas's *Star Wars* films, Han Solo, played by Harrison Ford, is being tracked through the galaxy by Boba Fett, purportedly a veteran of the Clone Wars and quite deadly. We don't see Fett until the end of Episode Five, *The Empire Strikes Back* (1980), when Darth Vader hands Solo over to him. In *Return of the Jedi* (1983), Solo is rescued by his friends, and Fett is killed. Almost 20 years later Lucas began the saga from the beginning, starting with Episode One. In the following film, Episode Two, we meet Boba's father Jango Fett, who is working with shady characters connected to the emperor-to-be. Thousands of warriors have been cloned, all using his likeness, and his ability as a fighter cannot be questioned. He battles Jedi Knight Obi Wan Kenobi to a draw, only to be later killed in the final scenes, ironically enough, during an attack by the clone warriors who look like him.

The interesting aspect of bounty hunting in Lucas' vision of what is to come is that the mores of the past now inhabit the future. No police are seen. Only storm troopers. Every planet runs things the way they want. On some, like Annakin Skywalker's, slavery is an acceptable practice. In the planet city where the senate convenes, drugs are sold in the open. Like the bounty man of the Old West, someone has to help clean up the frontier, in this case the various worlds of outer space. Whether intentional or not, both the Republic and the Empire in many ways seem quite libertarian when it comes to the law: if someone commits a crime or wrongs someone, it is perfectly acceptable to hire a bounty hunter to either kill him or bring him back. Storm troopers are not involved in such disputes. Taxes are paid for the maintenance of the military and that seems to be all. Lando Calrissian, Solo's buddy, is a wanted man running a mining operation. Vader is not concerned with the charges against him, only that he has not paid his taxes. In such an atmosphere, bounty hunters would not just be successful, they would thrive.

Logan's Run (1976) posits a future significantly different than that of Lucas. In the twenty-third century, people live a carefree life in a magnificent domed city. No one wants for anything—and hedonism is the rule, not the exception. Unfortunately for the people in this paradise, life is limited to 30 years, at which time they are destroyed. They have a biological clock in their hand which the master computer monitors. When their time is up, they are placed upon a carousel and tossed high in the air. Supposedly they are reborn, and few question it. Those who do become "runners"—that is, they attempt to escape the city. Bounty hunters called "Sandmen" track and destroy them. When the computer assigns Logan the task of breaking the runner's network, it adds four years to his life span, thereby making death imminent. He infiltrates the underground but, realizing the computer will not restore his years, escapes with a girl he meets in the network.

If the bounty hunters of Lucas' worlds are libertarian, the Sandmen are definitely the Marxist equivalent. Everything is provided to everyone in society, and the Sandmen are like the Party elite—getting even better treatment. Revelry runs 24/7. Feel like sex? Just input the girl (or guy) you want into the computer and they appear. The Sandmen never question their mission. With no God above, no Satan below, the here and now is all that matters. In fact, Logan is probably the only Sandman who questions what happens to the people on the carousel. They are supposed to be reborn and no one thinks twice about it but him. The fact that a computer can kill thousands of people each year to run society is no different than Stalin killing millions of people to do the same thing; the scale is merely grander in the latter case.

Logan escapes the city, and eventually brings down the computer. The free ride is over, people may live normal life spans, and they are amazed to see an old man, played by Peter Ustinov. On the surface, *Logan's Run* looks at one way a society imprisons itself once the world around it falls apart. However, it can also be viewed as the way a society preserves itself during the same trying times. The happy ending circumvents many unhappy questions: How do people fend for themselves when they don't know what to do? Is it right for one man (Logan) to decide for everyone that normal life spans are better than limited life spans when all the tradeoffs are considered? One characteristic that Sandmen share with other bounty hunters is a certain confidence in their abilities and decisions. It never occurs to Logan that some might like things the way they are. He makes the decision for them, which is the prerogative of the Sandmen.

Blade Runner (1982) is a deep film, moving in so many ways, that examines what it's like to be human, and to be a human who hunts others for a living. A box office flop when first released, it has gained cult-like status in the years since, and is consistently listed in various top film lists. Harrison Ford plays Deckard, a bounty hunter in 2019, hired by the police to track and kill androids, also called replicants, who are hiding in San Francisco. Because of problems with replicants in the past, they are banned from Earth. Deckard finds and eliminates the replicants one by one, only to have the tables turned when Batty, hardcore and combat-trained, hunts him through an aged, ragged apartment building.

The super-strong androids have only four years to live. Like the humans in *Logan's*

People must ride the "carousel" to be reborn after they reach 30 years of age in ***Logan's Run.***

Run, their span of existence is arbitrarily set by the overlords—in this case Cybercore, the corporation who built them. When Deckard falls in love with Rachel, a prototype replicant with a "normal" life span, things become complicated. Someday he might have to terminate her as well. The film was based on Philip K. Dick's *Do Androids Dream of Electric Sheep*, but unlike the novel, which deals with the nature of reality, *Blade Runner* examines the notion of sentience. The replicants look, act, feel human. They have false, implanted memories to give them some grounding in reality and, perhaps most importantly of all, they want a chance to live longer, something uniquely human.

As Batty taunts Deckard, busting him up, tossing the bounty hunter across the rooms and through the walls, we understand the driving force behind the replicant's killing spree. Like any other creature, Batty and the others use violence to survive. Even Batty killing his creator can be seen as a way to stop the man from making more androids. The themes of life, death and what it all means permeate the story, and Batty's poignant speech while dying in the rain is particularly powerful. With Deckard hanging off the building's edge, Batty lifts Deckard to safety, affirming life even as he dies.

The bounty hunter lives and hunts in a dystopic nightmare, polluted, and populated by those too poor to leave Earth for the off-world colonies. The streets are black, wet and steaming. Shadows alternate with bright, sourceless lights. Flying billboards and trash can bonfires compete for attention. The visuals are a seamless meld of science fiction and film

Logan (Michael York) and Jenny Agutter confront some less than friendly natives outside the city in *Logan's Run*. Is trading a short life in paradise for a normal life of hardship a good deal?

noir. As Deckard walks these streets, he takes the form of a '40s detective, rooting out evil, surrounded by corruption, yet seeking the truth. But what is the truth? And does he really want to know?

Deckard completes his mission, but as Batty saves him from death at the last moment, he has much to think about. The world is a poisoned place, not from replicants but rather from humans. Crime pays, again, not for replicants but humans. The androids have been manufactured to do the dirty work, from fighting their wars to serving as prostitutes. Human's steal and kill without purpose, and compassion died with the environment. The androids take care of one another, watch each other's backs, fall in love, even grieve.

Deckard returns to his apartment, where he finds Rachel asleep. He also finds an origami unicorn left by Gaff, a police detective attached to his case. In the director's cut of the film, Deckard had earlier dreamed of a unicorn. By Gaff leaving the origami figure, it is clear that the police know of Deckard's dreams, and his memories, pointing to the fact that he himself is an android. The argument over Deckard's humanity was finally confirmed by director Ridley Scott, who said during an interview in the magazine "The Blade Cut" that the bounty hunter was supposed to be a replicant. This places Deckard in the even more unenviable position of having killed his own kind. Escaping with Rachel, he has but a four-year life span, while hers continues indefinitely.

The common denominator among all these private law enforcers is their independent nature. These men, and now women, aren't bound by rules and regulations like the police, but rather fight for justice in their own way, and sometimes that way means operating just outside the bounds of law. Some, like the characters in Clint Eastwood's Westerns, are nothing more than criminals themselves. Others are more honest than the police, and are the only one's a victim can turn to when in need. Whichever the case, the profession continues to this day, and shows no sign of disappearing any time soon.

Deckard (Harrison Ford) tracks his prey through the nightmarish environs of a future Los Angeles in *Blade Runner*.

Sources

Brandt, James. *What Defines Human?* Bladerunnerinsight.com. 2000 *www.br*-insight.com/display.php?contents=article.009&cat=ANALYSI.

Cavagna, Carlo. *Blade Runner*. Aboutfilm.com. 2000 *www.br*-insight.com/display.php?contents=article.011&cat=ANALYSI.

Ebert, Roger. *Wanted: Dead or Alive*. Rogerebert.suntimes.com. 1-16-87 http://rogerebert.suntimes.com/apps/pbcs.dll/article?AID=/19870116/REV.

Gramstad. Thomas. *Humans and Technology, What Separates Them?* Bladerunnerinsight.com. 2000. *www.br-* insight.com/display.php?contents=article.010&cat=ANALYSI.

Harrington, Richard. *Wanted: Dead or Alive*. Washington Post. 1–17–87 www.washingtonpost.com/wp-srv/style/longterm/movies/videos/want.

Heilman, Jeremy. *The Hunter*. Apolloguide.com. http://apolloguide.com/mov_fullrev.asp?CID=3434&Specific=4134.

Hinson, Hal. *Midnight Run. Washington Post.* 7-20-88 *www.washingtonpost.com./wp-srv/style/longterm/movies/videos/midn.*

Johnson, Gary. *Thirty Great Westerns*. imagesjournal.com. http://imagesjournal.com/issue10/infocus/ridelonesome.html.

McLaglen, Andrew. *Chisum Interview*. The Western Channel. 5-16-2005.

Maloney, Frank. *Blade Runner*. IMDB Review. 1992 http://imdb.com/REVIEWS/15/1524.

Oscar Movies Review. *Logan's Run*. www.geocities.com/oscarmovs/logansrun.html.

Watson, Stephanie. *The History of Bounty Hunting*. howstuffworks.com. http://money.howstuffworks.com/bounty-hunting6.html.

VIII

Film Noir, Feminism and Private Heat

— *It's heavy. What is it?*
— *The stuff that dreams are made of.**

Like the bounty hunter, the private eye is an adjunct to law enforcement, helping out the cop on the street or the detective stuck at the station buried under reams of paperwork. During the '30s, some private eyes were sophisticated, like Philo Vance, whose run of mysteries began in the late '20s and ran 18 years, with different actors playing Vance. Often it was up to them to solve a crime or murder because the police were inept. These detectives were often dilettantes, moonlighting or dabbling in crimefighting while clad in tuxedos in between parties and European vacations. The *Thin Man* series focused on Nick and Nora, detectives whose cases sometimes bordered on screwball comedy.

With an influx of foreign directors, a world at war, horrors and death on a scale never before witnessed by any generations, and men in battle wondering what their wives and sweethearts were doing back home, the look of many films changed during the '40s, and a certain style became apparent: film noir. From the French word meaning dark or black, these films used deep shadows, night shooting, claustrophobic settings and unusual camera angles to accent anxiety or subversion. Within the police and detective narratives, the night and the shadows were indicative of the characters in the films: women whose hearts were in total eclipse, and men who found themselves both prey to these woman and victims of a world where traditional moral values left them ill-prepared to survive.†

Out of the Past (1947) is a good example, teaming Robert Mitchum with Kirk Douglas for the first time. Mitchum is Jeff Bailey, a tough but squared-away private investigator who takes a job from a gangster named Sterling, played by Douglas: find his girlfriend Kathie, who ran off with 40 grand of the crook's money. Bailey tracks the woman to Mexico, only to fall in love with her himself. He tells the gangster he lost her; now the two live on the West Coast, keeping a low profile, until they're spotted by Bailey's partner. The man follows Kathie, hoping for a cut of the money she grabbed from Sterling. He and Bailey fight, but Kathie shoots the man, killing him. They bury him deep in the woods, but Kathie

---

**Detective Polhaus (Ward Bond) and Sam Spade (Humphrey Bogart) at the conclusion of* The Maltese Falcon.
†*While a significant number of these films followed detectives or police, the style crossed genres, appearing in dramas, melodramas, even Westerns.*

takes off again — and Bailey finds that she did, indeed, steal the money. Bailey ends up in a small mountain town where he buys a service station. Just as his life begins turning around, Sterling reappears, and Bailey knows his life is on the line.

The key to survival is Kathie. Though Bailey is a straight shooter and plays things right, Sterling is an urbane sleaze with no problem killing anyone who crosses him. The two men couldn't be more different. But between them stands Kathie — and that's Bailey's ace in the hole. He realizes she is worse than Sterling could ever be, but he doesn't seem to fathom it. She shot Bailey's partner without hesitation or even blinking. When Bailey catches her across the border, she turns the tables on him, seducing him on the beach, surrounded by a huge fishing net, like a spider in her web. What Bailey didn't know then he certainly knows now: The woman is a psychopath who ensnared him, not the other way around. Burying his partner merely joined the two in murder — and the police would never believe she killed him, not alone anyway.

When Sterling gives him a new job to take care of, to steal some incriminating IRS documents, Bailey knows it's a set-up. His only chance is to do it, stay a step ahead of Sterling's scheme, and hope the cops get him — or to then take care of the gangster himself. Bailey survives Sterling's conniving; when he returns to Sterling, Kathie kills him. But Bailey still can't get by her. She kills him, too, as he drives toward a police roadblock, hoping to turn her in.

Jane Greer, who plays Kathie, has the face of an angel and the soul of Lucifer. Motivated only by money, she plays Sterling's own greed against him, then immediately sizes up Bailey, becoming the victim in need of rescue. After shooting Sterling, she shoots Bailey not in the chest but in the groin to make him pay for his double-cross. For the honest detective, his destiny came calling, as it were, out of the past.

Of all the films noir, those associated with novelist Raymond Chandler are perhaps the best, be they his Philip Marlowe detective stories adapted to the screen by others, like Jules Furthman and William Faulkner, or those written by Chandler directly for the screen, like his Oscar-nominated script for *The Blue Dahlia* (1946). In this film, Alan Ladd stars as Jimmy Morrison, a flyer whose cheating wife is murdered. Police suspect him for obvious reasons, but Morrison isn't the typical guy; he investigates the killing himself, taking and giving a number of beatings in the process. Once again teamed with William Bendix and Veronica Lake, Ladd exemplifies the tough guy who has to maneuver the mean streets with a pointless agenda: In this instance, solve the murder of his no-good wife. It's been said that the film's title inspired the media calling Elizabeth Short "The Black Dahlia." The film had been released in 1946, just months before her murder.

One thing is certain, the noir detectives had tough chins and hard fists, and were for the most part honest, particularly Marlowe, Chandler's L.A. knight who was surrounded by crooked cops and sleazy clients but never let any of it rub off on him. Many of these men *were* cops, but being on the take was the one line they wouldn't cross. They headed out on their own. The money may or may not be better, but it was theirs. As for a pension, well, they had to survive to get it, and the odds of that were not good.

One of the first noirs came from John Huston, who adapted the Dashiell Hammett novel *The Maltese Falcon* as his 1941 directorial debut, with Humphrey Bogart starring as Sam Spade, a cynical detective who is hired by a Brigid O'Shaughnessy to free her sister from an unwanted suitor. Spade sends his partner Miles Archer to handle the job, but he's murdered. Spade spends the rest of the film trying to catch the killers, all the while helping Brigid retrieve an ancient treasure shaped as a black falcon. As the detective worms his way out of a number of jams, he obtains the Falcon, only to find it a fake.

Spade is a jaded man, not prone to sentimentality. Even after his partner is murdered, he holds back information from the police, merely telling them they were working a case. He doesn't identify his client, and when he confronts Brigid, she tells him that *her* unwanted suitor probably killed Archer. But the suitor is dead, too. Who killed *him*? Spade runs across a number of other people looking for the Falcon, either trying to kill him, or buy him off. Though Spade plays fast and loose with the law, he keeps them updated, and always stays a step ahead. It's not so much that the police are a problem as much as they are a distraction: Spade will take care of the situations he faces himself. He works alone and likes it that way. He also wants the money the Falcon is worth, but there's another motive: his partner's death. As he tells Brigid after calling the police to take her away for murdering Archer, it's his partner, and it's his responsibility to do something about it.

Spade is clearly an anti-hero: He drinks like a fish, and hard liquor at that. He forces Brigid to give him all her money, and takes pleasure in pushing people around or humiliating them. If he can find the Falcon and make some serious cash, so be it. He gets down in the dirt and partners up with a group of people so mercenary to almost be caricatures of greed. One man is so fat, the gluttony hangs off him like pork from a meat hook. The other's face is nervous and shifty, like a rat trapped in a corner by an alley cat. Even Brigid, who says she loves Spade, in many scenes is surrounded by prison-like evocations, whether it's her striped clothes, furniture, even light cutting through the window blinds (Cinebooks, n.p.). Considering she's a double murderer, the ambience is certainly appropriate, foreshadowing what Spade will do once he solves the case.

James M. Cain's works personified the words *hard-boiled*. His characters were nasty and treacherous. If Marlowe was an honest Joe, and Spade straddled the middle ground, Cain's protagonists sat at the other end, mired in their own slime, none more so than those in *Double Indemnity* (1944). The film follows Walter Neff (*Huff* in Cain's novel), an insurance salesman who is persuaded by the wife of a client, Phyllis Dietrichson, to help her murder her husband so as to collect on an accident policy which Neff and Dietrichson obtain unbeknownst to the victim. The husband is killed and Neff makes it appear as if he fell from a moving train. Though the plan initially succeeds, it eventually unravels as the insurance company's private investigator Keyes digs into the incident, forcing the two killers to turn on one another, which they do with startling rapidity and brutality.

Double Indemnity exemplified the "ultra–femme fatale," where her scheming and tawdry wickedness is interesting not only for its riveting narrative content but for its subtextual reenactment of the Oedipal Complex and its ultimate subordination of Woman to the Patriarchal social order. The film also lends itself to conventional analysis: Neff and Dietrichson become mirror images of one another in their cupidity and willingness to kill, commented upon by the film-novel's title — "doubles" in their moral dissipation whose ultimate indemnification is death. Detective Keyes, though a moral force, is so callused by the nature of his work as to be a direct reflection of the seedy environs through which he navigates, ferreting out scam artists and liars to the point of completely dehumanizing himself. However, feminist views of the narrative's Patriarchal transgressions and Oedipal trajectory are even more fascinating.

Emblematic of the Law, Keyes functions as the seeker of Truth, the repository of moral values. Neff's friend, he also serves as his symbolic Father, that which gives Neff a sense of identity. To succeed in the murder-insurance scam equates to Neff succeeding the Father, in this case outwitting Keyes. If sexual repression is the key to gaining entry into the symbolic realm of Patriarchy, then Neff's sexual relations with Phyllis Dietrichson squarely posits him outside its bounds.

For her part, Dietrichson is treacherous and lying, one who not only kills her husband, but also his first wife in order to marry him, and perhaps some children when she was a nurse. Using her sexuality as a weapon, she is both physically dangerous and psychologically deadly. As a living, breathing reminder of "lack," that is, her missing penis, which serves to threaten the male with symbolic castration, she must be either fetishized, to make her sight pleasurable, or investigated and punished, to assuage the male fear.

Hence, when first meeting Neff, she is observed in a bath towel; later, in coming down the stairs, the camera follows her legs, particularly her gold anklet, establishing an "excess" of eroticism. Later, when she meets Neff at his apartment and they consummate their illicit relationship while planning her husband's murder, both offend the male social order, though after the homicide only Dietrichson is investigated.

To make the murder appear to be an accident, Mr. Dietrichson is killed first; then Neff takes Dietrichson's place on the train. In assuming the role of the husband, he also becomes the symbolic father of Dietrichson's stepdaughter, Lola, sacrilegiously reconstituting the family unit which he and Dietrichson had destroyed. Claire Johnston, in her essay on *Double Indemnity*, notes,

> In destroying the family unit, in testing the Law, Neff has entered an impossible family, a family explicitly based on a sacrificial murder, and thus socially censored [Johnston, p. 108].

When Neff dates Lola to distract her from her suspicions of Dietrichson, it becomes both a symbolic incest and a paternal act — the care of the "daughter," further commenting on the baseness of this "other" family.

Neff (Fred MacMurray) and Mrs. Dietrichson (Barbara Stanwyck) plot murder in *Double Indemnity*. Note how Dietrichson's light clothing belies her dark intentions, one of the ironies of film noir.

Though Detective Keyes "knows" that Dietrichson is guilty, and that she has an accomplice, he is blindsided by the revelation of Neff's involvement, the "Father" never suspecting the "Son." When Neff and Mrs. Dietrichson shoot each other, and the dying Neff makes his confession on the company Dictaphone, the sins against Patriarchy have been rectified, the offenders punished with death, and Lola and her paramour Nino, whose heterosexual relationship is central to the social order, are remanded into the custody and protection of Keyes, thereby reestablishing the patriarchal balance.

In Cain's novella, Neff (Huff) and Dietrichson do not die at each other's hands, though the latter does make an attempt to kill the former. Instead, they are allowed to "escape," which in a sense strengthens Johnston's (and other feminists') reading. Neff, having confessed to Keyes, is banished by the Father — as is Dietrichson — into the "wilderness," allowing them to leave on a cruise ship to Mexico, where, as Neff (Huff) realizes, the omniscient Keyes knew they would have no choice but suicide.

The film's original ending had Keyes watching as Neff was brought into the gas chamber. Wilder has said that it is among the best and most powerful work he has done; unfortunately the footage was thought to be too harsh, too realistic, and so it remains in the Paramount vault to this day. Too bad.

The following year, Cain's *Mildred Pierce* was adapted for the screen. It combined a melodrama with a hard noir murder mystery in which the cops have to break down the title character to find out just what happened. Joan Crawford plays Mildred, a simple but persevering woman who rises in the "man's world" of business, only to be toppled by those closest to her — primarily another woman. In Michael Curtiz's film version, Mildred still meets with a similar fate, only this time at the hands of men, underscoring a rather overdetermined message that it is best for women to desire little or nothing lest they risk punishment from a male-dominated society, like Mildred did.

As a happily married *wife* and *mother*, Mildred Pierce seems more like Suzy Homemaker than the shrewd businesswoman she will eventually become. Her wants are general and benign: success for her husband, the best of all things for the children. She even goes so far as to tell the detective investigating her second husband Monte's murder that she was always happiest "in the kitchen." Yet, there's the catch: She is really *mother* then *wife*, her relationship with older daughter Veda becoming an unnatural barrier between her and her husbands — unnatural to the extent that if Veda was a boy, it might appear incestuous. Hence, by placing her children first, ahead of her husband(s), Mildred commits her first transgression against the Patriarchal order.

Later, after her split with first husband Bert, she changes, and begins to "want" for her own success, no longer content with the kind of life she once led. Reserved yet persistent, Mildred longs for a different, better life, as much for herself as for Veda, as well as for an identity of her own. The more she does, the more she learns ... the more she experiences, the more she wants to do. In essence, she becomes ambitious, a trait highly regarded in men but considered unbecoming, even dangerous in women.

However, if in her rise to successful entrepreneur Mildred repeatedly violates the male social order, among her most telling "offenses" occurs at home, while still married to Bert. Just after his housing development goes under and their economic prospects worsen, Mildred nags him to get a job, directly affronting his status as breadwinner. Bert takes "solace" from the widow Biederhoff, which sparks a fight between him and Mildred. Rather than accept her husband's infidelities, which are the sole purview of the male, she sends him packing, in effect taking the place of the father, or Man, whom she has now overthrown.

As Mildred scrambles to find work, she must also fend off the unwanted advances of Wally, Bert's ex-business partner. This incident underscores the difference between novel and film, pointing up the importance of Patriarchy in the latter. In Cain's work, Mildred gives in to Wally almost immediately after Bert leaves, with no negative consequences. In fact, she goes on to get the job at the diner, which leads to her big business break.

However, in Curtiz's version, Mildred is initially the "good girl." She resists Wally's advances but later gives herself to Monty, a wealthy ne'er-do-well who serves as the counterpart to the widow Biederhoff. Hence, both Bert and Mildred become mirror images of one another, each in like relationships, seeking comfort and satisfaction outside the bounds of marriage. Yet it is Mildred's adultery which draws the immediate sanction, for when she spends the weekend with Monty at his beach house, her younger daughter Kay is suddenly stricken with pneumonia.

The irony of Kay's death is compounded by the involvement of the widow Biederhoff.* In the novel she is never seen, only referred to, usually as Bert's "friend." In the film, the ill Kay is sheltered in her house, where the widow has obviously taken great pains to care for the young girl. Biederhoff is now transformed, acquiring the characteristics of a caring and decent person, not a home-wrecker, an image directly contrasted with Mildred's "friend," the devil-may-care Monty, who lightly dismisses Kay's death with a casual "sorry" upon seeing Mildred again at the opening of her restaurant.

Thus, while Kay lays dying and Bert reaches a momentary personal (not financial) zenith as the figurative "head of the house," surrounded by wife, *mistress* and children, Mildred drops to her nadir, and must stand in the unpleasant light of her own iniquity. Had she been less headstrong; had she been a dutiful wife who overlooked her husband's philandering; had she spent less time developing her business; had she not broken her marriage vows—she might have noticed that Kay was ill; might have taken her to the doctor sooner; might have prevented her daughter's death. She becomes a pathetic figure, personally indebted to the "good widow" who broke up her marriage but tried to save her daughter, while socially (sexually) reliant on a rakish consort who increasingly uses her for her money.

Mildred quickly rebounds from Kay's death by concentrating on the restaurant. Soon it is a success, and she expands it, fully entering the world of business, a domain to this point dominated by men. If any man can be president, any woman can be the president of her own company, and Mildred proves it, discarding the parasitic Monty in the process. Yet, like the wound of the Fisher King, her first offense against Patriarchy continues to plague her, for Mildred's usurpation of the father's role results in a convoluted relationship with the daughter.

The hallmark of the Cain protagonist is to achieve what they covet, only to have it all blow up and unravel before their very eyes. In Veda's struggles for financial independence, she becomes a twisted version of the mother, going from bad to worse, first enlisting Wally's aid in the sleazy shakedown of a wealthy Hollywood movie producer, then leaving home to sing in Wally's bar. As Mildred rises to the pinnacle of financial success, Veda sinks into depravity, and Mildred, like Orpheus, must descend in order to save her.

Thus, to bring her wayward daughter back, Mildred enters into a marriage of convenience with Monty, whom Veda adores. She gives Monty a cut of the business, and when Veda returns home, daughter and stepfather become lovers, forming an illegitimate reconstitution

---

**She is in fact no widow at all, with Bert eventually finding out that she has a husband off somewhere else.*

of the family unit. They conspire against Mildred, in league with Wally, and bankrupt Mildred; in a twist on the legend, Mildred remains in "Hades," having *apparently* murdered Monty, while it is Veda who ascends out — if only temporarily.

Hauled in by the police for questioning, Mildred confesses to killing Monty, but the detective knows better, and forces her to tell the truth. She implicates Veda, whom the police had already captured trying to flee the country. Now broken, Mildred is reunited with Bert and the male social order is restored, the sin against the Father being avenged by the daughter while the Truth is established before the Male representatives of the Law.

At the time of *Mildred Pierce*'s filming, the war was winding down, and the countless thousands of women who had taken up the slack for their men in uniform by building tanks and planes and ships had to be "repatriated" to the home so that men could reclaim these jobs. In its not-so-subtle message about the dangers of overstepping bounds, *Mildred Pierce* fortified this effort, in effect "instructing" women that home and hearth was their proper place, *not* the workplace.

Curtiz shot the film in two distinct styles, dark, shadowy light for the "crime" parts while using high-key, cheery lighting for the flashback "home" sequences, hence successfully blending film noir with melodrama. The war's influence could also be seen in the "retooling" of the Bert character, who in Cain's novel is shiftless and without ambition. In Curtiz's work, Bert becomes a supervisory type at "Condor" Aircraft, a solid, responsible

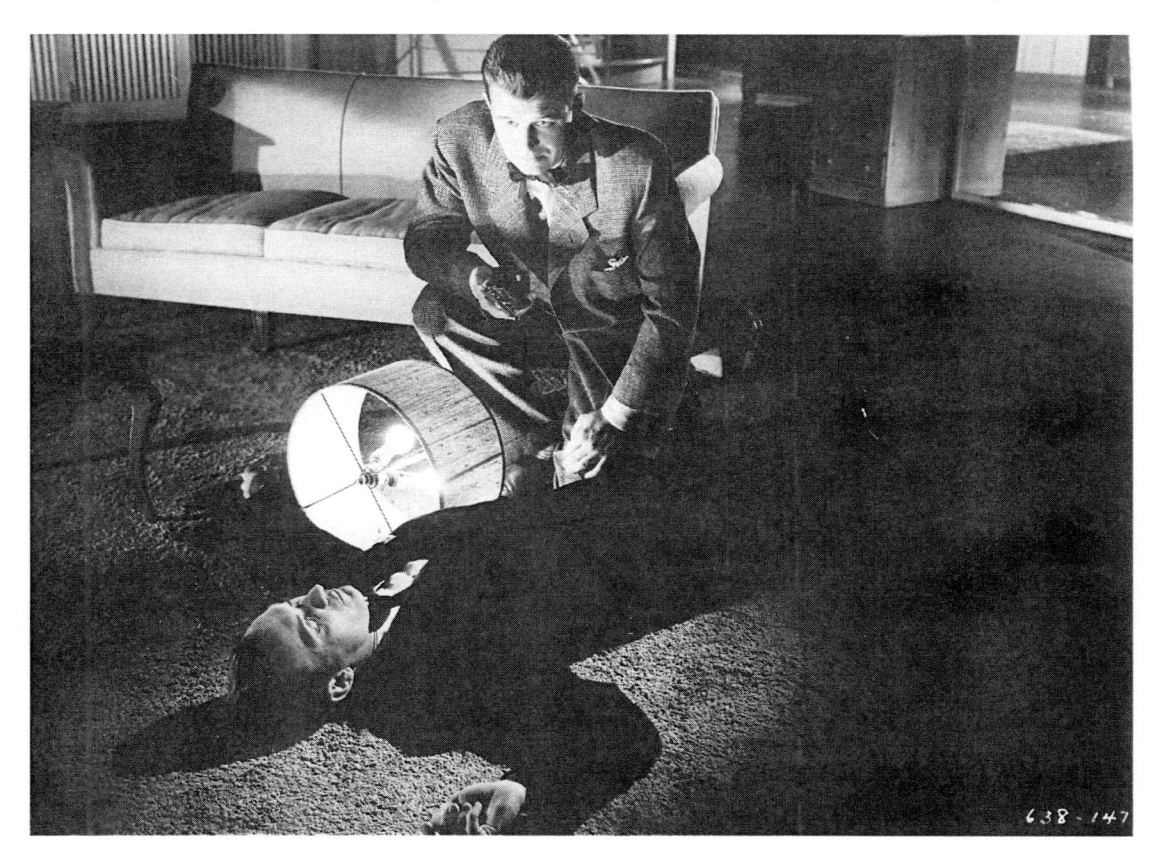

Wally Fay (Jack Carson) discovers the body of Monte Beregan (Zachary Scott) in *Mildred Pierce*.

middle-class citizen who implicitly rejects Mildred and Monty's lifestyle in the scene where he visits their mansion to bring Veda her birthday present. So much for literary license.

In 1944, RKO took a gamble on musical star Dick Powell, casting him as the tough-as-nails Philip Marlowe in *Murder, My Sweet*, an adaptation of Chandler's novel *Farewell My Lovely*. The film was a huge success, and vaulted Powell into the ranks of tough guy roles he'd play for the next decade. Marlowe is hired by Moose Malloy, an ex-con just released from a long stint for bank robbery. Malloy wants Marlowe to find his Velma, a slutty ex-girlfriend he had before he was sent up. Marlowe remains his scrupulous self even when insulting others, like a cowardly homosexual who wants to hire him to broker a stolen jewelry buy back. During the narrative Marlowe is beaten, drugged, strangled and sapped over the head, even temporarily blinded, but he perseveres and finds Moose's Velma. Unfortunately, the woman is married to a rather wealthy man and doesn't want Moose around to mess things up. He solves a number of murders even as Velma, her husband and Moose kill each other. In the end, Marlowe is no wealthier for his trouble, but he kept up his end of the bargain, which is more than anyone he ever runs across does.

Farewell My Lovely was redone in 1975, this time with Robert Mitchum as Marlowe. Once again he's on the trail of Velma, working for Moose, this time played by ex-boxer Jack O'Halloran. Mitchum runs up against the same walls as Powell did, only there's a weary quality about Mitchum's detective: older, dingier, but still dishing out the truth along with his swinging fists. As he sits waiting for the cops to arrive, with neon blinking on the streets outsides his window, Marlowe seems the last honest man in a city on the take. He knows he's a fool, but he's his own fool, bought and paid for by no one.

Lady in the Lake and *The Big Sleep* both hit the screen in 1946, and both were unique for very different reasons: The former film starred and was directed by Robert Montgomery, and he used the camera in such a way that it became Marlowe's eyes. In other words, the camera was Marlowe. The only glimpses seen of the character came when he passed a mirror. The technique was striking yet puzzling, but the audience was more confused by what they were seeing than the actual murder investigation. Howard Hawks' *The Big Sleep* was shot in his conventional style, leaving no artifices for the audience to even think of the director, but the narrative was so confusing no one, not even the actors, could figure out who killed whom. Instead it's a joyous ride of snappy dialogue and great action, with Humphrey Bogart playing Marlowe as he attempts to solve a number of murders linked to a general's promiscuous daughter.

The most bizarre adaptation of Raymond Chandler's novels comes in *The Long Goodbye* (1973). Director Robert Altman's version of the story is a significant departure from the norm, portraying the private eye as a more cerebral, pacifistic type, to the point where he exists in the vacuum of an identity crisis. Chandler's character is a big, beefy fellow with a degree in literature and a past stint as a district attorney's investigator, a man as comfortable reading poetry as he is trading punches. Altman's Marlowe is a man adrift, living in the wrong time, the antithesis of the hard-boiled detective.

Chandler's Marlowe is cast in the formal mode, that is, an ordinary man with ordinary abilities, albeit brighter than most and as tough as they come. Altman's protagonist is firmly grounded in the ironic, an ordinary guy with less than ordinary powers who is unable to cope with the many demands of his profession, let alone life. That Marlowe is out of touch with himself and his times can be seen in his style of dress and means of transportation; though it is 1973, he drives a 1948 Lincoln Continental, and no matter where he goes, is always in a dark suit. Considering this was a time noted for polyester leisure suits and the advent of casual wear, the contrasting images of Marlowe with others at a beach party underscore the former's social anomie and set him apart from those with whom he interacts.

Marlowe is investigating a murder, a missing friend, and an alcoholic writer who appears to be a lot like Hemingway, only weaker, as if someone was trying to say maybe that's how he was in true life. Be that as it may, Marlowe's real investigation is about who he is. It comes to the surface during his time in police lock-up. The detectives use rapid-fire questioning to confuse him and elicit information about Terry Lennox, whom they suspect of killing his wife. To one of the questions regarding his identity, Marlowe replies, "I don't know..."; to another he volunteers, "I'm from a long time ago..." As the sham investigation wears on, Marlowe uses the ink from his soiled hands (he had just been fingerprinted) to paint his face and mimic Al Jolson, a subtle metaphor about the duality of identity, Jolson being a white man who found success singing in blackface.

Marlowe, however, is not the only character experiencing identity problems. In fact, mistaken, confused or unknown identity is a predominant theme within the work. Terry Lennox, Marlowe's so-called friend, is also his "other," that shadowy figure which can mirror what someone is not. Where Marlowe is unkempt and introspective, Terry is outgoing and neat, a fastidious dresser; Marlowe is honest and reliable, Terry is deceitful and crafty; where Marlowe believes in loyalty to one's friends, Terry uses that loyalty to his advantage; while Marlowe "exists," Terry "lives"; and, most significantly, where Marlowe is an individual without a figurative identity, Terry is a man without a literal one, having been dead and buried as far as most are concerned.

Private eye Philip Marlow (Elliot Gould) questions Eileen Wade (Nina Van Pallandt) in *The Long Goodbye*.

Other characters follow suit. Roger Wade is really named Billy Joe Smith, and is described by his wife as alternately a kind man and a "monster," an individual who is someone else much of the time, to the point of her not recognizing him. The security guard for the Malibu Colony spends much of his time impersonating famous actors for the people entering and exiting ... an imitation Jimmy Stewart ... Cary Grant ... Walter Brennan ... yet, we never learn his real name or anything about him.

Similarly, the hood following Marlowe is young and inept (and, like Marlowe, living in the '70s but looking at the '40s as his model of "gangster" life). The young women who live next to Marlowe are druggies who parade about much of the time semi-nude, semi-conscious and semi-seriously searching for some kind of meaning, some inkling as to who they are. As Marlowe inquires about his runaway cat, they ignore him, engrossed in yoga, their "leader" chanting to them about who and what they are. Even the prisoner with whom Marlowe shares a cell claims to be something other than what he is, in this case a convicted criminal, but in his own mind an innocent man, a victim of "the system."

Altman also uses visual motifs to emphasize lack of identity. After the gangster Marty Augustine confronts Marlowe in his apartment regarding Terry Lennox's disappearance and alleged suicide, he confides to the detective that he is a wonderful family man, a loving father, in effect, nothing one would expect a loan-sharking thug to be. He then smashes a Coke bottle against his mistress' face, dramatically revealing what he really is. The next time the mistress is seen, her nose is held together by a metal rod which obscures her features, eerily distorting how she looks.

Later, after Roger Wade dies, Marlowe chases Mrs. Wade down the street, attempting to clear up some loose ends regarding her husband's and Terry Lennox's suicide. He is hit by a car and ends up in a hospital, sharing a room with a patient whose face is completely covered by bandages. When an entering nurse asks the fleeing detective if he is "Mr. Marlowe," the detective refers to the unknown bandaged patient.

Stylistically, the film revels in elaborate camera movements and cinematography which heightens the distance between the viewer and Marlowe, just as he himself is distanced from those around him. Early on, Altman starts the camera panning ... tracking ... cutting ... always moving ... rarely settling on Marlowe long enough for the viewer to be comfortable. When the detective is taken into police custody, being questioned about Terry Lennox, the camera pulls back to a point where not only can Marlowe be seen through a two-way mirror but so, too, can one of his interrogators, who is watching from another room; later, as Marlowe plays on the beach, the Wades argue in the house, and the camera again is positioned in such a way as to reveal both images, the startling effect serving to highlight the detective's fringe status as an outsider.

At the film's beginning, Marlowe is awakened by his hungry cat, whom he is truly attached to, and attempts to feed it; yet, the cat will not eat what he has prepared. When Marlowe tries to trick it into thinking the food it is about to consume is the "gourmet" brand it is accustomed to, the feline immediately ferrets out the ruse and leaves him — not to return. In a few short minutes, then, Altman has deftly set up his characterization of Marlowe as a borderline loser — a man who cannot even fool a cat! — a man living in the margins of life.

However, by film's end, Marlowe comes full circle, in a most abrupt manner, his slowly dawning realization of being duped forcing him to live up to the "code" of the P.I., triggering a violent reaction — his extermination of Terry Lennox, which Altman emphasizes by abruptly changing from a florid to classic shot–reverse shot style. Hence, as the film opens against "grain" with a whimper, it closes with a bang — all the more effective because it, too, is against the grain of Marlowe's expected behavior, his anticipated low-key response.

Whether Marlowe is a changed man is unclear. His last act was more one of personal need than professional necessity, although the code did call for it. Like Sam Spade, who sent Brigid to the electric chair for killing his partner, Marlowe had to square things, and in taking action, dubious as cold-blooded murder is, he remained a P.I to his own way of thinking.

Devil in a Blue Dress (1995) examines a black private eye roaming the postwar streets of Los Angeles, the same ones being walked by Philip Marlowe, with mixed results. At a pivotal moment in Carl Franklin's screen version of Walter Mosley's detective novel, the protagonist, Easy Rawlins, confronts the Jennifer Beals character about who she really is. Like *Chinatown* and *The Long Goodbye*, both of which were acclaimed critically, *Devil in the Blue Dress* is a period piece *revolving* around the question of identity — not only Beals but that of Easy as well.

In Roman Polanski's *Chinatown*, ex–LAPD detective Jake Gittes is something of a sleaze, a private investigator whose primary work comes from divorce cases, a depth to which Raymond Chandler's stalwart detective hero Philip Marlowe will not lower himself. Though Gittes is good at his craft, it is not until he tries to help Evelyn Mulwray find her husband's killer that he finds out how powerless he is against politically connected, socially

Private eye Jake Gittes (Jack Nicholson) finds himself getting deeper into an investigation he hadn't counted on in *Chinatown*.

upstanding citizens. This reality is underscored by the time in which the story is set — 1930s Los Angeles, a period noted for egregious municipal corruption.

As he investigates what begins as an individual case of murder that ends with a horrific revelation of moral turpitude, Jake simultaneously unravels a plot against the public domain, a diabolical financial scheme that will negatively affect the lives of Californians for generations to come. In breaking the case, Jake learns the true identities of everyone he's involved with — that Hollis Mulwray is not the unscrupulous public official he's made out to be but rather a kind and considerate man, one dedicated to serving the public honestly and with great integrity; that his wife Evelyn is not a murderess, only a woman victimized by a past depravity; and most importantly, he learns what Noah Cross is and his fiendish plan, as well as the true identity of Evelyn's "sister."

Fast-forward a decade... Easy Rawlins is an aerospace worker who is hired by an aide to a mayoral candidate to find the candidate's missing girlfriend, one Daphne Monet. He solves the mystery, but in the worst way, amatuerishly bungling his way into discovering the truth, which leads one to ask, "What are his qualifications?" He is black and unemployed, and able to enter the world of black nightlife — clubs and jazz music — that the missing girl is supposedly partial to. The author and director go to great lengths to portray the racist nature of Los Angeles in the '40s. But in doing so, they undercut the story and the main character, for how can one be a detective, a seeker of truth, when he can't even leave the city's black district without fear of being hauled in?

Jake may not always know what he is getting into, but he does know how to search for it, and in putting together what Hollis Mulwray was working on, discovers that Noah Cross is dumping water during a drought so as to force the city to build a dam —

on property he is quickly buying up under false names. Easy locates Daphne, only because *she* contacts him, and she eventually admits that she is really being sought by a rival candidate, because she possesses compromising pictures of him with little boys.

Where Jake is beaten by thugs to stop his investigation, Easy is beaten by the police because he is black; where Jake links together each piece of the puzzle, researches and investigates leads, Easy is directed which way to go; where Jake *finds*, Easy *learns*, his name appropriate to his style. While major points in both films show the detective resorting to violence to uncover the female protagonist's "secret," only Evelyn Mulwray's revelation parallels the dirty nature of the case which Jake solves. Daphne's confession that she is part-black is anticlimactic, only important in narrative terms to explain why the "good" mayoral candidate won't marry her at the film's conclusion.

Essentially, where *Chinatown* posits a private investigation which reveals public malfeasance, *Devil in a Blue Dress* begins with a future public official seeking a private investigation to avoid a personal scandal, a dichotomy that mirrors the author-director's inability to decide whether the film is primarily a mystery or a social commentary, whether Easy is a black man or a detective, categories which are not necessarily mutually exclusive but which appear to be so in the film.

On the one hand we see that black people like Easy own their own homes, pay their bills on time, go to church on Sundays, and live in clean, caring neighborhoods just like their white counterparts. We are shown that blacks suffered from police harassment, that oppression lurked everywhere, and that blacks were victims of all manner of discrimination and bigotry.

On the other, we are supposed to believe that this man Easy, with his slight Southern accent, mild-mannered ways and terrible shooting skills, can maneuver through the treacherous, noirish maze of big city corruption to solve crimes which even the police are afraid to touch. If Jake Gittes is a man who is sure of his own identity, one who seeks to discover the identity of others, to *solve* the mystery, Easy Rawlins is a man not only unsure of who he is but what he is doing, and in that aspect is quite similar to the Altman character of Philip Marlowe in *The Long Goodbye*.

That same schism exists in *Devil in a Blue Dress* though, unlike in Altman's work, it is not intentional. Easy must spend half his time both being a part of, and showing how, the black middle-class lives while dedicating the remainder of it to negotiating the twisting mystery of murder and deceit which a *noir* detective, which Easy is likened to, must be prepared to solve.

Easy Rawlins (Denzel Washington) searches for a missing girl in *Devil in a Blue Dress*.

Scenes of Easy doing domestic chores, such as planting trees in his backyard and helping out the neighbors, or having a beer with a friend on his porch, do not square with other scenes of him following leads in an illegal nightclub or shooting it out with the villains in a hillside hideout just removed from L.A. Easy may be a better detective than Altman's Marlowe, but it is only because the latter is completely lost while the former's identity merely wavers between two distinct poles: middle-class family type and hard-boiled loner.

A second element which gives credence to the film noir detective is a code of honor; Marlowe stood by his clients and his friends, and was respected as a man of integrity by both the police, who had little fortitude, as well as the criminals he did battle with; in fact, they were often one and the same. Sam Spade did the right thing, but first tried to milk whatever profit was in it for him. Easy certainly possess some of these qualities: His code opposes deadly force whenever possible, treats people with respect, and values above all his friends. However, Easy's relationship to Mouse, a cretin whose physical size and intellectual capabilities are signified by his name, strains the bounds of credulity, while Easy's sexual encounter with a good friend's girlfriend to obtain information was certainly questionable.

The private detective remains a staple of film and television to this day. While not a law enforcement officer, his duties are similar, and he is often able to accomplish more, with less, because, like the bounty man, the rules for him are different than for his sworn counterparts. However, the salad days of private investigation — where Marlowe and Spade hit the streets, gun under their trenchcoat — have long past. Most private eyes gather information, be it for divorce cases or traffic collisions. Some work for defense counsels in civil or even criminal trials, ferreting out facts that police or DA investigators might have ignored. But so long as there's film, the tough private eye will be around, doing the things the police can't or won't do.

Sources

Johnston, Claire. *Double Indemnity*. Women in Film Noir. Ed. Ann Kaplan. London: BFI, 1994.
The Maltese Falcon. Cinebooks. CD-Rom. 1994.

IX

Workin' for the Railroad

— They'll be waiting for us.

— I wouldn't have it any other way.*

The spread of railroads across the nation during the nineteenth century laid the infrastructure of what would become an economic powerhouse after World War II. And the towns connected by the tracks grew larger and more prosperous. As did the men who owned these conglomerates. The Vanderbilts and J. Pierpoint Morgan were just some of the industrialists who made fortunes in the industry. The railroads needed land to run their tracks across. Most of the time, they got it legally. Sometimes they employed questionable practices to obtain it. In an ends vs. means question, those involved in building a railroad saw themselves as making the country stronger by what they were doing. It became inevitable that some people would be hurt, though the vast majority would benefit.

As the various railroads made enemies (and became wealthier), they became a target for harassment and robbery by anyone with a grudge and a gun. Eventually, "railroad men" evolved from armed guards to actual police and detectives employed by rail lines to protect persons and property. Now, almost all railroads have a law enforcement department whose officers go through formal police training academies. A century ago, however, the railroads deputized whatever men they needed, and they operated with the authority of the law, though in many instances they were, more or less, bounty hunters. Jesse and Frank James found this out the hard way when the railroad land developers came calling at their farm.

Jesse James (1939)

The James brothers are perhaps the most recognizable outlaws from the Old West. They robbed banks, trains, fought as guerrilla partisans during the Civil War, and were responsible for many killings. Folk legends and, later, films glamourized these men and their exploits, though in real life they were brutal and mercenary. Jesse James was eventually shot in the back by one of his old gang members, Bob Ford, for the reward money. Frank James turned himself in to the authorities and was acquitted after two trials; other members of the gang were killed or arrested after a failed bank robbery in Northfield, Minnesota.

**Dutch (Ernest Borgnine) cautioning Pike (William Holden) about what they can expect when they head back across the border in* The Wild Bunch.

In this film, Tyrone Power stars as Jesse James, a peaceful farmer, who along with his brother Frank minds his business as they tend their farm. The railroad sends out its man, Barshee, a big, free-wheeling type who deals with an iron fist in a leather glove. When he talks to the farmers about taking their land, he punches them as he shakes hands. Trying that tactic with the James brothers gets him knocked on his rear end. The escalation between the railroad and the James brothers leads to them becoming outlaws. The film makes it appear that Jesse and Frank were ill-advised and wouldn't have gone wrong except for men like Barshee and the railroads.

Once the James boys go bad, the railroad brings in a United States marshal to stop them. The marshal is a sympathetic to Jesse and Frank, but he's committed to bringing them in for their crimes just the same. Where Jesse is bold, uninhibited, aloof and willing to uphold the code of "frontier justice," the marshal remains pragmatic, respectful, gregarious and committed to codified law. While outlaw hero Jesse's spontaneity assured him of audience popularity, the marshal had to rely on discerning viewers whose identification might waver depending on what next atrocity was committed by the railroad against the James brothers.

Once Upon a Time in the West (1968)

Henry Fonda is Frank, a gunman the railroad uses to "clear the tracks" of anyone who doesn't want to sell their land — cheap. Frank massacres a whole family, including children, to get his employer a piece of prime property where a train station can be built. Frank didn't get the wife, who was not at home, and now she owns the land and is not selling. The Harmonica man, played by Charles Bronson, arrives in town. He has an appointment with Frank, and intends to kill him. Frank sends his henchmen to take care of Harmonica, but they are no match and Harmonica kills all three of them. Harmonica teams up with Cheyenne, something of an outlaw, to protect the widow so she can build her train station in peace. Doing that means going up against Frank and the railroad.

Seeing Henry Fonda, almost always a hero, and Charles Bronson, up to that point generally a villain, switch positions was a surprise to most American audiences. In Europe, the film was a great hit; in the U.S., it tanked. Frank, as the railroad's enforcer, is both the creation of and the destroyer of Morton, the cripple who owns the rail line. Morton uses Frank and his gang to enforce his laws, and to get the company the land they need to expand. Without someone like Morton, Frank has no purpose. Morton's way is the future. He deals in money, land, water rights and transportation. Frank's only use is behind a smoking gun. Soon Frank's time will end and Morton's will begin. The fact that Morton's a cripple merely shows that physical strength is no asset in the world of big business, which is quickly coming.

Frank thinks about moving Morgan out of his position and taking over the railroad himself. But it's not to be. Harmonica is literally a ghost from Frank's past — and he has to reckon with it. Harmonica's real name is never mentioned. He has no past — except for Frank killing his brother — and no means of support — except for whatever he carries with him. He has no job, except to track Frank. He even helps Frank when Morgan hires henchmen to get rid of him. It's quite apparent that he wants Frank alive to satisfy his own revenge. Neither Frank nor Harmonica has a place in these changing times. Frank kills his creator and then goes to face his past, a younger version of himself. He meets Harmonica

Harmonica (Charles Bronson) outdraws Frank (Henry Fonda) in *Once Upon a Time in the West*. Both men are anachronisms in a time of rapid industrialization.

at the train station that the widow is building. It will be finished shortly, and she and the new owners of the railroad will certainly have a very lucrative partnership. After Harmonica kills Frank in the final showdown, he rides into the desert and disappears as quickly as he arrived.

The Wild Bunch (1969)

The film is set in Texas, c. 1913, and opens as Deke Thornton's old partners, led by Pike Bishop, enter a town to rob a bank. Deke has been plotting the Wild Bunch's moves and figures they'll hit the place, so he and his men lie in wait, and the Bunch is ambushed. In the ensuing battle, many people are killed and wounded, mostly bystanders marching in a church temperance parade. Bishop's gang is also decimated and what's left is forced to retreat into Mexico.

Though Westerns had always been a favorite national genre, this film signalled a change, for its protagonists were harsh, brutal men, unrelentingly violent. Up to this point, the myth of the "Outlaw Hero," so prevalent in American cinema, had acted to mitigate the nature of such characters, so much so that even the worst, most psychotic gunmen in the history of the West were reborn on the silver screen, be they John Wesley Hardin or Billy the Kid. As Robert Ray notes in his *A Certain Tendency of the Hollywood Cinema, 1930–1980,*

> The American mythology's refusal to choose between its two heroes (outlaw/official) went beyond the normal function attributed to myth by Levi Strauss... Part of this process involved blurring the lines between the two sets of heroes. First, legends often brought the solemn official heroes back down to earth... On the other side, stories modified the outlaw hero's most potentially damaging quality, his tendency to selfish isolationism [Ray, p. 64].

To be sure, none of the Bunch can be mistaken for traditional heroes. Killing is second nature to them, and they are good at it. In the initial shootout, they purposefully use the church parade as human shields, unconcerned by the fact that innocent people will be slaughtered in the withering crossfire. As they flee, a wounded comrade lags behind and calls out to Bishop for help — but Bishop shoots him point blank in the face. Later, two of the men dicker with a prostitute they had just shared simultaneously, arguing over whether they have to pay twice or once for services rendered. Such naturalism was a stark departure from the prototypical John Wayne period piece, yet it was not merely one-sided, as director Sam Peckinpah shows some of the men's good qualities—few that they have — without getting soft.

Pike Bishop is the glue which keeps the bunch together. Approaching 50 and past his prime, he nonetheless is a man to be reckoned with. After the surviving members make their way into Mexico to divide the loot from the bank heist, the men discover that they have been duped — their saddle bags contain steel washers! As they begin to turn their anger inwards, a stand-off develops between the Gorch brothers and Angel, who is backed by the old man, Sykes. Just as it looks as though the Bunch will finish itself off, Bishop intervenes: He will lead the gang or he will end it — right there. Later, as they travel deeper into Mexico, Sykes guides the bunch into a sand trap, almost killing them as they topple from their horses. The Gorch brothers, Lyle and Tector, immediately move to kill the old man, but Bishop again asserts his authority: "You're not killin' anybody... When you side with a man, you stick with him, 'til he's finished, otherwise you're no better than an animal..." These words are prophetic, for they presage the Bunch's last stand.

Despite Bishop's formidability, he is saddled with self-doubt. He has been living off the strength of his reputation, but his decisions have become increasingly ill-advised. The Gorch brothers openly question his leadership, as does Bishop secretly, recognizing that he has repeatedly jeopardized the safety of those closest to him. His bad leg is the result of an adulterous affair wherein the offended husband caught him off guard and wounded him, though killing the woman. The failure of the bank heist was in part due to his lack of foresight, as is the death of Sykes' grandson — a member of the Bunch — whom Pike forgot and left behind during the shooting.

Deke, once Pike's partner, leads the railroad men. He was caught and imprisoned because of Pike's overconfidence and poor planning. Where Pike wonders if he can lead his men, Deke has no such doubts. His men are gutter trash, but he knows what he's doing and he's patient. He will catch Pike if he bides his time — and if it means crossing the border into Mexico, he'll do that too. Deke is a match for Pike in every way, and he hasn't lost a step, which is something Pike can't claim. The best of friends are now the worst of enemies, and so long as the railroad is pulling the strings, Deke will keep on coming.

Sykes also knows that Deke is coming for them, and that if Pike doesn't pull himself together, their former partner will track them down. As for Pike, his negative self-view is reinforced by his realization that he has wrecked everything good in his life, from his friendship with Deke to the woman he loved. But Pike, and the other outlaws in the Bunch for that matter, clearly mirror the agents of law and order who chase them. The bounty hunters are despicable examples of white trash, indiscriminate murderers who shoot at anything moving, then steal everything imaginable from the body, be it money, boots, even gold fillings. The railroad men are no better; it is Harrigan, the head agent, who orders the bounty hunters to commence firing on the Bunch even though they have blended in with the church parade, thereby massacring scores of women, children and elderly.

Similarly, while both groups in *The Wild Bunch* are superficially alike, in effect, two sides to a counterfeit coin, what separates the outlaws from the railroad men is their sense of honor and commitment to each other. They may kill, but they don't kill without reason or provocation, though their reasons may not be valid to most other people. The same cannot be said for Deke's men. While he himself has a sense of honor and integrity which prevents him from doing the things they do, they still kill anything, any time — with the railroad's backing. When the Bunch encounters Mapache, a bloodthirsty Federale General who represents the "law" south of the border, Bishop jokingly compares the outlaws to the soldiers, and is swiftly rebuked by Dutch, his second in command: "No, sir, Mr. Bishop, we ain't nothin' like them at all. We don't hang a man." Clearly the bunch does not hold many of the conventional values associated with a "civilized" society, but they do assign importance to their own ethical code, which in some instances is superior to that of the society against which they rebel. Deke has the same values, but his major handicap is dealing his men, who have no values at all.

Another dominant theme of the Peckinpah film is that of lateness, or the closing of the West. As for the Bunch, their story takes place on the eve of World War I, the first technologically advanced conflict in modern history. They have outlived their time, as Pike sagely notes: "We gotta start thinking past the ends of our guns; those days are closing fast."

Like the outlaws Butch Cassidy and the Sundance Kid, the Bunch travels south to find an operating area less confined by law and the advent of "civilization." While they arrive on horseback in Aqua Verde, the general enters town in a motor car, surprising the men, who have rarely if ever been close enough to see a car, let alone touch one. Even their weapons are anachronisms, with Pike using a semi-automatic pistol during the bank robbery but reverting back to his old-fashioned, pearl-handled Colt six-shooter once on the trail. John Belton, in his *American Cinema/American Culture*, observes in this regard:

> A handful of Westerns, made in the 1960s and early 70s and set in the period after the closing of the frontier ... feature legendary characters who have outlived the heroic gold, silver, and bronze ages of the West and who are regarded as either curiosities or unwanted embarrassments by an indifferent or openly hostile twentieth century society... The suicidal resistance of these western anti-heroes to the values of modernity lies at the heart of several Sam Peckinpah Westerns [Belton, p. 221].

Eventually, the outlaws come to Mapache's attention, primarily through the actions of Angel, who kills the general's girlfriend as she lie in his arms; Angel is upset because the girl was once his fiancée. The general's advisors, German military personnel, end up hiring the Bunch to steal some advanced U.S. Army rifles being transported by rail along the border. The mission is a success, though not without a hitch: Deke Thornton once again has anticipated their actions and he and his men are waiting on the train. He chases the bunch into Mexico, though most of his men have been killed. He stays hot on the outlaws' heels, waiting out of range to pounce.

Pike and his men deliver the guns to Mapache, but he keeps Angel as a prisoner, having discovered that one box of rifles was "stolen" and given to Angel's village so they could defend themselves against raids by Mapache's troops. As the entire Bunch returns to

Mapache's town to avoid Thornton, they see Angel being tortured. This presents a final moral quandary for Pike Bishop, one which will determine not only his own fate and that of his men, but which also affords him an opportunity to redeem himself in his own eyes. This dilemma is better understood in light of Pike's earlier exchange with the usually agreeable Dutch after Thornton's men wound Sikes. Bishop, in keeping with nineteenth century character, holds that Thornton has to keep pursuing them because he gave his "word" to the railroad; Dutch, on the other hand, less rigid and more pragmatic in these modern days, fires back that it is *who* one gives his word to that really matters.

As Pike views it, then, the rifles Mapache is upset about were given to Angel as his "cut" of the job; therefore, Angel could have implicated the rest of the men to save himself, but he didn't. Bishop must now decide if those words he spoke earlier about sticking together had any meaning. Eventually he decides they do, and the bunch acts to get back their comrade, regardless of the consequences. They move through the town, armed to the teeth, and, in the final savage battle, Pike finally lives up to the creed he's always held but never fulfilled. Their final shoot-out is the one most prominently associated with Peckinpah. Louis Giannetti writes,

> When violent scenes are photographed in slow-motion, the effect is paradoxically beautiful. In *The Wild Bunch*, Peckinpah used slow motion to photograph the grisliest scenes of horror — flesh tearing, blood spattering, horses toppling, an almost endless variety. By aestheticizing these scenes of ugliness, Peckinpah demonstrates why the men are so addicted to a life of violence when it seems so profitless [Giannetti].

Members of ***The Wild Bunch*** (Ben Johnson, Warren Oates, William Holden, Ernest Borgnine) head into the eye of the maelstrom, confronting the Mexican Army to rescue one of their comrades. How does this scene compare to others in ***Tombstone*** and ***Wyatt Earp***?

Structurally, the film is circular in fashion, beginning and ending in ultra-violent shootouts, with Peckinpah deftly utilizing symbolism to convey meaning. As the story opens, the Bunch ride into town dressed as soldiers; they pass some children playing with a box at the side of the road. As the camera moves into the box, we see thousands of red ants stinging some scorpions to death, a motif repeated at the film's end as the Bunch take on Mapache's army in a fight to the finish. Again, the juxtaposition of the innocent (children) with the sadistic (torture) works to level the differences between those like the Bunch and the rest of society. Not coincidentally, as the Bunch unloads on the Federales, Pike is eventually felled not by a soldier or bandit but by a child — a follower of the general who shoots him in the back as he wields a machine-gun.

As the Bunch travels further south, they cross a river and enter Angel's village, where they are "reborn" — heroes to the oppressed peasants. During their stay, the men are like children, happy, carefree, their violent natures seemingly washed away. Later, after the men are spent in the fury of battle and the dead and dying are littered throughout the town square, a solitary figure in black picks through the remains, as if the Reaper, a windstorm following on her heels. And when Pike Bishop first enters the bank in San Rafael, Texas, he tells his men regarding their hostages, "If they move — kill 'em..." His face is partially shaded, one side dark as if to show the duality of his nature; at the film's conclusion, he looks around the whorehouse, sickened by what he sees, by what he has become. He decides to get back Angel and finds his men, saying only, "Let's go...," his face again partially shaded.

However, much of the film's negative criticism was generated by Peckinpah's very treatment of these men and their deadly ways: In attempting to deglamourize violence by showing it in a horribly gruesome way, realism was replaced by a martyred sense of beauty. Other criticism was generated over his depiction of women. As earlier noted, Pike's initial wound was ultimately caused by his dalliance with a married woman; during the final shoot-out, he is shot in the back by a whore he had just spared. Angel, meanwhile, learns a lesson about women when his fiancée gives herself to Mapache because of his wealth and power. Later, as the Bunch delivers the rifles to the general, Angel is betrayed by the mother of his fiancée, whom he had earlier killed, thus setting in motion his capture and torture, and the Bunch's revenge. Hence, even if women do not have a large role to play in this film, as in Peckinpah's vision of the world, it is apparent that they are responsible for most of the trouble, at least indirectly, and these images do add up to a distrust, and even a dislike of women (Tuska, p. 306).

Deke and what few men he has left ride into the town. Pike and the Bunch have decimated the army, and the survivors are walking into the desert. Deke sees Pike, hand on the machine-gun, dead. Whatever hate, whatever vengeance he held evaporates like the lives in front of him. He takes Pike's pearl-handled Colt; it wouldn't be right for anyone outside of the Bunch to have it. His men load the bodies of the Bunch on their horses, but Deke is not returning. He kept his word, he hunted the Bunch, and he forced them into the battle which caused their death. He sits and watches as his railroad men ride off to Texas. A few hours later, Sykes and the men from Angel's village make it to the town, but they are too late to save the Bunch. They have already killed Deke's railroad men, and Sykes asks Deke if he wants to ride with them. It may not be the same as before, he tells him, but it beats nothing. And Deke agrees — it does beat a life of nothing.

Sources

Belton, John. *American Cinema/American Culture*. New York: McGraw-Hill, 1994.
Giannetti, Louis. *Understanding Movies* 6th ed. Upper Saddle River, NJ: Prentice Hall. 1993.
Ray, Robert B. *A Certain Tendency of the Hollywood Cinema, 1930–1980*. Princeton, NJ: Princeton University Press, 1985.
Tuska, Jon. *Encounters with Filmmakers: Eight Career Paths*. Westport, CT: Greenwood Press, 1991.
The Wild Bunch. Cinebooks. CD-Rom. 1994.

X

Vigilantes with a Badge

I know what you're thinking. Did he fire six shots or only five? Well, to tell the truth, in all this excitement, I've kinda lost track myself. But being that this is a .44 Magnum, the most powerful handgun in the world, and would blow your head clean off, you've got to ask yourself one question: Do I feel lucky? Well, do ya, punk?*

As defined by Merriam-Webster, a vigilante is "a self-appointed doer of justice." Vigilantes watch for crimes to happen, but if that's all they did they wouldn't be considered vigilantes. In 2005, President George W. Bush, in a patently obvious attempt at pleasing Mexican President Vicente Fox, referred to members of the Minuteman Project as "vigilantes."† The Minutemen, who were watching the Arizona-Mexico border to spot illegal aliens crossing into the States, merely watched the aliens and called authorities. They did not confront the lawbreakers. Considering many of the minutemen were Vietnam-era vets, a distinction claimed by the president but certainly up for debate, Bush's attack was ill-conceived, if not preposterous.

By their very definition, vigilantes circumvent the law, usually pronouncing a severe judgment and following through with an even hastier sentence. Lynch mobs have operated throughout American history, generally saving their vitriol for minorities, though some whites have found themselves dangling from the end of a rope as well. After the Civil War, blacks were often hung for various crimes by mobs which formed after a trial. Murder, or raping a white woman, was a charge that could get them hung *without* benefit of a hearing before a judge.

As hate groups like the Ku Klux Klan became powerful in the 1920s, blacks continued to be targeted. In attempting to gain respect for their pseudo-political limericks, some rap shouters have featured the macabre and grotesque photograph of whites gawking and pointing at the abject figure of a black man hanging from a tree during an early twentieth century lynching. The utter depravity of such a scene should be enough to stop anything like that from happening again in a civilized society, but as this chapter will show, the idea of what's civilized is a tricky notion to nail down.

Vigilante films usually feature a number of generic conventions, most or all being present in the narrative which drive the story forward. A law (or many laws) have been broken, and the authorities are powerless to stop the criminals, either because the authorities themselves are corrupt or because some aspects of the justice system coddle the criminal. The

---

*"Dirty" Harry Callahan (Clint Eastwood) laying down the law to a bank robber suspect in *Dirty Harry.*
†More specifically, Bush was asked by a reporter what he thought of the project and said he didn't approve of vigilantes.

hero is an isolated figure, or a loner, though not always, but he possesses strength, courage and intelligence which set him apart from others. Either the hero's family, or someone close to him, has been killed or otherwise hurt by the malefactors, and when he is pushed so far that his back is against the wall, the hero will act with decisiveness and brute force, "upholding" the law by breaking the law. For the peace officer, one other condition is added: His actions occur behind his badge, which he sometimes finds to be a hindrance.

Dirty Harry (1971) featured Clint Eastwood as "Dirty" Harry Callahan, a San Francisco police inspector assigned to the Scorpio shooting murders.* Callahan is one of the department's best detectives, in part because he never lets the law stand in the way of a good bust, and stopping the Scorpio killer tops his list of good busts. That Callahan is defined by action and not words is set up immediately. As Harry eats a hot dog, a bank across the street is being robbed. Chewing his food, Harry calmly walks out to the street and dispatches all of the robbers, who happen to be black. In one of the most famous scenes in cinema history, Harry tells a wounded robber thinking of reaching for a shotgun that he (Callahan) might have fired five rounds or six, but because his handgun is a .44 magnum and could blow the robber's head off, the robber has to ask himself if he is feeling lucky. The robber decides not to gamble and Harry picks up the shotgun. The black man says he "gots" to know, so Harry sadistically pulls the trigger of an empty revolver which is pointed at the man's head.

In a time when white male dominance was under attack by Affirmative Action and pressure from civil rights groups, Harry establishes that he is not only unafraid of minorities, in this case blacks, but will take whatever measures are necessary to uphold the law and his own place in society. As Pauline Kael notes, Harry is a single-minded attack on liberal values.

After the shooting, Harry takes a helicopter ride through the city, and director Don Siegel sets an eerie backdrop as police snipers cover the roofs trying to pick off Scorpio. After Harry is congratulated for another fine bust, he is paired with Chico, a Mexican-American college graduate. Harry prefers to work alone because his partners always get killed or hurt badly. One of the other detectives tells Chico not to be too upset, that Harry hates everyone — niggers, Kikes, honkeys, etc. We find that Chico and Harry are a good pair. Both disparage many of the same groups, Chico calling the homosexuals they drive by during patrol "fruitcakes" and wishing the weirdos would disappear.

Harry breaks laws to catch Scorpio. In one instance he stands on some boxes and looks through a window, only to find a fat prostitute servicing her john. Harry himself is set upon by vigilantes, dockworker types fed up with scum and perverts—they think Harry is a peeping tom. Chico wants to haul them in, but Harry lets them go, understanding why they did what they did. During the next phase of the film, Scorpio continues to outwit the police and kill. Everyone, from the police chief on down, bemoans how powerless they are — that dirtbags like Scorpio can do anything while the police are literally handcuffed. The city is in a panic and something has to be done. But what? Before the police can figure their next course of action, Scorpio strikes again: He kidnaps a young girl, rapes her and buries her alive, sending the police a tooth he pulled out of her mouth with pliers.

Harry is chosen to deliver Scorpio's ransom. It becomes almost a quest, with Harry running from one end of the city to another, facing criminals who stand between him and gaining the girl's release. Harry's intensity regarding saving the little girl borders on

---

*During this time, the Zodiac killer was operating in the Bay Area; he shot people at random and to this day has never been captured.

obsession. When he delivers the money, Scorpio slams him against a concrete cross and strangles him. The crucifix doesn't save him, or Harry's partner, whom Scorpio severely wounds with a machine-gun, but Harry stabs Scorpio with a knife and the murderer flees. Harry tracks him to the football stadium where he lives in the basement. A detective tells Harry it is illegal for them to go in without a warrant, but the girl will die otherwise so Harry hops the fence.

Harry finds Scorpio and shoots him in the leg with his magnum, but the killer won't tell him where the girl is buried. Scorpio taunts Harry, tells him he has rights, that he wants his lawyer, telling Harry to leave him alone. Harry uses more force to find the girl. But she is dead, and for the first time we see Harry has some emotion as the coroner takes her body away. The next day, the district attorney tells Harry that they have to let Scorpio go. The search of the killer's apartment was illegal, as was torturing him to find where the girl was buried alive. The D.A. cites cases like Escobedo, and Miranda, and the Fourth Amendment — all of which Harry violated. Harry rejects the legal mumbo-jumbo and we find out why they really call him "Dirty."

Harry follows Scorpio on his own time. He is ordered by the department not to, but he shows no signs of giving up. When Scorpio kidnaps a bus full of kids and the mayor wants to pay him off, Harry takes matters into his own hands, waiting for the bus to pass and forcing it off the road. He and Scorpio shoot it out, and Harry finally kills the psycho. But, in a scene reminiscent of *High Noon*, Harry throws his badge into the river. Unlike Will Kane, who did not believe the town deserved a lawman, Harry thinks just the opposite, that San Francisco definitely needs lawmen — but our judicial system prevents it.

"Dirty" Harry Callahan is the prototypical vigilante cop. Roger Ebert called him a fascist. Either way, in the topsy-turvy world of the '70s, with serial killers, mass murderers and courts seeming to release criminals on technicalities daily, everyday Americans, particularly the white middle-class, felt threatened. Hollywood, never too far behind the popular animus, followed the trend with such films as *Death Wish* (1974), *White Line Fever* (1975) and *Defiance* (1979), all featuring ordinary folks taking the law into their own hands. But Callahan did it with a badge — and personified the belief that the only thing wrong with the law was too much law. Common sense and maximum force was all that was needed by police when confronting the crime wave sweeping the nation.

In *Dirty Harry*, Eastwood is the sole steady character when measured against the other people he works with and among. The victims mean something to him. They are not a number, they are a name, and they had a family and a story and a life. He doesn't forget it, though the others do. The mayor, who runs the city, is only worried about votes — what will happen to him if the children are harmed on the bus. The police chief is only worried about policies and procedures — such as why Callahan circumvented his orders and took his partner along when delivering the money to Scorpio. In fact, when Callahan tells him that he prefers a magnum weapon because of its power, the chief replies that no one should be thought of as an animal, clearly conflicting with the actions of Scorpio, who is worse than any animal ever conceived. Harry's partner Chico is promising, but after he is wounded, his wife wants him to quit and become a teacher. Getting shot at to protect people who call him pig isn't worth it, she tells Harry. The district attorney and an Appellate court judge brought in to review Harry's actions are as bad as the religious elite who crucified Jesus. The symbolic nature of the cross where Callahan was almost killed comes into play again. The D.A. and judge are only concerned with the letter of the law — whether it's no miracles on the Sabbath or no violation of search and seizure clauses — and Harry's the one left crucified this time.

Harry next appeared in *Magnum Force* (1973), this time battling, of all things, a group of vigilante cops! Before this can happen, though, Harry runs across a hijacking in progress at the airport, where he's eating a hamburger prepared by the ex-cop who runs the stand. Callahan puts on a pilot's uniform, boards the plane and then guns down the Arab-looking terrorists. Having firmly established his credentials and dominance once again, Harry spends the rest of the movie chipping away at the fascist exterior established in the first film: His partner is black, his girlfriend is Japanese, and when the vigilantes mess with them, they find themselves in big trouble.

Again, Harry is positioned in the middle ground most identifiable by audiences. Willing to bend the law, even break it if necessary to nab a killer, Harry is a man of force and action, but not lawlessness. The opening scene depicts a Mafioso (charged with murder) getting released on a technicality. The crowd outside the courtroom erupts in a fury, almost a riot, upset about such outrages being allowed by the judicial system. Acting on those feelings, a mysterious motorcycle cop kills the Mafioso and his bodyguards. Caught between the criminals and the vigilante cops, who almost appear like Hitler Youth, Harry again takes the common sense approach, exposing their operation and then gunning them down.

In 1976 Eastwood came back for one more go-round as Harry in *The Enforcer*. This time he has a plain female partner and he's on the hunt for brutal urban terrorists. The supporting cast has returned, too, giving the film some continuity, as though five years had not passed from the first installment. Harry kills but his vigilante cop routine seems stuck in neutral, in part because the story sags, and without Don Siegel directing, the film lacks the fast-paced quality of the first.

No one would have expected Eastwood to resurrect Inspector "Dirty" Harry Callahan after three times, but in 1983 he produced and directed *Sudden Impact*, which was a massive hit. Harry is as tough and ornery as ever, only now he's faced with his mirror image — a dirty "Harriet" who takes the law into her own hands to avenge a brutal sexual assault. Harry's opening shootout, which has become his stock in trade, takes place in a coffee shop he frequents. After dispatching the miscreants, he tells one of them to make his day! The saying became so popular it was used by such politicians as President Reagan when threatening to veto legislation.

The crime paranoia which drove the Dirty Harry films of the '70s was replaced by the conservative trends of the '80s. The film was more humorous than prior episodes, and by now Harry had become an icon; bending the law was expected of him. However, in this film, as he unravels the murders, he has to protect his fellow vigilante from not only the people she was killing but the police, who are hot on her trail. Harry is able to cover for his protégé, and by film's end, everyone who should be punished, is. It finally looked like Harry had a female love interest with staying power, but five years later Harry returned in *The Dead Pool* (1988) and started all over, this time romancing a reporter.

"Dirty" Harry Callahan's Southern counterpart is Sheriff Buford Pusser, a literally larger-than-life Tennessee lawman who waged a real-life one-man war on a gambling-liquor mob operating out of his county. Pusser was a big man, almost 6'6" and 250 pounds. He did a short stint in the Marine Corps and wrestled professionally, actually defeating a live grizzly bear in a match (Buford Pusser, n.p.). Pusser returned to his home in McNairy County and ran for sheriff in 1964. He was elected at the age of 27, served three times consecutively, and was eventually termed out. According to Pusser's Internet biography, during his time as sheriff he was:

X. *Vigilantes with a Badge*

The calm before a storm: A tender moment for Buford Pusser (Joe Don Baker) and wife Pauline (Elizabeth Hartman) in *Walking Tall*.

- Shot eight times
- Knifed seven times
- Fought off six men at once, sending three to jail and three to the hospital
- Destroyed 87 whiskey stills in 1965 alone
- Killed two people in self-defense
- Hopped on the hood of a speeding car, smashed the window and subdued the man who had tried to run over him

If the real-life Pusser was afraid of anything, he didn't show it. The people he was attempting to put out of business were ruthless; unfortunately for them, so was Pusser. Late one night in 1967 he was responding to a disturbance — his wife insisted on going with him — when the two of them were ambushed. Pusser's wife Pauline was killed and he had his jaw shot off.

The film *Walking Tall* (1973) is based on some events in Pusser's time as McNairy County Sheriff, and considering what Pusser had been through, he gave Hollywood a lot to fictionalize. Ironically, Pusser died in an automobile crash after he was set to play himself in the sequel. The authorities concluded it was an accident. Conspiracy theorists think otherwise.

In the film, Pusser and his family return to Pusser's childhood home in Tennessee, where he goes into business with his father. He has given up the violent life of wrestling and now runs a saw mill. One night he's set upon by goons who work at the gambling roadhouse. He takes on all comers but eventually they cut him up and leave him for dead. When Buford heals, he cuts himself a piece of wood and goes back, tearing up the roadhouse and anyone who gets in the way. Pusser is tried for the crime, but when the jury sees the scars on his body, they acquit him. He runs for sheriff and wins. That's when the fun really begins. Fist for fist. Knife for knife. Shot for shot. Buford Pusser will not back down. He attacks the moonshiners selling rot gut whiskey which kills young kids; he shuts down the gambling houses which cheat the customers, and whore houses where the clients are robbed. He hires the department's first black deputy, and relies more on his stick than a gun (but he *will* shoot). At last Buford cleans up McNairy County, but the personal cost is high. His wife is dead. His children are frightened. He's been disfigured. But justice prevails.

The difference between Dirty Harry and Buford Pusser can be imagined as the difference between dawn and dusk. Similar, but also poles apart. The men are physically large, and take the law into their own hands even though they both wear badges. But Harry's badge is too heavy — and Buford's too light. The people in San Francisco worry so much about the law, they forget about the victim. McNairy County doesn't have any law. The badge means nothing. The courts are crooked. The sheriff is corrupt. Payoffs are the order of the day. The gamblers and moonshiners run their business everywhere. When Buford confronts the dirty sheriff, he tells him how he admired him as a kid — how he used to think he "walked tall." When Buford becomes sheriff, walking tall becomes priority one. He fires the dirty deputies, replacing them with honest ones. He enforces the law equally for all people, no matter what their color. He puts the judge's chambers in a bathroom to show him what he thinks of his integrity. And most important is the stick — the symbol of what comes to those who transgress. Buford isn't afraid to use it.

Dirty Harry was a high-budget picture. *Walking Tall* was low-budget. They both appealed to the same fans even though the characters operated in different spheres. Harry wore suits and shot a lot of people. Buford wore jeans and beat up a lot of people. Both were after the bad guys and neither allowed little things like legal technicalities to stand in their way. But Harry was a more ambivalent figure. He wanted law and order, but didn't extend it too far into a person's personal affairs. His own morality was unconventional, and even though he smirked at homosexuals, he had a "to each his own" philosophy. Put another way, Harry split personal, private conduct from what should be done publicly.

In some ways, Harry's life mirrored that of Eastwood, whose public persona as one of the greatest actor-directors of all time has been cemented firmly in cinema history. Yet his private life, while generally quiet, has not been free of scandal. Pusser is a more conventional hero. Happily married, he loves his wife and children, lives with his folks in an extended family, and resists the charm of a prostitute helping him get the goods on the mob. Harry's long hair is not within department standards. Pusser is no hippie, and embodies a Southern traditionalism still reflected in the society today. Harry takes aim at the abstract — various segments of society thought to be troublesome, be it minorities, hippies, peaceniks. Pusser stands up against the concrete — a clearly identifiable menace like drugs, gambling, prostitution and their by-products.

If Harry is a libertarian, then Buford's a conservative. They accomplish the same things for many of the same reasons, but Harry is the less scrupulous of the two. Harry might break a law in private which he enforces in public. Buford would not. In *Magnum Force*, the ex-wife of a friend comes on to Harry. He does not resist — only a phone call from his superiors stops him. Pusser doesn't fool around though he has opportunities, and his off-duty life revolves around his family.

Another thing both characters had in common was sequels. *Part Two: Walking Tall* (1975) followed Buford's further exploits cleaning up McNairy County. This time Joe Don Baker, who played Pusser in the first film, was replaced by Bo Svenson, who follows the trail of syndicate types up the ladder to find who ordered the assassination of his wife. What is bizarre here is that the real Pusser had died the year before — so the story's ending is reduced to an anticlimax since we know what eventually happens to Buford. That doesn't stop the car chases, shootouts and stick-wielding. Film critic Roger Ebert liked the film and its view of the modern South. The folks Pusser is going against are not hillbillies but outlaws operating throughout a number of states.

Buford Pusser (Bo Svenson) changes faces, but the violence quotient remains the same in *Walking Tall Part 2*.

Walking Tall III (1977) carried on after Buford left office. He was not allowed to run again for sheriff, though his prospects appeared quite good, all things considered. He had a hit movie about his life, and was scheduled to star in the second film. The trilogy ended here, with Pusser's death, but the very next year Brian Dennehy picked up the wooden stick and served notice to McNairy County in the television film *A Real American Hero* (1978). The franchise was revisited with real-life wrestling star The Rock in 2004 — *Walking Tall* was still about Pusser's life, but the name had been changed to Chris Vaughn. The fighting intensified because of The Rock's physicality, and while some of the brutish elements were gone, there was still the kernel story of breaking up the syndicate-drug operation being run out of Indian casinos.

A wounded Buford (Bo Svenson) prepares to go into action. Is it ironic that Buford was killed in a traffic accident of his own doing? Or did his enemies finally get him?

Charles Bronson had a long career in film, but didn't get into major starring roles until the '60s, when he was in his late forties. Bronson is probably the most readily identifiable face attached to *the* vigilante, mostly because of *Death Wish*, a very depressing and violent look at New York City, and what happens when good people seem to disappear into the cracks. The film was a huge hit and boosted Bronson into superstardom. Like Dirty Harry and Buford Pusser, Paul Kersey, the architect-turned-vigilante, appeared in a number of *Death Wish* films, but only once as an agent for the police. In *Death Wish 3* (1985), Paul Kersey returns to New York City to see an old friend. When he gets there, he's stunned to find the neighborhood a war zone, and his friend murdered by gang members. Kersey is busted by NYPD, who find him with his friend's body. He is thrown into a holding tank with gangsters and thugs, but rams one punk's head through the iron bars when the man messes with him. Like Harry and Buford, Kersey is not a man to be taken lightly.

A police commissioner recognizes Kersey, and in return for not prosecuting him for his past activities, makes a deal: Kersey can clean up the neighborhood — his way — but he has to keep the commissioner informed of his actions. Kersey makes friends with the residents of the apartment building, protects them and, by film's end, leads a neighborhood attack against all the gangs. As the battle goes district-wide, the police move in to back up the neighborhood folks. Kersey and the commissioner fight side by side, and then he allows Kersey to escape quietly into the landscape.

Reportedly, after the second *Death Wish*, Bronson was tired of the vigilante films. However, gunplay in a New York City subway by a commuter sparked a resurgence of interest and support for vigilantism. In a nutshell, a group of black youths intimidated the shooter, who opened fire. Backing for the vigilante swelled, though he received a minor sentence. His popularity encouraged Bronson to sign up for his third *Death Wish* film. But even more interesting is that the Paul Kersey character is actually quite liberal. He was a conscientious objector during the Korean War; hated guns; and did not blame the police for his problems or the justice system. He was an environmentalist. He would not build a project in Arizona unless it was friendly to nature. His initial vigilante acts were more pathological: With his wife murdered and his raped daughter in an insane asylum, he felt personally relieved after taking some type of violent action against criminals he ran across.

Unlike Harry Callahan or Buford Pusser, Kersey does not have an agenda. Callahan goes after unpopular groups. Pusser establishes law where before there was corruption. (Pusser does have some revenge elements imbued in his quest for justice, but the people he is after are involved in the syndicate controlling the county.) Kersey merely protects his family and friends. In this instance, as an agent of the authorities, he's after a neighborhood gang that the police have problems corralling. Unlike in the first two films, Kersey has a sense of humor, and some scenes are funny even considering the violence that accompanies them. Kersey's love interest, a public defender, shores up his liberal credentials, and it's only after she is killed that the film kicks into high gear.

Ten to Midnight (1983) featured Bronson as an LAPD detective investigating a series of killings by a psycho who murders women who have rejected or somehow maligned him. Bronson interrogates him and, using a ruse to gain access to the man's bathroom, finds a sex perversion device. After the man is released for lack of evidence, Bronson speeds up the wheels of justice by planting blood evidence on his (the psycho's) clothing, but his young partner refuses to go along. The man is freed and Bronson suspended — but after the killer calls Bronson and threatens him, Bronson turns the tables and starts shadowing him!

Like his *Death Wish* character, Bronson has no ax to grind. The police are fine. He has no problems with minorities or other people. He is strictly interested in getting this guy behind bars. The narrative is split between Bronson and his young partner, played by Andrew Stevens. Bronson is an old-time cop, Stevens is the new breed. Bronson's family suffered because of his dedication to the department. Stevens is a college graduate with new theories and ideas. Bronson is what LAPD was; Stevens is what it will be. Where they come together is Bronson's daughter. He is trying to reestablish his bond with her. Stevens is attempting a romantic relationship. Both rush to save her from the killer. Bronson finally shoots the psycho in the head, though the man is attempting to give up.

Bronson's actions were what the viewer expected, desired even. The killer, while not as bad as Scorpio, is damn close. He strips down naked before he murders, and savagely uses a knife to gut the women, sometimes while they are having sex. At the film's climax, he knifes a whole dorm room filled with girls, then runs naked across the campus as Bronson chases him. The differences between the heroes and killer become apparent immediately. The psycho is mentally inferior to the young detective, Stevens, and physically weaker than Bronson, though he masquerades as a stud. Bronson feels comfortable around women. Stevens is a little shy but affable. The killer is impotent without his knife. The women he works around all think he's a weirdo or, worse yet, a creep. Their reactions to Bronson and Stevens are warm and friendly. When Bronson kills the psycho, the relief in the audience is palpable.

Ten to Midnight was more exploitation than most other cop-vigilante films: The bloodshed was up-close and personal, and so were the naked women. But in many ways, that's the nature of the beast. Their emotional content makes it that way. Callahan hunts killers who prey on children, terrorists who hijack planes, urban guerrillas, rapists and mass murderers. The sadism presented in *Walking Tall* gave Sheriff Pusser all the cause he needed to be just as savage. Bronson's quarry is even sicker, because the lower-budgeted films of Cannon (the producers of most of Bronson's '80s films) demand the violence be in the audience's face, as well as the naked female bodies that come with it. We know the celluloid lawman is right because the audience views the wrongs against him in their entirety. Watching them take care of business on screen is almost as good as them taking care of business in the field. Almost.

In real life, the line a vigilante cop must cross isn't so simple. When Harry tortures Scorpio to find the buried girl, most would agree. If he tortured a burglar to find some jewels, people might wonder. If he spray-painted the face of a tagger caught in the act, we might laugh. But what would we do if he stopped our uncle? Or our mother? The Rampart scandal of the early '90s weeded out LAPD officers who had framed suspects, planted evidence — robbed banks, even. Some of the suspects supposedly set up were hardened criminals with long records. Some were not. The catch for a vigilante cop like Dirty Harry is that he always knows who's guilty. And we know he always knows.

Sources

Ebert, Roger. *Dirty Harry*. *Roger Ebert's Video Companion*. CD-Rom. 1996.
Ebert, Roger. *Part Two: Walking Tall*. Rogerebert.com. 1–1–75 http://rogerebert.suntimes.com/apps/pbcs.dll/article?AID=/19750101/REV.
Kael, Pauline. *Dirty Harry*. *5001 Nights at the Movies*. CD-Rom. 1996.
Talentdisplay.com. *Buford Pusser*. 2005 www.talentondisplay.com/pusserabout.html.

XI

BAD APPLES

*I'm hell at whacking.**

The esteem or respect which a community affords to the police is dependent upon the honesty and integrity shown by the individual officers on the force. The old saying that a bad apple can spoil a whole bunch is never truer than when dealing with the justice system. Sordid stories of murder, beatings and rapes by law enforcement officials undermine confidence in those who are entrusted to protect society. Wearing the uniform entails great responsibility. The line between right and wrong may appear thin and hazy to an officer benefiting from the authority granted him by the public. In for a penny, in for a pound. The badge is never more tarnished than by those officers attempting to rationalize their own misdeeds, or, as seen in the following films, believing themselves to be beyond the law.

Touch of Evil (1958)

Orson Welles directed and starred in this film about Hank Quinlan, a corrupt detective working the rundown border town of Los Robles. When a car bomb detonates, killing the car's occupants, Quinlan finds a suspect — a young Mexican man in the company of the daughter of one of the victims. Mike Vargas, a Mexican narcotics officer working with his American counterparts, sees the explosion and offers his assistance in the investigation. Quinlan, an obese, bigoted detective, has a reputation for doing whatever it takes to get his suspect. Many suggest he plants evidence to make sure his suspects are found guilty. Vargas, who goes with Quinlan on a search of the suspect's house, believes Quinlan placed a bomb in a shoebox to frame the man. No one takes Vargas seriously — except Quinlan. When Vargas starts investigating Quinlan, the fat detective retaliates, using a local drug dealer whom Vargas had targeted in the past to threaten Vargas's wife.

The film's narrative is based on a novel entitled *Badge of Evil* and, as written by Welles, is ironic to the point of melodrama. Quinlan's wife was murdered years before, strangled, but no one was convicted. Quinlan's observation of the guilt of others is sharp; if he's framed suspects, he's always been right. But perhaps that's because of his own sense of guilt. Later in the story, Quinlan strangles the drug dealer he's been working with. He appears quite

---

*John Book (Harrison Ford) to the widow Rachel (Kelly McGillis) about what he's good at.

proficient at it, and the possible connection to his own wife's death hangs in the air. Vargas, who involves himself in an investigation which is really none of his affair, pushes a confrontation that might never have happened otherwise. At the film's end, after Quinlan has been killed, word comes that the Mexican suspect is indeed the killer who planted the bomb. The fat detective had the right man after all.

The observation that Quinlan was a great detective but a lousy cop is probably the biggest irony of all. Unlike most other crooked cops, where money is what tempts them, Quinlan's motives are more complex. If Quinlan didn't kill his wife, then framing suspects he believes are guilty means that's one more criminal who won't get away. If he did kill her, then perhaps each man he puts in prison makes him feel less guilty. Whatever Quinlan's reasons, in the final moments of the film, he floats dead in the filthy water of a canal, a fitting end to a man whose good work was overshadowed by the touch of evil which infected his soul.

Welles used all the cinematic resources at his disposal: He filmed in black and white; used canted and unorthodox camera angles; loud music during scenes of violence; in one scene, where Quinlan strangles the drug dealer, a caged bird goes crazy during the frenzy. Janet Leigh, who plays Vargas' wife, is almost treated as a doll by Quinlan, who has her drugged, posed on a bed in a white gown for the viewer to appreciate, and eventually arrested. The racial dynamic between her lily whiteness and her Mexican husband is somewhat assuaged by the fact that all–American Charlton Heston is playing Vargas, but it still remains in the background: Was she really incarcerated for marrying outside of her race? Lighting in the film is baroque — shadows and shades of gray throughout, and of course, Welles' massive bulk, his face puffy and blotched. The noir style, which Welles had been a part of since his masterpiece *Citizen Kane* (1941), is taken to extremes in this film. Though most noirs had petered out by the early '50s, one would not know it by watching this.

True Confessions (1981)

This dynamic film spotlights police corruption and the wheeling and dealings of politicos in the City of Angels during the 1940s — all as a bad cop trying to walk the straight and narrow investigates a savage killing. While the case is called something else, it is clearly the Black Dahlia, a tragic murder which was one of the most horrific in the city's history.* The victim was Elizabeth Short, a wannabe actress who made the rounds in Hollywood until she ran into the wrong man. One evening she left the Biltmore Hotel to meet a date; the next time she was seen was in pieces. Literally. She was cut in half, posed and abandoned in a dirt field. It was almost as if Jack the Ripper had crossed the pond and wanted to leave a calling card. The killer — or someone who found Short's purse — wrote to the newspapers, taunting the police (similarly, the Ripper mailed London police items belonging to the young woman).

Much has been written about the murder, the subsequent investigation and the various suspects and confessions. What hasn't been clarified is who the victim really was.

---

*Released information shows that the LAPD did an exhaustive investigation into the woman's murder which spanned years. One of their own detectives, Steve Hodel, wrote a book in 2004 called *Black Dahlia Avenger,* in which he names his father as the Black Dahlia's killer. His father, a noted doctor, pedophile and pervert, left the United States to avoid further police attention.

Popular belief held that Short was a prostitute, out to con any guy she could, and would do anything to get into the movies. In reality, nothing could be further from the truth. Short was born with a congenital defect that made conventional sex almost impossible. Any career as a streetwalker would have been short-lived. From her friends and women she roomed with, LAPD learned that she dated many men but was not intimate with any of them. Most of the time, she was looking for a free dinner and some laughs.

The media's fancy with the case passed after a few months, but LAPD continued to dig. False confessions poured in. Some were from drunks; others mentally ill. As in the Whitechapel murders, where London police had pinpointed a number of men likely to be Jack the Ripper, LAPD had a group of people under suspicion and observation. But no more killings followed — the leads eventually hit brick walls, and the Black Dahlia was largely forgotten except when resurrected by tell-all books claiming to know the identity of the killer. To this day, Elizabeth Short's murder remains a mystery, and while a savage killer walked away from his handiwork, cinema portrayals of the case and the officers pursuing her killer(s) usually solve the murder and provide the justice her brief life and brutal homicide demand.

In *True Confessions*, one of those dedicated men is Tom Spellacy, an LAPD detective who used to be a bagman for Jack Amsterdam, a large postwar builder in Los Angeles. Amsterdam is connected to Spellacy's younger brother Des, an up-and-coming priest who serves as advisor to the cardinal. In the world the brothers inhabit, vice and virtue are turned on their heads. Spellacy's badge used to be for sale — he ran the whorehouses for Amsterdam before the latter was a respectable construction tycoon. When Amsterdam sets up one of his madams to be convicted for his prostitution business (a fall that Spellacy and Amsterdam could have taken), the cop takes a long hard look at his life and goes straight.

Des goes the other way, falling as his older brother is rising from the muck. Des steers the archdiocese construction needs to Amsterdam despite the scandal surrounding the man. In return, Amsterdam pulls favors for the church, like getting certain land deeded over to them at a fraction of its real cost. Spellacy used to think that graft was owed a cop. Des seems to think that cutting corners and doing business with criminals is fine so long as it benefits the church. He associates with a number of businessmen who support the archdiocese, even though the men break every commandment they can and Des knows it.

A classic ends-versus-means dilemma develops, until a young woman is found cut in half and abandoned in a vacant lot. Spellacy pushes the case, even though his partners and supervisors slough it off, believing the girl to be a whore. The newspapers call her the "virgin tramp." No one cares except Spellacy. When he finds that both Amsterdam and his brother Des are connected to the girl, he has a tough decision to make.

As things stand, Spellacy can barely make it on his salary. His car is on its last legs, and he lives in a dump. Des, who's sworn to a life of poverty, lives in a mansion. Roles are reversed. At one time he was a simple priest; his mentor, Father Fargo, is an old-fashioned priest running a school. He clashes with the cardinal, and Des fires him. When Spellacy hounds his brother about dealing with Amsterdam, Des tries to extricate the archdiocese from doing business with him, not because it's morally wrong but to save the church from scandal. Only after it becomes apparent that Amsterdam may very well be the Black Dahlia's killer does Des come around, but by this point it's too late for him.

Spellacy's investigation leads him into a dark maze of sleaze and filth, and some old friends from his bag man days. The madam set up by Amsterdam is out of prison and, like the detective, barely making ends meet running a $5 whorehouse. Even though it's clear the feelings the two had for one another were strong, Spellacy let the woman take the rap. Still, she gives him information regarding the victim, tying her to a vicious stag film director. Eventually the woman kills herself, unable to live like she does. Spellacy's sense of guilt spurs him on even more, almost to obsession as he looks for a way to pin the murder on Amsterdam.

Spellacy solves the crime — the girl's killer is the pornographer, but he was killed in a car accident just after he murdered her. His "film studio" is an empty hangar in El Segundo, and Spellacy finds the tub where the killer cut her up and drained her blood. The detective arrests Amsterdam anyway, knowing it will ruin his career and his brother's, but more importantly it will put a stop to Amsterdam and his dirty practices. The builder is eventually released, but the scandal destroys him — as it does Des, who is dismissed by the cardinal. Spellacy never advanced further in the department, though he still had many years left before retirement.

Des takes a position in a poor desert parish, working alongside Father Fargo, learning how to be a real priest. Things aren't so good for Spellacy. His partner is still dirty, taking payoffs from Chinese restaurants and building a hotel with the money. His supervisors and fellow detectives remain on the take, and all Spellacy can do is handle things day by day. An honest cop in a crooked department, Spellacy's road is just as hard as his brother's, though both men have now regained their integrity.

Detective Tom Spellacy (Robert Duvall) and his partner Frank Crotty (Kenneth McMillan) investigate a savage murder in *True Confessions.* In 1940s Los Angeles, it's easy for a good cop to go bad.

Witness (1984)

An Amish widow and her young son are taking a train trip. During a layover in Philadelphia, the little boy walks around the station and is amazed at "modern devices" like a drinking fountain, something he's never used or even seen. He marvels at the paintings on the wall and ceiling — and when he uses the rest room, he witnesses the most brutal murder imaginable. Within a few hours, the widow and her son have been exposed to the best and worst of progressive society, and long to return to the safety of their Amish community in rural Pennsylvania.

Hard-nosed cop John Book, played by Harrison Ford, investigates the murder. He shows the boy lineups and mug shots, and even takes him and his mother through a ghetto to check out a prime suspect. The boy cannot identify the killer. While browsing around the police station, however, he sees the killer's photograph in a trophy case. Book, knowing the danger the boy is in from the crooked cops, goes to his supervisor, who tells him to remain quiet. Book is soon ambushed and wounded. Figuring the crooked cops will be coming after the boy next, Book picks up the mother and her son and drives them back to their home, where they can safely disappear among the thousands of Amish in the countryside.

In the big city, the Amish mother and her little boy were small fish in a large pond, and were certainly out of their environment. When Book is betrayed by his supervisor and

Detective John Book (Harrison Ford) gets physical while looking for a cop killer in *Witness*.

the other dirty cops, he takes refuge with the Amish to recover. Now the tables have turned — he is out of his element, only he's a shark in a pond full of goldfish. The narrative revolves around a series of contrasts. The Amish live in a world suspended in a time warp. No electricity. No indoor bathrooms. No cars. No fancy clothes. No modern medicine. Book is completely modern. He's never been in a prolonged environment without electricity, bathrooms, medicine or cars. When milking a cow, he tells the widow's father-in-law he's never held a tit that big.

The Amish are non-violent. Book is good at what the widow calls "whacking," their term for fighting. The disparity is apparent when tourists come to town. They bother, hinder and become nuisances to the Amish, who only want to go about their business. The Amish ignore them, but when a group of young men taunt one of Book's friends, he "whacks" one of them good in front of a crowd of shocked witnesses. The Amish don't believe in firearms. Book carries a .38, and when the little boy picks it up, his mother is livid. To blend in with the Amish, Book dons their simple clothes. Good at carpentry, he helps in a barn raising, symbolically blending the two ways of life, if even for just a moment.

The dirty cops have stolen from the police evidence warehouse barrels of a chemical which is needed to make narcotics. The man they killed in the rest room was an undercover cop trying to bust them. Schaeffer, Book's supervisor, heads up the criminal ring; he's a family man, happily married with children. Whenever talking to Book's friends, he uses a family analogy regarding the police department. Book is single, lives fast and easy, but wouldn't fit in with Schaeffer's world or with the other dirty cops. When Book falls in with the Amish, he becomes a family man, in effect, a surrogate father to the little boy. The

Detective John Book (Harrison Ford) says goodbye to the Amish boy (Lukas Haas) in *Witness*.

dirty cops, who act as family men, are killers. Book, who is honest, lives up to the ideal of the "good" cop most people think of: dedicated to family, job and doing the right thing.

The longer Book stays with the Amish, the more he respects them and the way they live. He falls in love with the widow but there is no sugary ending. Both are products of their own environment. The widow cannot enter Book's world of corruption any more than he can bring the evil of his world into hers. They go their own ways.

Witness was an interesting and, at times, a hypnotic film, with tall wheat waving in brisk wind to an enormous barn going up before our very eyes with a huge blue sky as the backdrop. The openness of the country clashed with the squalor and claustrophobia of the city, and until the dirty cops come looking to kill Book, one almost forgets the trouble Book, and the little boy, are in. Almost, but not quite. Every so often, Book calls Schaeffer to remind him that he will be coming back to get him soon. But Book's actions are both rash and futile. How deep the corruption goes is anyone's guess. The cops murder Book's partner, cover it up, yet Book is the only one who knows they did it. By coming to kill Book and the little boy, they publicize their own guilt. As Schaeffer rants to the Amish about being a police officer (all the while preparing to kill the little boy), the term has sadly lost all meaning.

We never know why the cops have sold out. Schaeffer makes a very comfortable living, supplying his wife and children with the best things money can buy — but nothing elaborate or what can't be bought on his salary. Drugs and the allure of easy money seem to be the incentive. Book makes the narcotic connection when telling Schaeffer about the cop whom the little boy identified, but nothing is spelled out beyond that. In one chilling scene, Book calls Schaeffer and asks why he went bad. While Book carries on, the family is having a party or barbecue, and one can see Schaeffer's nervousness — a man living two different lives, with each about to implode on the other. Schaeffer never answers Book, so why he and the other men crossed the line can only be surmised. Whatever the reason, they are a disgrace which Book eventually overcomes.

Above the Law (1988)

Steven Seagal burst onto the movie scene in this film about police duplicity and cover-ups, which he co-wrote and co-produced. Seagal plays Nico, a Chicago cop and family man who finds the CIA interfering with his investigation by protecting drug dealers. Nico himself was once a CIA operative, working in Vietnam during the war. He recognizes some of the players involved and, while uncovering the corruption surrounding the case, discovers the drug dealer is plotting to assassinate a crusading senator. Seagal, a master in Aikido, fights his way to the truth rather than using any brain power. Unlike most martial arts heroes, Seagal is solidly left-wing, and his film was a slap at the Reagan Administration, which was connected to the illegal support of Central American countries involved in a fight against Communism.

Seagal's narratives often revolved around police corruption and conspiracies. In *Hard to Kill* (1990), Seagal played an honest cop who exposes Mafia ties with a politician, and is killed by dirty cops on the politician's payroll. Only he really isn't dead — just in a coma. When he awakens, he goes after the dirty cops with a vengeance, using his martial arts to kill, maim and savage anyone in his way. Seagal's following films, such as *Marked for Death* (1991), which doesn't point to police corruption but rather their incompetence, and *The Glimmer Man* (1996), which reintroduces CIA interference with police investigations, validated the martial artist's liberal stance.

An Innocent Man (1989)

Tom Selleck is Jimmie Rainwood, an American Airlines mechanic charged with keeping the company's aircraft safe at LAX. He has a great job, a loving wife, and his life couldn't be any better — but it could get worse. When two dirty cops bust into his house by mistake looking for narcotics, then shoot him, they frame him as a drug dealer to cover their tracks. Convicted, Rainwood is sent north to prison and finds out just how bad life can get.

As the title says, Rainwood is an innocent man. The police are the ones who are guilty. But the world in which the mechanic finds himself is twisted and unrecognizable. The prison is a divided war zone. Blacks stay with blacks; whites stay with whites; Hispanics with Hispanics. The guards have heard every story a thousand times, and in a prison filled with people who say they didn't do it, their efforts are confined to keeping the perception of peace, not protecting inmates from one another.

Rainwood is targeted by the Black Guerrilla Family, in part because he refuses to harden into the usual convict. He's beaten almost beyond recognition by them, then thrown into solitary by the warden when he refuses to say who attacked him. The Aryan Brotherhood tells him he had better stick up for himself — or else. Another convict, Cane, attempts to school Rainwood in how to act in the joint. Rainwood refuses to listen, preferring to maintain his live-and-let-live beliefs — that is, until his tormentors show him some black Muslims raping a prisoner and then tell him he's next.

The narrative seems to be saying that such a tragedy could befall any of us. However, the cops are so unbelievably sleazy that it defies any logic that Rainwood could be convicted, let alone that the department wouldn't have caught on to these guys a long time ago. Working on tips from "confidential" informants, they burst into the apartments and houses of drug dealers, arrest or kill the suspects, then take some money and dope off the top — the latter gets re-sold back on the street. No one, including the judge in the mechanic's trial, seems to ask if the officers ever got a warrant, or why two officers are busting into these places without sufficient back-up.

The real lesson here is the nature of corruption, and the definition of what constitutes crime, particularly in the upside-down world that Rainwood's been thrust into. The cops who busted him are nothing more than felons with badges. What about the prison guards? All disturbances of the peace are dealt with quickly and with maximum application of force. The warden knows the BGF is responsible for almost killing Rainwood; he also knows that for a prisoner to "snitch" on another prisoner is a death sentence from all the groups in the yard. Throwing Rainwood into solitary confinement is tantamount to punishing the mugging victim while the muggers walk free.

The prison rules seem saner, simpler, even fairer than the laws governing the outside. You stick to your own kind, and take care of your own problems. For Rainwood, it means killing one of the BGF members. Otherwise, he knows what's coming. He stabs the man with a knife made out of sharpened Plexiglas, breaking the blade off in his gut. Everyone knows Rainwood did it, including the warden, but no one saw anything. Now he's established and the blacks back off. In Rainwood's environment, did he commit a crime? Should the warden investigate the murder?

Rainwood is eventually paroled, which essentially means he's walking a tightrope the police can cut at any time. In prison he had earned respect; because he was permitted to hang out with Cane, who was something of a legend, others knew that Rainwood was not one to mess with. Now he's back in the real world, where things should be better, but once again they're upside-down. The dirty cops are leaning on him — will they frame him again? In prison, blacks were the enemy. On the outside, a black internal affairs detective is the only person who can stop the rogue cops. Once again Rainwood needs Cane, who was also set up by the same cops years before.

Rainwood eventually clears his name, and the cops are busted by the department. But the happy ending belies some not-so-pleasant particulars. If the yards of a prison can be a more rational place than the city he once lived, hope that society can ever evolve into a better place is certainly dim. Roger Ebert calls the film's lesson fascist — the victim must protect himself with force when society can't — but that seems more like common sense. The real lesson is: When cops go bad, they need to be dealt with quickly. When prisoners have a higher moral code than outside society, the world truly is upside-down.

Internal Affairs (1990)

Dennis Peck is a highly decorated veteran of the Los Angeles Police Department. He's been on the job a long time and earned the respect of everyone, from the chief down to the boots just coming out of the academy. He's not a sergeant, he's not a two-striper, he's just an officer working day after day on the mean streets of Los Angeles. But therein lies part of Peck's problem. His partner is being investigated by Sgt. Raymond Avila from internal affairs. The fact that Peck is such a hero in the department but hasn't been promoted makes Avila suspicious. He believes that Peck is involved in criminal behavior, both off- and on-duty. By remaining a street officer, Peck can fly under the radar and do what he wants. And he does. Peck provides the often cash-strapped officers with off-duty gigs at a fancy mall. He talks to supervisors on behalf of other officers. He has a string of ex-wives children, and lovers across the city. And he's available for any number of criminal jobs, off- or on-duty.

Peck's partner Van Stretch feels the heat from I.A. and is about to crack. He tells Peck he's going to name names to try to save his job. Peck arranges for some illegal aliens to kill his partner while they are on a vehicle stop; he's worried what his partner will say about him and his activities. Avila turns his attention to Peck, whom he believes killed Van. Peck, knowing that I.A. is after him, watches his back, but continues on with his activities. He's hired to kill an elderly couple by their son, who wants them out of the way so he can modernize their business. Peck kills the man's parents, but is eventually tracked down by the I.A. officers and killed. Yet Peck's death leaves a strange void for many because he was not a one-dimensional, cardboard character like Book's supervisor, Schaeffer. On the one hand, he is a horrible man, one who killed his partner, and who also works as a hit man. On the other, he's a loving parent, a brave man, and someone respected for his past heroism.

Like *Witness*, this film works off a set of disparities. Peck is a man who has proved himself in the street — no easy desk jobs for him. He commands respect from everyone. Avila works in an office setting, in suit and tie. He stays away from the hard part of the job, and as an Internal Affairs investigator is hated universally among rank and file officers. When the two men get together, it becomes a boxing match, both figuratively and literally. Peck, cagey and streetwise, senses trouble in Avila's life. He investigates a little, and finds out that Avila is having marital problems. In front of City Hall, Peck comments about Avila's wife. The I.A. investigator punches him. Peck is now under his skin and has the upper hand. Later, Peck arranges a meeting with Avila's wife, knowing that Avila is following him. It appears from a distance they might be having an affair. As Avila comes out of an elevator, Peck is waiting, and decks him. He throws Avila's wife's panties in Avila's face and tells him to clean up. Peck has now established himself superior to Avila, both physically and mentally.

Unlike John Book, who is strictly honest, Avila is not. In fact, it's Peck's superiority which pushes Avila to be dirty, too, to push what he is doing beyond the law. Peck's supervisors examine the evidence against Peck, find nothing serious and do not approve any further investigation of him; Avila keeps going anyway. At that point, Avila has nothing solid and should leave Peck alone. However, he follows Peck off-duty, investigates on Peck's ex-wives and family, and eventually runs an illegal financial check on Peck, which leads to the discovery of Peck's criminality. Avila begins searching for the illegal-alien killer of Peck's partner, hoping he might provide information about Peck. To back him up, Avila uses some gun-toting relatives, who are no better than gang members and criminals. At one point, Avila becomes so unglued that he assaults his wife in a fancy restaurant while she's having dinner with a co-worker.

In *Witness*, the motive for the cops to become dirty is assumed to be drugs and money. In *Internal Affairs*, it's all too clear that Peck is supporting tons of children, all of whom he loves, and ex-wives, who all still love him. Money obviously drives him as well. When Peck crossed the line in the first place isn't addressed. And, for that matter, it wasn't with Book's supervisor Schaeffer, either. What makes a man who has done so much good become so bad? Neither film provides a clear answer as to when the cops first went down that road, disgraced themselves, and sold their integrity at wholesale prices.

Officer Dennis Peck (Richard Gere), left, confronts IA investigator Raymond Avila (Andy Garcia) in *Internal Affairs*.

Bad Lieutenant (1992)

A nun is raped in a ghetto church. The Mafia posts a reward. And the lieutenant assigned to investigate the crime is arguably worse than the rapists or the mobsters. Such is the case of the bad lieutenant, a man so warped we never learn his name—and never want to.

Like Schaeffer and Peck, the lieutenant lives a double life. At home he's a family man—but barely. His life away from home is mostly a drug-induced haze. Addicted to coke, alcohol and any other mind-numbing substance he can get his hands on, the lieutenant must use every ounce of his diminishing sanity to remain calm at home. When the nun is raped, the lieutenant interviews her, but she has already forgiven her attackers, leading the lieutenant to wonder about his own redemption.

Unlike the protagonists of *Witness* or *Internal Affairs*, the lieutenant has no good characters to play off of. Other officers are as cynical as he is, though perhaps not dirty and certainly not addicts. Like Orpheus descending, the lieutenant visits prostitutes, secretly watches the nun strip down during her rape physical, even stops some teenage girls from driving without a license and masturbates in front of them and ordering them to watch. His anger rages as well. He is in debt to the mob for losing bets during the World Series; at times he's so furious he fires his gun and curses the Dodgers, on whom he has bet. At the film's end, the bad lieutenant is well over his head in debt, but he's caught the rapists. In a bizarre turn of events, he frees the criminals as a way to find some personal salvation.

If the bad lieutenant is "bad" for himself, he is even worse for society. His sanity is in question. Are the things he sees real or delusions? He pays prostitutes just to feel a human touch, robs thieves for extra cash, and sees Jesus, but in his wasted state of mind, it could be the Zig Zag Man. He just doesn't know—but he does know he can't go on. Having captured the rapists, he lets them go. Looking for the same type of serenity as the nun, and perhaps a sense of deliverance, he saves them from the horrors to come, either prison or the mob. But, in reality, he's released two criminals back onto the street, two monsters who are likely to menace communities over and again until they are caught and imprisoned. Ultimately, the bad lieutenant receives his redemption from a bookie, who fills him full of holes during a drive-by shooting. Perhaps not what the dirty cop desired, but probably the only way any salvation was coming to a man like this.

Dark Blue (2002)

Two cops—one trigger-happy and having no remorse pulling it, and the other possessing a lingering bit of conscience, which makes him weak in a department where strength is valued above all. *Dark Blue* is a police corruption film that used the Rodney King beating debacle of the early '90s as a backdrop. The attachment is tenuous at best, and the sleaze almost cartoon-like. Kurt Russell stars as Perry, an LAPD detective assigned to Special Investigation Section (SIS), an elite division tasked to hunt down the most infamous criminals in the city. The SIS's history has been a very successful, if equally controversial one. Officers in the unit stake out and follow high-risk felons, waiting for them to commit serious offenses. They've been known to allow the suspects to commit low-grade crimes without taking action, preferring to catch them doing something serious. Because of the dangerous nature of their work, the unit's officer-involved shooting ratio is much higher than other divisions within LAPD. Many claim that the officers are merely cowboys with a Wild West attitude, shooting first and making up the answers to the questions afterward. Those victimized by the criminals taken off the streets by SIS would argue differently.

Russell's character is burned-out, his personal life a mess. The job is a different story: It gives him a purpose to keep going and it's the one thing he remains good at. Unfortunately for those around him, he's a time bomb ticking, someone who's suspected of routinely killing the felons he catches. His guardian angel is Van Meter, an old-school dick who goes back decades and decades to the '50s. He's worse than Russell, and often tells his protégé which felons or criminals he wants offed. Russell blithely kills those in need of disposal, until he's faced with a dilemma: Van Meter has his partner killed because he's weak and ready to talk. Russell now must decide if there's enough cop left in him to confront Van Meter and make him pay.

Dark Blue takes a shotgun approach to the narrative, hitting a number of issues and moving on. LAPD, like any police department, has its secrets and its cliques. Van Meter's power is that he knows where the skeletons are buried, and has probably planted a few himself. He helps his people move up the ladder, and uses blackmail and intimidation to keep his enemies down. Holland, a deputy chief, wants Van Meter out of power — not because he's necessarily corrupt or a killer but because the chief heads up the "black" faction which wants to take control of the department. Van Meter stands in his way.

The film's depiction of racial polarization within LAPD is clearly more interesting than that of police corruption. Russell's character, which represents a good cop turned bad, kills people most citizens would say good riddance to. His baseness is not exactly riveting. But the struggle between the aging white warhorses running the department, and Chief Holland and his followers trying to pull a coup, *is*. At a major department function, Russell comes in and exposes Van Meter in front of everyone, clearing the way for Chief Holland to take over. However, even more compelling was the response of the officers and supervisors sitting in the auditorium to the Rodney King verdict. When the white officers speak highly of the accused and are happy they are not convicted, Chief Holland and other blacks remain silent. The same division of opinion split officers everywhere, mostly along racial lines.

The film ends with the city in the beginning stages of a riot. Chief Holland and Russell talk as they look out from atop City Hall at the spreading flames. Neither man seems all that concerned with what is happening. For Russell's character, who's about to go to prison for a long, long time, it might be understandable. For Chief Holland it's inexcusable — or is it? While the real LAPD Police Chief Daryl Gates was popular with his officers and with much of the city, Mayor Bradley and others wanted him out. The riot hastened his departure, and the city's first black police chief, Willie Williams, was appointed afterward. Williams' credentials were rather threadbare, and many of the candidates who tested for the job were of the opinion that the city fathers were going to pick him regardless. Nero supposedly fiddled while Rome burned — Chief Holland may very well have been thinking the riot was the best thing going with regard to promotion.

Sources

Ebert, Roger. *An Innocent Man*. Rogerebert.com. 10–6–89 *http://rogerebert.suntimes.com/apps/pbcs. zd11/article?AID=19891006/REV*.

XII

Keystone

It's true what they say: Cops and women don't mix. It's like eating a spoonful of Drano: sure it will clean you out, but it will leave you hollow inside.*

You're a disease, and I'm the cure.†

Comedy is a funny thing — no pun intended. It is perhaps the most difficult genre for the writer to write and the actor to act. There's dry humor, where the wit is carried through the dialogue and the way the actors deliver it. There's slapstick, with lots of physical activity. Think the Three Stooges. When Moe slaps Larry, who then slaps Curly, who then slaps Moe ... well, you get the picture. Parody and sight gags play what is seen by the audience against what is supposed to be happening. Mack Sennett's Keystone Cops and the *Naked Gun* films are good examples. And, of course, there are jokes and wisecracks, which characters reel off to comment upon their situation.

Police "humor" seems a little like a contradiction in terms. Most cops find some comedy in their daily duties, though perhaps, like coroners, it may be a little unusual. How many police films depict one of the partners hungry after paying a visit to the mortuary and watching an autopsy?

Even television commercials have gotten into the act. One, for Outback Steak House shows two police officers enjoying a hearty Code 7 (lunch), laughing, sharing stories, the older one presumably passing on his knowledge and experience to the younger one. The scene is lit with an abundance of earth tone hues, browns and golds, to reinforce the heart-warming aspects of two men bonding over the great food available at the restaurant. A later shot shows the two officers walking side by side, satisfied at their great meal and the close attachment they have formed. The older man, wearing sergeant stripes, is a mentor to the younger one. The commercial cuts to the men getting into their black-and-white squad car. In the back seat, in the built-in cage, sits a prisoner, who is upset with the officers — but is it because they left him? Or because he didn't get to eat, too? Both officers just laugh at him.

The officers are presented in a semi-serious way, symbols of the law. When we see they left a prisoner in the car to eat, two ideas are imparted: one, that the steak house serves such good food that the officers would risk their jobs by eating there, prisoner or no; and two, that the prisoner probably deserves that kind of treatment. Viewer

---

**Frank Drebin (Leslie Nielsen) in* Naked Gun: From the Files of Police Squad!
†*"Cobra" (Sylvester Stallone) warning any number of the scum in* Cobra.

identification is already established with the officers. What does it hurt if they eat, especially at a great place like Outback? The real comedy here is the fact that most officers don't get paid enough to eat at a place like Outback Steakhouse, at least not for lunch on a regular basis.

Genre Characteristics

In gritty or violent police films, like any other kind of movie, flashes of humor may help move along a story. In *Death Wish 3*, Paul Kersey, working for the NYPD, purposefully parks a nice car in front of his apartment in a bad neighborhood. He has dinner with the elderly residents of the building. When he hears the local gang breaking into the vehicle, he walks out to see what is happening. The punks ask what Kersey wants and he says that it's his car; then he calmly shoots them.

In *Cobra* (1986), Sylvester Stallone plays the title character. A raving maniac has taken over a supermarket, shooting women and children, and holding hostages. The police send in Cobra, a one-man killing machine, to confront him. The maniac tells Cobra he is going to blow up the supermarket — to which Cobra replies something to the effect, go ahead, I don't shop here anyway.

Actual police comedies vary in degree and intensity. Some are very broad in their humor, and concentrate less on the police aspect; some vice versa. But a number of distinctions remain common throughout, though not all will be present in any one film:

1. The police are not held responsible for their outrageous actions. In many films, lawmen will commit shocking deeds for which there are no ramifications. In *Police Academy* (1984), a number of bizarre and unsuitable trainees are hired by a police department. Despite the fact that none of them could really be hired, their antics are beyond the pale. In one scene they hire a prostitute to hide inside the podium and perform — well, you get the idea — on the police chief who is making a speech. In another they set up their nemesis — the sergeant — in a gay bar, with the requisite encounters that follow. Of course, the cadets get away with all of it and are soon on the streets, protecting the fine citizens of the city.

2. The peace officers are hardly competent, but often don't realize it. Some narratives place a tenderfoot as the marshal, or a rank amateur as the sheriff. In *The Outlaws Is Coming* (1965), the Three Stooges head west with Adam West, a photographer for an Eastern newspaper. The local kingpin wants to control the town so West becomes sheriff. The only problem is that he can't shoot. Annie Oakley, who secretly loves West, stands in the shadows and shoots down the bad guys for him. The kingpin hires every bad man ever shown in movies, from Johnny Ringo to Cole Younger, to face the sheriff, and it's up the Stooges to become deputies and keep their friend out of trouble.

3. The lawmen have little or no effective supervision. In committing their antics, the peace officers have no one to reel them into reality or put the brakes on their manic actions. In *Naked Gun 33 1/3: The Final Insult* (1994), Lt. Frank Drebin, played by Leslie Nielsen, comes out of retirement at the behest of his supervisor, played by George Kennedy, to catch a mad bomber. To do so, he infiltrates a sperm bank (!) and the Academy Awards, among other places, and Kennedy can't restrain Drebin from making a shambles of the ceremony. The jokes about the movies being nominated, such as a musical about Mother Teresa, provide almost as many laughs as Drebin's tricks.

    4. *The heroes often find themselves in extreme or otherwise preposterous situations.* How these people get where they are is often unexplained or is ridiculous in and of itself. In the opening scene of *Naked Gun* (1988), Drebin breaks up a conference of evildoers and then returns to the good old U.S. of A. The waiting crowd cheers as he gets off the plane, but we find it's not for him but, rather, Weird Al Yankovic!

    5. *Justice prevails, though police work, or for that matter logic, has nothing do with it.*

In all of the *Naked Gun* films, Drebin saves the day, but how he got from point A to B, while certainly side-splitting, is completely without reason. In *Loaded Weapon I*, a take-off on the *Lethal Weapon* films, how the detectives bust the villain, played by William Shatner, is incomprehensible. Of course, with one joke being followed by another, the audience doesn't really care. In one scene, taken right from the *Weapon* films, Samuel Jackson is sitting on a toilet. His partner, Emilio Estevez, fearing something is amiss, busts into the bathroom and asks what's wrong. Jackson replies that he's taking a sh —.

Lt. Frank Drebin (Leslie Nielsen) displays proper eating habits in ***The Naked Gun 2½.***

Lt. Frank Drebin (Leslie Nielsen) protects Jane Spencer (Priscilla Presley) in *The Naked Gun*.

Kindergarten Cop (1990) is a fine example of many of the elements discussed above. Arnold Schwarzenegger plays a hard-boiled detective who has to teach a kindergarten class while conducting a murder investigation. During the opening act, Schwarzenegger arrests a murdering drug dealer he's been pursuing for almost half his time on the force. He arrests the man, but his witness won't cooperate. Schwarzenegger follows the woman to her drug hangout. Using a police riot gun, he blows the place to smithereens, shooting everything

Arnold Schwarzenegger disciplines his class in *Kindergarten Cop*.

in sight. After all the other drug addicts have fled, he takes a seat next to his witness and lets her know that unless she cooperates, he is going to hound her night and day. The next scene shows her identifying the murderer.

Schwarzenegger's violent and unlawful outburst is not even addressed in the story. He could have killed someone, but the scene is treated in a comical way, with Schwarzenegger beating one suspect, and scaring others, and this is *before* he shot up the drug house. Being a comedy cop has advantages.

Schwarzenegger is quite competent and effective as a police detective. He's in shape, deadly, and ready for action. But as a teacher, he's in way over his head, especially with a bunch of six-year-olds. He finds himself in an absurd position. Without warning he's teamed with a female partner and they're sent off to Oregon, to an elementary school in Astoria. Just a few days before, he was shooting up a warehouse full of drug addicts—now he's taking care of little children. And a thousand miles from Los Angeles, neither he nor his partner have any supervision. Schwarzenegger solves the case, but not by anything he or his partner does. The murderer is released from prison after the witness against him is killed, and he comes to Astoria to kidnap his son from his ex-wife. How the killer knew which school to check out is never revealed. Arnold kills him, but is also wounded. But perhaps the most comical thing of all is that he remains in Astoria to become a real kindergarten teacher.

Going back some years, in *Destry Rides Again* (1939), James Stewart plays the title character, the son of the famous marshal who in his own right has established quite a reputation as a man with a gun. The town of Bottleneck, which is being run by the infamous saloon owner Kent, is almost completely lawless. The town sheriff has been killed by Kent for trying to stop him stealing other ranchers' property through crooked games of poker. In a cruel and sad joke, Kent and his partner, the judge, appoint Wash as the new sheriff. Only Wash is the town's drunk. He plays his banjo in the saloon for drinks. Wash used to be Destry's deputy but had fallen on hard times when the famous lawman left town. When Wash finds out he's been made sheriff, he swears off the bottle and calls for Destry's son to be his deputy. He's very surprised, as is the town, when Destry arrives wearing no guns and carrying a woman's parasol. The son put away his guns when his father, the older Destry, was back-shot by villains and killed.

The film has all the makings of a serious story, and in some ways it is. Destry has to get the goods on Kent and the crooked judge, and return the ranches to the victims who have had them stolen. But how? He's foresworn carrying six-shooters or rifles. The town thinks he's sissy or, worse yet, a coward. Wash is near tears, and Kent humiliates Destry in front of everyone in the saloon. But the deputy has a plan — find where they buried the body of the sheriff they murdered, and then he and Wash can put them behind bars where they belong. To help their cause, they enlist another "misfit," Callahan, a Russian immigrant who's so bullied by his American wife that they call him by her name and not his own. So the town's law is set: one expert with firearms who won't carry them; one ex-drunk who can't shoot any more; and one foreigner who doesn't know anything about a gun. Kent thinks he's got the town wrapped up just the way he wants it. Only he underestimates Destry...

When Destry arrives in town, he isn't wearing a firearm, something everyone carries, even if they can't shoot one. Callahan's the only one who doesn't carry one and that's because his wife won't let him. That very fact is outrageous. The entire town knows he is coming to take on Kent, and without a gun he should be easy pickings. But Kent and the others merely laugh and humiliate him. Frenchie, the saloon girl, gives him a bucket and a mop and tells everyone that's how Destry must have cleaned up all those wild towns. Kent's men and the rest of the saloon are splitting a gut. When Destry goes into Kent's saloon to have a drink, he orders milk! More laughter. Destry's actions have made a mockery of himself and Wash, who was bragging all over town about how he was going to take care of business when his famous deputy got there.

Destry, like Wash and Callahan, appears inept, but he's not. He's smart and knows the key to busting up Kent's racket is to find where the gambler buried the sheriff's body. By playing the fool, Kent and his men underestimate Destry. Wash, however, means well but can barely get his gun out of the holster. Callahan doesn't know what a holster is! When some ruffians start shooting up the town, Destry confronts them. Of course they laugh at him. But when the deputy borrows their guns and puts on a shooting display that would impress Wild Bill Hickok, the men back down, and many in the town begin thinking there's more to Destry than meets the eye. Later, a huge, bullying cattleman tries to take the law into his own hands but Destry kayoes him with one punch.

How Destry ends up in this outlandish situation is touched upon but never explained. We know he gave up wearing a gun after his dad was shot in the back, but how did a seasoned lawman think he could tame a town whittling shower curtain ringlets? Wash as sheriff is the most ridiculous thing going — except perhaps the Three Stooges as Adam West's deputies. Callahan can barely speak English. He spends half the film trying to steal other people's pants because the saloon girl Frenchie won his in a poker gang. Like *Kindergarten Cop*, the film gets somewhat serious at the climax, when Kent's men murder Wash. Destry straps on his guns to confront Kent, as the women of the town march on the saloon where Kent is holed up with his men and attack them. Destry kills Kent but only after Frenchie sacrifices her life to save his.

Unintentional Comedy

Sometimes movies are supposed to be serious, or action-packed, but instead come across as so ridiculous that they really are comedy, only no one told the director or the actors. *Cobra* falls into this category. Cobra is assigned to investigate a serial killer terrorizing the city. He has no leads, but suspicion is on a Satanic cult working to bring about the end of the world. A high-class model leaving from a late-night photo shoot sees the killers at work. At another photo shoot a few days later, the cult tries to kill her. She survives the attack and is moved to the hospital, where police have a 24-hour guard on her. They try again but Cobra is too fast and thwarts them. Finally, Cobra takes the model on a ride across country to protect her, only the Satanists find him and he has to battle the whole coven.

Cobra provided plenty of action, but so much inadvertent comedy that it ranks as one of Stallone's funniest films, which surely was not the intent. The humor starts with the opening sequence in the supermarket, and only gets better as the minutes pass. Though the market is surrounded by SWAT and patrol officers, the captain decides to call in "The Cobra." Stallone arrives in a hot rod, goes into the building all by himself and liquidates the cultist. Later scenes of the cultists show them in some kind of warehouse, smashing together their medieval weaponry in almost a techno-dance. The cultists try to kill the model a number of times but it never occurs to anyone to give her more protection than just the Cobra and his partner. Finally, when the Satanists catch up to Cobra and the model, he dispatches them almost by his lonesome, then goes to fight the head cultist, who likes to do the weapon-smashing techno-dance the most!

The film's intentional comedy — that is, what the director put forth — relied a lot on sight gags and wisecracks. In the supermarket, trading shots with the cultist, Stallone picks up a beer. At his home, he opens the refrigerator and pulls out a pizza box which contains his gun-cleaning kit! The parking structure chase between the bad guys and Cobra is enough to put one to sleep, except for the fact it's obvious Stallone isn't driving the car. When Cobra goes home at night, he has to use his car to push low riders away from the curb so he can park. When they surround him, he grabs one of the men and pulls his shirt down, telling him to buy some new clothes.

Cobra operates on many of the same principles as *Kindergarten Cop*, though Schwarzenegger's movie is supposed to be a comedy while Stallone's is not. Cobra employs extreme uses of force but there are no repercussions, except by a high-ranking police official who hates Cobra and wants him cashiered. Cobra's captain is a loudmouth who really gives him no guidance, except to tell him to go find the killers or some such nonsense. Cobra certainly finds himself in a ridiculous predicament when he takes the model on a road trip to protect her. Can one really be protected driving around sightseeing? In the end, Cobra saves the day, but not by anything he did: The cult finds them, not vice versa, and at that it takes Cobra and his partner forever and a day to realize they've been double-crossed by the female officer who is on the road with them.

Not to be outdone by Stallone, Steven Seagal throws his weight around, which by that time had been increasing, as "Gino," the most feared cop in Brooklyn, in *Out for Justice*

(1991). Gino's partner Bobby, another Italian, is gunned down in the street in front of his wife and children by Ritchie, a childhood pal of Gino's. Gino spends the entire night prowling the streets of the city with an unmarked police car, his 9mm and a riot gun. He rousts Ritchie brother, sister, even the man's parents. He meets with old pals from the neighborhood, rescues a cute puppy thrown from a moving car, even finds time to talk to the streetwalkers.

Gino finally tracks down Ritchie at the apartment of an old girlfriend. The killer and his gang have called up for some hookers and are having a party. Gino moves in quietly and then shoots up the place. When only Ritchie is left, he pummels him using his skills in Aikido. The brutality of the fight alone is almost more than anything seen in the prior 80 minutes of the film. Every time Ritchie gets up, Gino savages him again, until he slams a corkscrew into the slime's brain.

Seagal's performance in the film was something of an acting stretch for him: In some parts he spoke his dialogue in both Italian and Spanish, and his New York City accent was convincing. Also, many of the film's songs were written by him, including the closing tune (sung by Greg Allman), a great bluesy rocker. Where things went wrong was the actual story — a New York City cop on a seek-and-destroy mission, sanctioned by the department, and nothing secret about it. The revenge aspect of the plot is the same as a million other films of the same ilk. In cinema, cops often take revenge on their partner's killers — but most attempt to remain within the bounds of "Hollywood realism." Seagal is so flamboyant that any sense of reality is jettisoned within the opening sequence, when he jeopardizes a $3 million drug deal just to beat up a pimp slapping around one of his girls.

Where much of the action in *Cobra* is cartoonish, Seagal's brand of action goes the other way, bordering on sadism, and the violence itself is piled on so high and thick it becomes sickly comical itself. When Bobby is gunned down, Gino arrives on scene amidst much hoopla, police cars everywhere. Gino wears a beret of some kind, probably military, signifying his war service. Everyone knows him. Gino tells his captain he'll find Ritchie and, like that, without any direction or guidance, he is turned loose on the city with only one goal — kill Ritchie. As Gino moves through the neighborhood, he gets into a number of altercations. In a deli, some of Ritchie's men attack him. He meat-cleavers one of them, and then incapacitates the rest with various gruesome bone breaks. He leaves the scene of the attack without even calling the situation into his station, and nothing is even mentioned. Later, while Gino is talking to his wife, they are attacked by Ritchie's thugs, and Gino kills five of them. Or maybe six. By a certain point, Seagal kills so many bad guys that accurate numbers became hazy. He then calls the station, tells them what happened, and is on the road again.

Gino visits Ritchie's brother's pool room. He beats up a whole division, each victim getting it in a "funnier" method than the last. One guy says he's a boxer so Gino knocks him out. Another guy talks smack so Gino breaks out his front teeth. Fortunately for this fellow, his missing teeth do not prevent him from joining Ritchie in the hooker party at the end of the film. Obviously, if one can't find a good dentist, well, a good prostitute will do. A few other guys playing pool get hit with a cue ball wrapped in a towel. An Asian guy called "Sticks" begins swinging cues around but Gino merely plays with him, then breaks his jaw. When Gino leaves, no one is left standing — but he still doesn't know where Ritchie is.

Then there's the Mafia. They want Ritchie, too. He's brought shame to them, along with some bad publicity, so they're hunting him. Gino meets with "the don" in a tiny deli, to pay his respects. Later, the don wants to see Gino. He instructs his men to "tell" Gino — then stops and rephrases: "*Ask* Gino," he says, to meet with him at his favorite restaurant. Gino is so feared and respected that even the mobsters don't mess with him.

Gino saves the most humorous for last. After busting up the party and shooting the riot gun in the midst of rooms filled with hookers whose only crime is a questionable occupation, Gino gets the girls out and kills all of Ritchie's henchmen. He tosses Ritchie into any number of pieces of furniture; whenever Ritchie gets up, he looks worse and bloodier. Thrown into the kitchen, Ritchie grabs a stick. Gino takes it away and uses it on him. Ritchie picks up a knife and Gino breaks some bones. Ritchie says he likes the pain, and finally moves up the chain of household weapons to the corkscrew, which Gino firmly embeds into his skull. Each time Ritchie gets up, there is that sick chuckle which comes from knowing one shouldn't enjoy seeing gruesome pain inflicted upon another person, yet enjoying it anyway because that person is despicably psychotic.

Invasion USA (1985) puts Matt Hunter, played by Chuck Norris, in the unenviable position of having to save the country from terrorists plotting to overthrow it. As a retired federal agent, he's re-enlisted to stop an actual invasion of Florida. The story, while ridiculous, certainly comments on the state of the nation's border security. Estimates in 2005 place over 11 million illegal aliens in the country. Otherwise, *what were the producers thinking*? Hunter lives in a swamp, in a shack, isolated from everyone and everything except animals and insects. When the terrorists land on the beaches of Florida, actually using amphibious vehicles, the government gives Hunter a blank check. Wherever he finds terrorists, or people he thinks are terrorists, or even people who might know terrorists, he kills them in a variety of ways, the more gruesome the better. No matter what Hunter destroys, he never has to account for it, be it a busy mall or huge buildings.

Of course, since Hunter insists he work alone, he has no one to really look after him or supervise what he's doing. He drives his pickup right into a crowded mall, then shoots up the terrorists before disappearing. Hunter is certainly good at what he does; there's probably no one better. But can anyone really believe that terrorists land on beaches like the marines on Iwo Jima? That they come out into the open and kill and maim people? That only Hunter and his faithful truck can find them? The only people in a more preposterous situation are the audience watching it.

XIII

The O.K. Corral

The law is coming! You tell them I'm coming. And Hell's coming with me. You hear? Hell's coming with me!*

During the latter half of the nineteenth century, Western figures such as "Wild" Bill Hickok, Buffalo Bill, even Billy the Kid became famous, or infamous, mostly due to the advent of quickly written and wildly inaccurate exploitation stories, often called "dime novels," which heralded the likes of this person or that. In John Wayne's last film, *The Shootist* (1976), he plays an ex-lawman turned gunman dying of cancer. One of these so-called writers desires to do justice to Wayne's character's life, even though he knows nothing about him. Wayne refuses when he finds out the man intends to make up most of the stuff as he goes a long.

In Eastwood's Oscar-winning Western *Unforgiven* (1992), a morally ambiguous film, a dime novelist first latches on to one gunfighter, and then the sheriff, who bluntly tells the man his books are lies. The writer watches as Eastwood savagely guns down the sheriff and almost the entire town in a fit of drunken anger; now, having seen what a real "gunslinger" is like, he retreats quickly to the safety of his make-believe stories.

Arguably the luckiest if not most widely known lawman of the day was Wyatt Earp. In all his gunfights, Earp was never wounded or even nicked, though the same cannot be said for those he faced. Earp's older brother Virgil was generally thought to be a better lawman, and more honest. But whatever the case, cinema has glorified Wyatt Earp and his shootout with the Clanton gang at the O.K. Corral more than any other true-life Western peace officer.

Historically, the real Wyatt Earp (1848–1929) had been a marshal in such places as Wichita and Dodge City, where he became a prominent lawman-gambler. He was effective if not heavy-handed, and he applied force quickly without thinking twice. Having turned in his badge, Earp and his brothers moved in 1879 to Tombstone, an Arizona Territory boom town which, by all accounts, was wild and lawless. Though the family had come west to mine silver and gamble, eventually they ended up where they were most effective, as lawmen, with Virgil becoming town marshal.

Wyatt furthered his reputation as a gunfighter, first as deputy sheriff of Puma County and later as deputy U.S. Marshal for the entire Arizona Territory (Encarta, n.p.). Along with his brothers, Wyatt obtained a financial interest in one of the gambling establishments, and he renewed his friendship with Doc Holliday, a sometime killer and full-time

---

**Wyatt Earp (Kurt Russell) to Ike Clanton (Stephen Lang) in* Tombstone.

gambler. Before too long, the Earps and the Clantons butted heads, neither side being "good" though the Earps were arguably the better of the two.

The situation eventually exploded into violence, with the two groups squaring off at the O.K. Corral. Later, after his brother Morgan was murdered and his brother Virgil was incapacitated, Wyatt became obsessed with his vendetta against the Clanton gang and deputized a number of unsavory characters to assist him in his pursuit of them. Not only did Wyatt and his "posse" gun down Frank Stillwell, a former deputy sheriff sympathetic to the Clanton faction, but Indian Charley Florentino and Curley Bill Brocius as well. Years later Earp is thought to have returned to Arizona to finish what he started, killing Johnny Ringo,* among the most infamous of the Clanton gunmen (Ball, p.125).

The remainder of Wyatt Earp's life was uneventful, and he might very well have faded from memory after he died if not for the moving picture. *Law and Order* (1932) and *Early Arizona* (1938) featured events leading up to *a* shootout with criminals in Tombstone *without* Wyatt Earp. Why the studios told these stories using the Earp character but calling him something else isn't clear. *Frontier Marshal* (1934) was remade five years later with the same name, this time starring Randolph Scott as Wyatt. The Tombstone sage is there, with the usual suspects and heroes. In 1942, *Tombstone, the Town Too Tough to Die* was released. Earp, Holliday and the O.K. Corral finally appeared, and in all three films the distinction between right and wrong was clear and distinct: The Earp faction represented good, the Clanton faction evil.

Of the countless movies about Earp that followed, or which involved Earp, or even about his friend Doc Holliday in which Earp appeared, the most critically acclaimed yet least accurate was John Ford's *My Darling Clementine*. In 1946, Ford set out for Monument Valley, Utah, to direct the film, with many of his stock actors in tow, including Henry Fonda as Wyatt Earp and Ward Bond as his older brother Virgil. Ford looked at the movie as a fairy tale, a way to finish his contract with Fox, to whom he owed one more film, and he elevated lawman Earp to mythical status: The fastest gun. The hardest fists. Brave. Resolute. Simple but uncompromising enforcer of the law. To do this, Ford completely sidesteps history and reworks the Hero-Quest Legends to depict the civilizing of the West, with Earp encountering what Joseph Campbell, the noted authority on mythology, identified as the Monomyth, or six stages common to the quest: *The Call*; *The Other*; *The Journey*; *Helpers and Guides*; *The Treasure*; and *The Transformation*.

In the first stage, the hero is on the brink of great change. He is called to duty, to perform a task, to spring into action, the directive coming from any source: friend, relative, even a stranger (Schecter, Semeiks, p. 8). He (or she) may answer it willingly, or they may be reluctant, hesitant, initially refusing to heed the call, like Wyatt Earp is.

When we first encounter Wyatt, he is on the trail with his brothers, driving cattle to California. Pa Clanton attempts to swindle Wyatt out of his cattle but is rebuffed. Later, he goes to Tombstone for a shave and is almost shot when a drunk starts shooting up a saloon. Since everyone is afraid to take action against him, a disgusted Wyatt clobbers the troublemaker with a rock. The authorities ask him to be the new marshal but he refuses. When he returns to his youngest brother James, whom he left to guard the cattle, he finds the lad dead and the cattle stolen. Wyatt returns to Tombstone and becomes marshal, intent on bringing his dead brother's killers to justice.

Recently some scholars have split on the cause of Ringo's death. Some hold it was not Earp who killed him but rather Doc Holliday. Others say it was suicide.

The Other is a hidden aspect of the hero, an opposite, perhaps a stranger, perhaps a friend, perhaps a darker side which the hero must confront if he is to increase his own self-awareness. In Jungian terms, the other can be seen in "the shadow," that portion of the conscious mind containing the hidden, repressed or unfavorable aspects of the personality (Jung, p. 110). For Wyatt, Doc Holliday is that person. Doc is demonstrably violent, yet educated and urbane, while Wyatt is usually passive, bright (in a common-sense fashion) and from the frontier. Doc is sickly, compulsive, seemingly suicidal. Conversely, Wyatt is the picture of health, patient, appreciative of life. Where Doc is bullying, Wyatt is anything but, to the point of appearing almost afraid of Doc.

When they first meet, Doc is clad in dark clothing while Wyatt wears light. Yet, when Wyatt is forced to use his gun, he, too, is dressed like Doc — in black. Both men are outsiders, estranged from the community, yet they are linked by a shared moral code which sets them apart from the other townspeople (Place, p. 70). However, when it appears that Doc is responsible for James' death, Wyatt must confront him. Wyatt chooses to overcome Doc by shooting the gun from his hand (!); having "conquered" his darker side, Wyatt can now embrace Doc again and bring him back to his world.

The quest necessitates a journey for the hero, be it figurative or literal, one strewn with obstacles and filled with danger. Wyatt's journey is twofold. Before he can get to California, he must bring his brother's killers to justice, a concrete physical obstacle which culminates in the deadly shoot-out with the Clantons at the O.K. Corral. Yet, in doing this, he also brings the law to Tombstone, a much more abstract concept and one which places him smack in the middle of two competing, mutually exclusive convictions— that of nature and the frontier opposed to culture and civilization.

Though Wyatt had served in the past as an official hero, that is, as a representative of civilization, in *My Darling Clementine* he is introduced as a man between two worlds, a former lawman now a cattleman, a man on the trail, a part of nature. It is only when he enters Tombstone — a "frontier town" in which the elements of culture and nature uneasily coalesce — that he is drawn into their conflict. As he seeks his brother's killer, Wyatt straddles the line between the two ideals, the town becoming a hall of mirrors, each side reflecting off the other.

At one end of the spectrum are the Clantons, vicious criminals preying on weaker folks like Wyatt's young brother James, men who answer only to nature's law. On the other stand men like the parson, the mayor and the nurse Clementine, who are determined to bring order to the chaos. Doc, the outlaw hero, is, like Wyatt, also a man caught in the middle, originally hailing from the East, possessing a medical degree, but with a distaste for any regulation and a predilection towards violent confrontation, attributes better suiting him to the wilds of the West.

Their partnership is symbolic of the ultimate reconciliation of nature and culture, of the frontier's evolution into civilization. Robert B. Ray observes that "*Clementine* achieved much of that [reconciliation] by blurring the lines between outlaw and official hero so that their surface disagreements would only emphasize their essential similarities" (Ray, 224). When the Clantons kidnap and make sport of a Shakespearean actor, it expresses their rejection of Eastern values, of culture. Likewise, when both Doc and Wyatt rescue him, it is not only emblematic of their cooperation, but of Wyatt's support for the budding civilization.

However, such a journey has costs, and Wyatt pays the bloody price with the loss of two brothers, and later a good friend. Their killers, the Clantons, await him at the O.K. Corral; yet Wyatt remains true to the law, first attempting to serve them with arrest warrants.

When they refuse to give up and begin shooting, Wyatt, Virgil and Doc return fire, eventually killing them, though Doc also loses his life in the process.

To successfully complete his quest, the hero will often need helpers and guides to see him through. Doc and Virgil are Wyatt's obvious partners, but so is Clementine, whose influence brings Wyatt over to the side of civilization. The "treasure" Wyatt gains is twofold, both the affection of Clementine and the establishment of a more civilized order in Tombstone, which results from Wyatt bringing the Clantons to justice.

When the hero is somehow changed by his quest, when his experience results in a rebirth of sorts, an inner liberation, he is considered transformed (Schecter, Semeiks, p. 9). Wyatt's transformation does not result in a marked internal difference, since he was once a part of the civilizing movement, but rather is linked to that of Tombstone. Just as the town is changed by the establishment of law and order, which facilitates the onset of culture, Wyatt is changed by both his appreciation of such an evolutionary process, as evidenced by his promise to one day return to Clementine and Tombstone, and his temporary refusal to join it. As Place notes, "Wyatt's inner solitude cannot be healed by the town, and in leaving he legitimizes the myth through his sacrifice" (Place, p. 70).

Though *My Darling Clementine* corresponds to Campbell's Monomyth, Ford's work also exhibits a number of other mythic strains, particularly with regard to the Grail Legends. Wyatt Earp appears as a western Parsifal, searching for his Holy Grail. Like Parsifal, he is of humble origins. On taking the job of marshal, he begins a quest yet, like the knight, is resourceful. Johnson notes in *He*, "Parsifal subdues many knights in his career but none are killed" (Johnson, p. 220). Likewise with Wyatt, who doesn't kill unless he absolutely has to. On arriving at Tombstone, he clobbers the rowdy drunk with a rock rather than confronting him with his gun. Later, he contends with Doc Holliday, though he is not wearing a gun. When Doc pulls his, Wyatt introduces Holliday to his brothers Morgan and Virgil, who have the drop on Doc. When the Clantons are holding the Shakespearean actor hostage, Wyatt clouts one of the boys and then merely wings another who has drawn on him.

Ford reportedly did not want to make the film, so he shot quickly, in 45 days, and was quoted as saying, "I knew Wyatt Earp, and he told me about the fight at the O.K. Corral. So in *My Darling Clementine* we did it exactly the way it had been" (Cinebook, n.p.).

Historical accounts differ from Ford's statements, and the film remains much closer on every level to the fairy tale he wished to tell. Of all the Earp films, it's more legend and myth than truth, but every Wyatt Earp film that followed borrowed something from it. Wyatt Earp's next appearance on the big screen came 11 years later. John Sturges' *Gunfight at the O.K. Corral* (1957) starred Burt Lancaster as Wyatt and Kirk Douglas as Doc. The film ended with the shootout, yet added nothing to the accuracy of Earp's role as town deputy marshal. The film was tedious in parts, and Lancaster was so stolid as to be almost unbelievable. Douglas came off as a more enjoyable character yet (in following the precedent Ford set in *Clementine* by using the powerfully built Victor Mature as Doc) was much too virile to be a dying man. The shootout was unrealistic by any standard. The only new innovation to the legend came with Wyatt befriending, and then having to kill, a young member of the Clanton gang.

Hugh O'Brian's immensely popular television series *The Life and Legend of Wyatt Earp* ran for six years, 1955 to 1961, and contributed to keeping the Earps' mythical status alive more than any one film. The series merely showed Earp besting all villains and hardships in over 260 episodes, few if any of these things ever really occurring. A whole generation of kids recognized the handsome, athletic O'Brian as *the* Wyatt Earp and he appeared over the next 30-plus years in cameo roles as Earp and guest spots in other television shows, such as 1989's *Paradise*, where the lawman came out of retirement to partner up with other legendary gunmen to break a friend out of prison. In 1994 he saddled up in *Wyatt Earp: Return to Tombstone*, in part to capitalize on the Earp craze in Hollywood. The film utilized clips from the past show, and found Wyatt traveling to Tombstone toward the end of

Burt Lancaster's turn as Wyatt Earp in *Gunfight at the O.K. Corral*.

his life, having to face down one more outlaw challenge.

In *Hour of the Gun* (1967), John Sturges picks up where his *Gunfight at the O.K. Corral* ended. Lancaster and Douglas are replaced by James Garner and Jason Robards, Jr., respectively. Up to this point, Earp films generally followed Wyatt's keeping the peace in Tombstone and ended with the O.K. Corral. Sturges goes beyond to the trial of the Earps and Holliday for the shootout, their acquittal and the subsequent killing of Earp's brother Morgan and the maiming of his brother Virgil. Garner's Earp tracks those he believes responsible and for the first time viewers see not only Garner playing a character with a dark streak, but the first hints that Wyatt Earp was not the all–American lawman he's been made out to be.

Hugh O'Brian was television's Wyatt Earp.

Garner reprised his Earp role later in *Sunset* (1988), as a pleasanter character who is now a movie advisor. He teams up with star Tom Mix to find some killers. Earp is at the end of his trail, hence the title, but he and the celluloid Earp, played by Bruce Willis, have to face down and shoot it out with the thugs *a la* the O.K. Corral. The entire film has a bizarre quality to it: The supposedly "real" Earp (Garner) is really an actor playing Earp in this movie, while Tom Mix (Willis) is an actor playing Earp in a silent film (within this movie). Hal Hanson of *The Washington Post* accurately pointed out that the pairing of Earp and Mix allowed viewers to imagine the comparison between a real deal Western lawman and the Hollywood copy (Hanson, n.p.). Sadness marks the film as well: Anyone knowing anything about Earp knows he passes away in the year the film takes place — 1929. So as he rides away on the train at the film's conclusion, we know it is the end, literally.

The United Artists production *Doc* (1971) was clearly influenced by revisionist Westerns coming of age in the late '60s and was as inaccurate as Ford's in the opposite direction. Like Sergio Leone's spaghetti Westerns, or even *The Wild Bunch*, the film was stark and bleak, and boasted no readily identifiable hero. With discontent raging throughout

American society between young and old, the Establishment was attacked daily by a counterculture definitely anti-police, and views of law enforcement were affected. Herein, the Earps were clearly the evil force oppressing the people, like many groups thought the police were doing then. The Clantons were more or less white trash just wanting to be left alone, living out in the desert like many who communed with nature.

Holliday, the main protagonist, is friends with Wyatt, but interestingly enough not enemies with the Clantons, something certainly not true in real life. Earp's ambition grows to becoming mayor of the town, though Holliday sees where it will lead: the O.K. Corral. For the first time on screen, the events at the shootout are not heroic. Roger Ebert notes they are "cold-blooded," and that the gunplay is "sudden, brief, and terrible" (Ebert, n.p.). Holliday

Wyatt Earp (Kurt Russell), Doc Holliday (Val Kilmer), Virgil Earp (Sam Elliot) and Morgan Earp (Bill Paxton) head for the O.K. Corral — and immortality — in *Tombstone*.

Wyatt Earp (Kurt Russell) lets one of the Clanton gang know he'll be coming for them.

backs the Earps and helps kill the Clantons, even brutally gunning down a Clanton boy he had befriended. Holliday's action or motivation is unclear. He could be symbolically killing himself, or he could be stopping Wyatt's political career by making the showdown so bitter for Tombstone that the people would never elect him. Either way, Holliday leaves, but the Earps still control the town, emblem of the police's unjust power.

More than 20 years passed before Hollywood resurrected Wyatt Earp and the events of Arizona in the 1880s. Kurt Russell played a very reluctant peace officer in 1993's *Tombstone*. In this version, Virgil becomes town marshal after seeing criminals rampaging through the streets of the boom town. The Earp-Clanton feud continues, and many of the conventions shown in Ford's *Clementine* are present, including the Shakespearean stage troupe. The film adds a fresh twist by tying the Clantons into a gang called "The Cowboys," clearly capitalizing on the anti-gang sentiment of the country. The story continues beyond the shootout in the corral and posits Doc Holliday as the killer of Johnny Ringo, a leader of the Cowboys. Wyatt hunts down those who killed his brother and the film adds its own contribution to the Earp myth by having him with Doc when the latter dies in a sanitarium in Colorado a few years later.

In 1994, Kevin Costner starred as the lawman in *Wyatt Earp*. The film was long and epic in scope, and attempted a more accurate depiction of Earp's life, starting with his stage-driving days, his bout with drunkenness and horse thieving, his time as a buffalo hunter and finally as a town marshal in Kansas. Costner's Earp was troubled and flawed,

Wyatt Earp (Kevin Costner) holds off a lynch mob in *Wyatt Earp*.

The march to the O.K. Corral from *Wyatt Earp*. *From left to right*: Dennis Quaid (Doc), Linden Ashby (Morgan), Kevin Costner (Wyatt), and Michael Madsen (Virgil).

and probably closer to the real Earp than any previous portrayals. The emphasis on family ties was an overriding theme in this story, and motivated almost all of Earp's actions, including his obsessive hunt for the Clantons in the last act of the film. By this time, however, the lawman's legend was ingrained in the public's imagination. Costner's most important contribution was humanizing the man, but not his accomplishments. Like in the movies before, Costner's Earp was sure-footed, a surer shot, and never one for indecision.

The face of Wyatt Earp changed with every actor and every film over the 75 years since his death in 1929. However, with only a few exceptions, his term as deputy town marshal in Tombstone is seen as a heroic struggle cleaning up a lawless place. The truth is not so clear or evident. The Earp-Clanton feud was just as much a political struggle between competing ideologies, with the Earps' upholding Republican land and silver interests while the Clanton's were free-ranging Democrats. The films, particularly *Tombstone* and *Wyatt Earp*, are not so easily read. Both support modern conservative values of law and order, taking direct action when challenged, and bearing personal responsibility for one's behavior. Yet they also back gun control, as the Earps demonstrate by prohibiting firearms within town limits, and support the gambling and prostitution industries. We will probably never learn everything about the Earps or Clantons, or the shootout at the O.K. Corral, but so long as Hollywood churns out movies, Wyatt Earp's legend can only build.

Sources

Ball, Larry D. *The United States Marshals of New Mexico and Arizona Territories, 1846–1912*. Albuquerque: University of New Mexico Press, 1978.
Ebert, Roger. *Doc*. Rogerebert.com.
Hanson, Hal. *Sunset*. washingtonpost.com.
Johnson, Robert A. *He: Understanding Masculine Psychology*. Revised ed. Berkeley, CA: Harper & Row, 1989.
Jung, Carl, M-L von Franz, Joseph Henderson, Jolande Jacobi and Aniela Jaffe. *Man and His Symbols*. New York: Dell, 1964.
My Darling Clementine. Cinebooks. CD-Rom. 1994.
Place, J. A. *The Western Films of John Ford*. New York: Citadel Press, 1974.
Ray, Robert B. *A Certain Tendency of the Hollywood Cinema, 1930–1980*. Princeton, NJ: Princeton University Press, 1985, p. 224.
Schechter, Harold, and Jonna Gormely Semeiks. *Discoveries: Fifty Stories of the Quest*.
New York: Oxford University Press, 1992.
Wyatt Earp. Microsoft Encarta. CD-Rom. 1995.

XIV

GUNSMOKE

Good evening. My name's Wayne. Some of you may have seen me before. I hope so. I've been kicking around Hollywood a long time. I've made a lot of pictures out here. All kinds. Some of them have been Westerns and that's what I'm here to tell you about tonight. A Western. A new television show called Gunsmoke. *When I first heard about the show* Gunsmoke, *I knew there was only one man to play in it. James Arness. He's a young fellow, and maybe new to some of you. But I've worked with him and I predict he'll be a big star. And now I'm proud to present* Gunsmoke.*

In the twenty-first century, television and DVD will continue to expand as giant screen monitors and surround sound systems allow for home theaters to reproduce much of the movie experience. With the cost of films skyrocketing along with the prices to see them, audiences are shrinking.† During the 2005 season, box office take was down 19 out of 20 weeks—midway through July—compared to the previous year's numbers (LaSalle, p.1). As television came to prominence in the '50s, a similar phenomenon occurred. Movie studios countered with big-budgeted pictures shown in widescreen, hoping to lure people from home and away from their small, colorless boxes. Low-budget producers such as American International Pictures (AIP) churned out exploitation films to bring in the teen crowd; there was nothing like a double-feature and a little quiet time for a guy and his girl.

Hollywood's current strategy to bring audiences back to theaters harkens to the '50s—big stars, great special effects and plotlines kept as simple as possible to appeal to the broadest audience achievable: *Independence Day* (1996); *Star Wars III* (2005); *War of the Worlds* (2005)—all of these films made hundreds of millions of dollars. However, for each one of them, how many films made little or no money? What does a studio do with *Waterworld* (1995) or *Troy* (2004) or *Cinderella Man* (2005)—films that cost huge amounts of money and brought back little from theatergoers?

Whatever the future course of cinema, television is not going anywhere, and depictions of police officers, detectives and private eyes in weekly series continue to be a staple of the prime time lineup: *Hill Street Blues, NYPD Blue, Law and Order, CSI* and so on. Despite the violent crime plaguing the nation—or perhaps because of it—the interest in law enforcement continues. But the interest started long ago, when television was a new

---

John Wayne introducing the first episode of Gunsmoke. *Wayne had worked with Arness in a number of his movies.*
†*Film revenues have been up the last few years; however, the audience has been decreasing. The increase money-wise is due to the ticket prices-over nine or even ten dollars in some markets. In 2005, summer movie attendance was down from that of 2004. If the trend continues of higher and higher ticket prices, even fewer people will be able to afford a trip to the show. Such a business superstructure cannot be supported indefinitely like this.*

thing, the pictures were black-and-white, and many shows were live! B film stars found themselves out of work as the double-feature faded with the studio's loss of its exhibition arm. However, television was a godsend: These stars were used to working quickly, on small budgets, so the transition was smooth for many. William Boyd starred in 66 Hopalong Cassidy films between 1935 and 1948 — an average of five films a year! He then moved right into television with the character. Roy Rogers, Gene Autry, even Gabby Hayes had their own shows.

In 1955, *Gunsmoke* premiered, starring 32-year-old James Arness as Matt Dillon, a United States Federal Marshal working out of Dodge City, Kansas. The show had been a success on CBS Radio, featuring William Conrad as the voice of Marshal Dillon between 1949–1960.* Critics contended that the radio episodes were more realistic than the television show, sometimes featuring villains who were successful with their crimes, which is often the case in real life (Wikipedia, p. 1). Conrad wanted the television job as well, but he didn't have the commanding stature of Arness, who was 6'6". CBS went with Arness for the television show, but Conrad continued with his radio duties, and many think of Conrad's voice as that of Marshal Dillon even as Arness is the physical incantation of the incorruptible lawman.

The opening of the show featured the marshal walking down Main Street while an outlaw heads toward him. The outlaw draws first, but Dillon is faster and the man crumples

The cast of TV's ***Gunsmoke*** (James Arness, Amanda Blake, Ken Curtis, Milburn Stone).

*Some sources, like Wikipedia, put the radio dates as 1952–1961.

into the dust. The marshal doesn't look pleased but rather slightly pained, as if wearing the badge gets a little heavier each day. Later, the opening changed, and Arness' co-stars were named first, and Arness came last. Like his character, who never pushed his considerable weight around, Arness was comfortable enough to share the spotlight with the cast, which stayed pretty much the same for almost the show's entire run. Miss Kitty (Amanda Blake), Doc (Milburn Stone) and Festus (Ken Curtis) remained the marshal's trusted friends, and Festus often accompanied Dillon when he went after a criminal on the lam.

Aside from the superb cast, much of *Gunsmoke*'s popularity stemmed from the way the characters mixed. Every week the marshal would be involved in the plot, but not necessarily as the main player. Sometimes he'd support the other characters as they worked their way through a problem or dilemma. Other times a guest star was the focus. The stories were also very well-written, and sometimes a reflection of their time. In one episode, Festus was watching a snake oil salesman hawk his wares. The man's young assistant, a supposed gunman, was shooting bottles out of the sky. Festus innocently pointed out that the gunman was using snake shot, not bullets, which meant a blind man could hit the bottles. The man challenged Festus, who didn't want to fight him. Matt broke up their squabble, but he warned Festus against fighting. When Matt left town, the gunman drew on Festus, who killed him. Afraid to put Matt in a bad spot, Festus ran instead of facing up to what happened.

Festus winds up broke and exhausted in a little hamlet miles from Dodge. The people there are less than friendly, and he's taken in by a widow with a young son, and her father. A sadistic family wants the widow's place and will do anything to get it. They don't count on Festus helping her. In the time-honored tradition of the Western, Festus shows the boy that sometimes you have to face up to your enemies. They beat Festus while he's still weak, but when he recovers he goes to town and protects the family in a shoot-out. Matt rides up to help. The boy learns that running away from a problem is never a solution — and so does Festus. Coming at the height of the Cold War, but with no reference to it at all, the story reinforces conservative notions that walking tall and standing firm is the American way.

In another story during the same era, Beau Bridges guest-starred as a guitar player so attached to his instrument that he kills anyone who tries to touch it. His father fought in Mexico during the war and married a Mexican woman. There he learned to play Flamenco guitar and passed it on to his son. With his family gone, the instrument is all he has left to remember them. When a man grabs it and begins plucking the strings, the young man stabs him, but before he can bury the body some drifters appear on the horizon. The young man rides to Dodge and finds a job playing in Miss Kitty's saloon. When the drifters arrive in Dodge, Matt arrests them for murder after finding some of the dead man's belongings in their possessions.

The young man throws the jail keys through the window of the drifters' cell so they can escape to avoid being hanged, but the men chase him through the woods, where they eventually kill him. Matt arrives to late too stop the fighting — but realizes that when men place too much emphasis on possessions or property, to a point where it is pathological, only conflict can come about. This pragmatic point of view doesn't conflict with the "walking tall" image from the other episode, but merely shows another side to the issue. When examining what situations are worth fighting about, be it personal property or missiles in Cuba, all circumstances must be considered in totality. Clearly, for the young man, a guitar was not a worthy trade for his and the other men's lives.

As with the radio show, *Gunsmoke* didn't always end on an upbeat note. In this respect, it was far ahead of other shows of the era, and the fully developed nature of its stories could be sad, brutal or both. In one case, a struggling dirt farmer living on the plains outside of

Dodge is continually insulted by his wife, who calls him a failure. The man leaves, swearing to make something of himself far away from her. He rides into Dodge, accompanied by his dog, the only comfort he really has. He sits in Miss Kitty's saloon, counting up his change for a drink of whiskey. She sits with him, recognizing that he needs someone to talk to. A bully goads her to sit with *him*. The farmer, already drunk, tells the bully to beat it, and Miss Kitty threatens to call Matt. The bully leaves and the farmer is hailed as a hero by many in the town for standing up to the brute.

The farmer sleeps in an alley, gets up the next day and is greeted by many people. He runs into the bully again and, now sober, realizes he is in big trouble. The bully humiliates him in front of everyone. Later, as the farmer walks down the street, no one talks to him and no one will hire him. Matt tries to console the farmer, who tells him that he'd like to be brave like Matt, someone people look up to. The marshal tells him to be himself and most folks will accept that just fine. At the end of the story, Matt is ambushed by some gunmen, and the farmer saves him at the cost of his own life. The wife never appreciated what a fine man her husband really was, and the farmer never had a chance to realize he was just as brave as he hoped to be. Only the man's dog was there to mourn what never should have happened in the first place.

As a federal marshal, Matt Dillon embodied the old-fashioned traits from the classic era of Westerns. He never drew first. Never started a fight. Never gossiped. Always faced a man head-on when he had something to say. While Miss Kitty's occupation of saloon owner and hostess was never elaborated on, Matt never did anything with her that would compromise his position as lawman. Even during the '60s, when society was in turmoil and ultra-violent, revisionist Westerns featuring anti-heroes like Clint Eastwood's Man with no Name and Sam Peckinpah's *The Wild Bunch* were the rage, Matt stood firmly entrenched as the traditional Western lawman, a television John Wayne.

Gunsmoke ran for 20 years. The first five featured 30-minute episodes. From 1960, it went to an hour long. The show's first ten years were filmed in black-and-white, the last ten in color. The show was almost cancelled in 1967, but viewer reaction persuaded CBS to keep the showing going in a new time period (Wikipedia, p.1). Later, James Arness repeated his role as Matt Dillon in a number of television movies. In 1987, much of the cast reunited in *Gunsmoke: Return to Dodge*, as Matt was forced to confront a specter from his past. Mannon, played by Steve Forrest, is released from prison, killing anyone connected with his lock-up, and Marshal Dillon is the last he has to square things with. Matt, who's now retired, is a trapper living alone in the mountains. He's ambushed coming down with a load of furs, but makes it into Dodge, shot up but still breathing. Doc is gone, as is Festus, but Miss Kitty returns to nurse Matt back to health. Mannon comes looking for Matt and holds Miss Kitty hostage. Many of the townspeople offer to help Matt go up against the gunslinger, but the ex-marshal declines and faces the man himself. One on one, face to face, Matt guns him down.

The narrative was unique, even by *Gunsmoke*'s standards. Much of Mannon's interaction with Miss Kitty borders on sexual anguish; at times he violently abuses her, even appearing to rape her, though it wasn't specified. He makes her get on her knees, in front of his crotch, to unbuckle his gun belt. Other times he brings her flowers, and speaks niceties. And still other times he discusses Dillon, how he is a better man than the marshal. But better at what? While Miss Kitty nurses Matt back to health, she mentions their past "relationship," how it never worked because he was always a marshal first and foremost. With Mannon lying dead in the street, nothing stands in the way of Matt and Miss

Mannix (Mike Conners) on the case.

Kitty getting together. Unfortunately, Amanda Blake, who played the saloon owner, died a couple of years afterward, so the relationship couldn't continue in the sequels.

The success of *Gunsmoke: Return to Dodge* spawned four more films. In *Gunsmoke: The Last Apache* (1990), Matt learns he has a daughter from a one-time love interest, and that the girl has been kidnapped by the Apaches. The producers brought back Michael Learned, who was in a *Gunsmoke* episode years prior, to recreate her character. Matt goes after the girl, *a la The Searchers*. In 1992, Arness returned in *Gunsmoke: To the Last Man*, where he finds himself tracking cattle thieves in Arizona.* In *Gunsmoke: The Long Ride* (1993), Matt's framed for murder and locked up. Perhaps because of his years living alone and not wearing a badge, Matt does something he would never have done when he was younger: He escapes to find the real killers—which he does. The last sequel was *Gunsmoke: One Man's Justice* (1994), where Matt helps the son of a dead friend track the gang responsible for killing the boy's mother. Since this last *Gunsmoke* film, Arness has not made any movies; however, that's not to say he won't. The show was the longest-running entertainment series in prime time, and the fan base is still out there. It's just up to him to get back in the saddle.

Another popular character was *Mannix* (1967–1975 CBS), a 1940s-style private eye working during the swinging '60s, a war vet who was tough but sincere, honest, yet not above possessing the little things that most men like, such as fast cars and beautiful women. Joe Mannix's loyal assistant was his secretary Peggy, a black woman with a young son, whom much of the audience was convinced he was having a sexual relationship with (www.thrillingdetective.com, n.p.). Whatever their personal "status," the two worked together like hand in glove. Peggy would often have to get Mannix out of jail or pick him up at the ER, while God help the crook or creep who threatened or otherwise bothered his loyal partner.

In the show's first season, Mannix worked for a hi-tech agency which relied on brains rather than brawn; Mannix was the black sheep of the firm, preferring to whoop copious quantities of behind to get the information he needed to solve a case. He finally broke with the firm and, at the beginning of season two, had his own agency. However, the same pattern developed. Peggy put her brain together with Joe's and sometimes pointed out things he missed— Mannix would then let his fists do the talking. The show ran eight years but, like Matt Dillon, Joe Mannix wasn't the kind of guy to stay down for the count. In 1997, Mike Connors reprised his role as the hard-as-nails detective in an episode of *Diagnosis Murder*. Honoring a promise he made to a little girl decades before, Mannix is on the trail of her father's murderer. Dr. Mark Sloan (Dick Van Dyke), star of the series, is an old friend of Joe's and agrees to help him work the case. Connors once observed that, somewhere out there, "Mannix is still working ... there was a decency and dignity about the man..." (www.thrillingdetective.com, n.p.).

Halfway through the 1974–1975 television season came *Baretta*, an unusual ABC cop series about a police detective who worked alone, was single but not a ladies man, and lived in a grungy hotel when not at work, which was most of the time. The unusual thing about the series was not so much the character but the man playing him: Robert Blake. Blake was an amazingly talented actor who had turned in outstanding performances in films such as *In Cold Blood* (1967), based on the Truman Capote book about the senseless murder of a family by some twisted youths, and *Tell Them Willie Boy Is Here* (1969), playing an Indian on the run after killing in self defense.

Blake made Tony Baretta come alive, literally. He talked hard and, though not as tall as some actors, he was in good shape. Some of his wisecracks were often repeated and mangled by wannabe tough guys, such as "You do the crime, you gotta do the time." Baretta was familiar with his city, knowing it inside and out. He worked undercover a lot, but his ties to the community made him popular with a lot of normal folks. In one episode, he has to convince a boxer friend it's time to give it up—which sometimes has to be shown rather than just talked about. However, Baretta's worst enemy was Tony Blake, as tempestuous and temperamental as he was gifted. The show ended in just two and a half seasons.

---

*Leonard Maltin reports the film was shot in 1990.

Blake's best cop performance came a year before *Baretta*, when he starred as highway patrol officer John Wintergreen in *Electra Glide in Blue* (1973). Wintergreen wants a crack at being a detective but he's got one problem: He's a little on the short side. In a memorable scene, the motor cops are standing outside, all clearly well over six feet except Wintergreen. It's played for laughs—but hollow ones. Wintergreen knows that being tall is an advantage, but he uses his head and eventually finagles his way onto a murder case, only to become disillusioned with the people he works with.

Baretta (Robert Blake).

Many of Blake's best films have a tragic quality about them, for both his characters and others. This was no different. An existential thread runs through the narrative, and in Wintergreen, for that matter. A man is murdered. No one really cares but it has to be investigated anyway. Wintergreen rolls up and down the endless highway day after day. He doesn't always write up speeders—sometimes he just talks to them. But why pull them over in the first place? The highway's a lonely place, and for Wintergreen it's going nowhere fast. The people come and go, and Wintergreen's stint as a detective is over almost before it begins. The murder is solved, but who cares? The highway patrolman is back on the blacktop, driving up and down. Ironically he's killed by the very people he often gives a break to: long-haired hippie types whom he attempts to treat fairly, unlike the other officers who encounter them. As Nathan Rabin writes,

> Alas, had the hippies looked beyond Blake's uniform and haircut, they might have recognized a kindred spirit, a good-hearted and surprisingly open-minded outcast determined to live by his own code, no matter the consequences [Rabin, p.1].

SWAT debuted on television in 1975; it only lasted a season and a half, in part because of network concerns about excessive violence. However, considering the show was based upon the Los Angeles Police Department's Special Weapons and Tactics unit, violence was the only thing they could expect. The team is part of Metro, an elite group of officers drawn from all over the city divisions. Metro officers are supposed to be the best of the best, and handle high crime areas or special problems occurring in various parts of the city. SWAT officers are drawn from those in Metro, and only those who meet the rigorous testing standards make it.

Because such units are inevitably called to handle armed, barricaded suspects, hostage conditions, even hijackers or terrorist situations, deadly force is often the outcome. The television show featured Steve Forrest as Hondo Harrelson, the commander of a SWAT unit based in a big city like Los Angeles. Every week the team would have to confront a problem involving some criminal menace, as well as whatever personal problems might be plaguing the guys at the time. They help each other work out the demons—they know that each of their lives depends on the others. Almost like clockwork, Hondo and his men would be called out at the show's end to strut their stuff against whatever is threatening peace in the city. The men respected their leader and got along well with each other, and with other officers in the department.

SWAT (2004), a full-length film, was based loosely on the TV series—very loosely—and follows Sgt. Hondo, played by Samuel L. Jackson, as he works his team to perfection. One of the men (Colin Farrell) is an outsider, blackballed by the department and stuck working in the evidence room. He tries out for the unit and Hondo is impressed enough to take him on, despite the division captain's resentment and animosity toward Farrell. The team's female member (Michelle Rodriguez) and Farrell seem attracted to one another; however, the story never pauses long enough for them to develop their relationship. The city has one of the most wanted men in the world in their custody, and it's up to Hondo and his team to get the man to a federal lock-up in the desert.

SWAT follows a by-the-numbers plotline present in many police and military films, where men have to come together to fight for a greater good. Nothing is really left to imagine. The few twists are not enough to develop the story beyond a high-energy action picture, but it does that portion particularly well, exploding trucks, crashing cars and shooting helicopters out of the sky. In forming his team, Hondo must:

1. Get the best people for the job. Considering the city of Los Angeles is an Affirmative Action employer (in real life—not just in Hollywood!), the team will mix across ethnic and racial lines to be politically correct and culturally diverse. While this is not the best or most effective way of picking a life-or-death response team, it does happen in many cities.

2. Train the unit until they work together as a team without thinking. This might include some of guys coming to blows before bonding. Farrell and one of his teammates almost do just that over the teammate's sister, who was dating Farrell at one time.

3. Test the unit before the big shots to show their value. Hondo's team assaults a jet with hijackers aboard while the command staff watches. The team improvises, and because of some tricks Farrell picked up when dating a flight attendant, the men enter the aircraft and dispatch the hijackers in less than four minutes.

4. A party to celebrate the unit's success. After impressing their superiors, the team goes out together to have a good time and cement their partnership. They are now a family whose lives depend on each other. At this point, Farrell and Rodriguez are comfortable with one another and he accepts her invitation to come to her daughter's birthday party.

5. In action! The team gets a call, comes together on their day off, and confronts a crazed man armed to the teeth and barricaded in his house. Once again, Farrell has an idea: They shoot a torpedo with claws into the house and pull down the wall, surprising the man.

6. The Real Mission. The county sheriffs are transporting a prisoner to court, but they are unaware he is among the world's most wanted men. His accomplices stop the bus and kill the deputies, but Hondo and his team respond to the call and thwart the breakout. It is now up to LAPD, particularly Hondo and his guys, to find a way to get the prisoner to the federal lock-up.

In *The Dirty Dozen* (1967), shot almost 40 years prior, the same matrix is followed. Major Reisman, assigned to form a team for a special mission, picks the best people he can find in an army brig, most facing hanging. He trains the men until they work together like a team. Before the unit goes on its mission, it must prove itself in a special test, which it does. Reisman throws the men a party, complete with prostitutes and liquor. The men are then sent on their mission: kill specific Nazi officers prior to D-Day, in order to weaken the German defenses. The formula can be seen over and again, but *SWAT*, with its high production values, never takes itself too seriously. By keeping things light until the story gets heavy, it's an improvement over the television series.

Sonny Crockett (Don Johnson) prepares to fire in ***Miami Vice.*** Observe the color coordination. Equally important to the show as its narrative was style. Without a doubt, Crockett is an MTV generation cop.

TV's *Miami Vice* (1984–89) was clearly influenced by the popularity of MTV. Don Johnson starred as Sonny Crocket and Philip Michael Thomas was his partner Ricardo Tubbs, undercover detectives handling a variety of crimes, from robbery to murder and, of course, vice stings, all the while trying to stay above the dirt they sometimes have to crawl in. The series relied on a thriving (mostly) rock soundtrack, with people like Phil Collins and Glenn Frey contributing. In many episodes, right, or good, was a situational proposition, and the detectives often had to check themselves before wavering too far off path. The same was said for the rest of the team, who found force in the cause of "right" a much more attractive proposition than arresting someone they knew would be out a few hours later.

The moral ambiguity of the series was associated with the hard-boiled world of Chandler and the film noir of theatrical cinema (Butler, p.2). Stories could be vicious, and often the more wicked a character the more he got away with — a sometimes fact of life in the real world. Olmos, who played the squad's supervisor, Lt. Martin Castillo, was a stern and demanding counterweight to the temptation his people were faced with, but at times the futility of their job also got to *him*. In an episode that typifies what *Miami Vice* was all about, a ghost emerges from Castillo's past — a past that none of the squad knows about. When he was younger, Castillo worked drug enforcement in South East Asia, but the CIA was protecting the biggest drug exporter because he was "anti–Communist." Castillo was separated from a woman he loved by the withdrawal of Americans from South Vietnam, and suddenly she turned up in Miami years later, married to the drug lord's son.

Even though the CIA attempts to monitor the family and stop them from dealing drugs, the younger men do what they know best, and soon Castillo's people are after them. The drug lord brought the woman with him for "insurance," knowing that Castillo was the one man he couldn't buy off — but the prospect of something happening to the woman would make him think twice before going after the family. The sickening sight of the family (particularly the young men's wives shopping with money made off the bodies of the overdosed across the cities) is palpable, and even the most jaded viewer feels some rage. The team supports Castillo in whatever he wants to do, but the CIA intervenes again, freeing the young men. The family is spirited away, including the woman, who chooses to stay with her husband rather than leave him.

Alone again, Castillo has to wonder: Was it a cultural thing? Or was she so addicted to the easy living that she was no better than the junkies her in-laws created? Either way, the shifting perspective on what exactly is right hits home. For the local cops, stopping the drugs is the number one priority. For the CIA, using the drug lord to help them in their battle against the Red Menace takes precedence. During this time, the CIA was accused of importing drugs and developing crack cocaine to sell in inner city neighborhoods to finance their war against Communists in Central America, a war that Congress had cut off funds to. While the agency *was* illegally raising money to support these endeavors, the drug accusations were preposterous, and when the government demanded proof, the accusers had none. Either way, for Castillo, the ghost had come and gone: the suppressed memories of a time long past, only repeated, and then vanished once again.

The success of *Miami Vice* for director Michael Mann led to another of his series creations, *Crime Story* (1986–88), which followed a Chicago Major Crimes Unit, headed by Lt. Mike Torello, as he wages a one-man war on the mob. Torello's nemesis is Ray Luca, a two-bit hood who rises up the ladder of Chicago's crime syndicate. When Luca moves to Vegas to run the operations there, Torello and his squad follow.

Every once in a great while, Torello and Luca would find common ground and work together from a distance. In one episode, a pornographer uses one of the old Mafia don's granddaughters in a movie. The girl's boyfriend, an innocent from Chicago, comes to find her. Torello and his men go into action and bust the pervert. To save the boy from unneeded anguish, they tell her his girlfriend is dead because the Mafia don would never permit their relationship. The boy leaves, and then Torello tells the D.A. to drop the charges against the pornographer. As the man leaves the courthouse, the Mafia don and his men are waiting. They nod their thanks to Torello. Some things both the cops and the criminals can agree on — the importance of family is one of them.

The series was a period piece set in the early '60s and it did a fine job of recreating Las

Vegas during that period. Many fine actors guest-starred, some of them going on to greater fame later, such as David Caruso, Ving Rhames and Julia Roberts. A theme present in this series, and in other Mann works such as *Heat* (1995), is that of doubles. Torello and Luca are the same but different in a way that is eerily familiar. They could easily trade places, the criminal become the cop and vice versa. Both Torello and Luca are Chicago tough guys; both have killed and will kill again; both are leaders with responsibilities, and matters of life and death are in their hands. Both break the law, Luca everyday, Torello when he feels forced. In one episode, the crew guards a Russian defector who is going to be traded for a captured American spy pilot. The defector doesn't know it, and Torello and his men at first could not care less. At the end they save the defector by double-crossing the Soviets, causing a potential international incident. Another story has Torello going to Mexico to kill a savage murderer being protected by the government. His men join him, risking their lives. It may be wrong, and is certainly illegal, but it has to be done.

In *Heat* we see the same breakdown. Al Pacino leads a squad of detectives in the LAPD's Robbery Homicide division, an elite group that investigates major crimes throughout the city. Robert De Niro leads a takedown crew so sophisticated, their plans are researched down to the type of metals that the men may have to drill through. The takedown crew blows up an armored car and steals the money, but one of the team compromises their identity, so De Niro's men gun the guards down. Pacino, like Torello, after Luca, goes about bringing De Niro down. Both Pacino and De Niro are consummate professionals, so much so that De Niro has no personal life and Pacino and his wife separate because he's never home. Both men lead a tight group of men loyal to one another. And both are at the top of their game. When De Niro's crew break into a warehouse to drill through the vault, he hears a noise, and sees some unfamiliar trailers in the junk yard across the boulevard. He stops the operation immediately, leaves his equipment, and backs out. Pacino, watching, orders his SWAT back up team *not* to arrest the men — he wants them for murder, not for a low grade burglary charge.

The two men's greatest similarity is also their greatest flaw — rigidity. Pacino, in failing to arrest De Niro and his men when he had the chance, allows them to regroup and plan a bank robbery, which goes haywire. The result is a reproduction of the North Hollywood shootout, with casualties everywhere. De Niro, on the other hand, gets away and has a private flight scheduled for New Zealand, where he plans to retire. During the course of the story he's picked up a girlfriend and he's taking her with him. However, he gets word that the man who snitched off his robbery heist to the cops is staying in a hotel by the airport. He could let it go and escape — or he could take his revenge. He goes after the snitch, the cops are waiting, and Pacino kills him in a shootout next to a runway.

Crime Story ends in a similar but more ambiguous way. Luca has fled to a South American country, just ahead of Torello, who was about to arrest him. Torello follows, but Luca is in effect running the country. When the president interferes with Luca's plan he shoots him, and promotes the vice president! As a plane barrels down a runway with Luca and Torello on it, they fight tooth and nail. When the pilot is shot, the plane plummets toward the ground but the men are locked in battle. Unfortunately, the series was not renewed, so the plane is still plunging ...

The longest-running modern police show of all time is *Law and Order*, which debuted in 1989. The series is actually become a "brand," spinning off a number of successful sequels such as *Law and Order: Special Victims Unit* and *Law and Order: Criminal Intent*. The website for the show claims a record number of 600 combined episodes (www.nbc.com, p.1). Generally the police handle the first half of the show, and the district attorney's office headlines the second. The detectives will investigate a crime, coming up with the suspect the evidence points to. The assistant district attorney then prosecutes the case. Many times the man is found guilty, but sometimes the suspect will walk, even when it's clear he's guilty. It's the way things go in New York City—and everywhere else in America.

One episode touched on a number of issues rolled up in the murder of a tourist. An Asian woman was killed on the streets and her husband was slightly wounded. The killer was a black man, but no one working that area saw any black people around. The detectives finally figure out that the husband had someone kill his wife and wound *him*—but by blaming a minority, as has happened any number of times in real life, he thinks the police would be more inclined to believe his story. However, these detectives are professional and they don't. He's arrested and prosecuted. Life and death goes on in the big city.

In 2004, HBO, a premium cable channel which features movies, TV series and original films of their own making, launched *Deadwood*, a Western unlike any other show previously featured on the small screen. The Deadwood of the title is an "illegal" city in South Dakota before it was white territory and instead belonged to the Sioux. A treaty forbid whites from crossing into the area, and the Army was charged with keeping settlers out. However, gold was discovered in the territory, the greedy rushed in and the town was established in the middle of nowhere. Too powerful for the Indians to attack, the whites used the city for supplies, carousing and whoring, then would go back to their mines, hoping the Indians didn't attack them, which they often did.

Deadwood is an adult western in all senses of the meaning. The f-word is used in almost every sentence, especially by people like Calamity Jane or Al Swearengen, who owns one of the town's major saloon-whorehouses. Completely unlike *Gunsmoke*, except in the strength of its stories, the subject matter turned off large numbers of traditional Western fans (who probably turned to the Western Channel instead for customary shows and movies) but attracted widespread new viewers who liked the graphic violence and sexuality. All manner of copulation is shown—frequently. Murder and mayhem is most gruesome, and never done in the usual Western style of two men shooting it out, face to face. Generally it's back-stabbing—literally. As well as ice picking and ax wielding and ...

Swearengen is by far the worst of all the characters in the town. In one episode he sneaks into the room of a man he had to give money to, and kills the drunkard with his knife. In another, he drowns a henchman who messed up a job by keeping his head down in the bathtub. Another henchmen who screwed up has his hand out to receive his payoff. Swearengen shoves his knife directly into the man's stomach, gutting him. A close second to Swearengen is Mr. Wu, the very silent head of the Chinatown section. Whenever Swearengen kills a man, or his lackeys kill someone, they take the body to Wu, who feeds it to some very large and voracious hogs.

A very few decent characters stand out, men and women who try to remain consistent with the values and morals of the time. The hardware dealers, Seth Bullock and Sol Star, run an honest business, do not jack up prices, and are not murderers, which is more than could be said for many of the townspeople. Bullock, who was a U.S. Marshal, quit the job to make his fortune in Deadwood. When the Army moved in against the Sioux and the town fell under U.S. jurisdiction, Bullock became the town marshal, much to the chagrin of shady dealers like Swearengen, who knows the man cannot be bought or bullied. Wild Bill Hickok, played by Keith Carradine, was a guest star in the first episodes. He was a former lawman like Bullock, and the two become fast friends. When Hickok is gunned down playing cards and the killer is set loose, Bullock goes after him to set things right.

Sometimes politicians ride to the town to get their share of the graft. Swearengen, who has a murder warrant from the states, pays thousands of dollars to one highly placed official and the warrant disappears. Because of the gold in the area, neighboring jurisdictions want to annex Deadwood, so the town's committee — mostly made up of cutthroat businessmen like Swearengen — look for the most profitable deal, not necessarily for the town but for themselves. Once the Army arrives and the town has to become a "real town," with fire marshals and welfare committees and the like, many of those chosen, even ones who are killers, actually become "concerned citizens" and do their jobs conscientiously!

The doctor in the town, a decent man with a good heart, helps everyone whether they can pay or not. But even he has a past: He was barred from practicing medicine for digging up cadavers for medical experiments. Seeing the immorality of most of the town's citizens, particularly its leading ones, jades him, but he continues to help people nonetheless. Bullock remains a moral force in the town. Before he was town marshal, Bullock and Wild Bill had to draw against a fiend who massacred some settlers and tried to make it look like Indians. Wild Bill asked his partner whose bullet hit the man first and Bullock said it was Wild Bill's. However, it was clear that both men were equally fast and their aim sharp and clear. Considering that Wild Bill Hickok was noted as the best shot among outlaws and lawmen, Bullock is in good company. Despite the town's depravity, its marshal remains constant and unbending, just like Matt Dillon, so perhaps in that respect it's not too different from *Gunsmoke* after all.

Television has a great impact on the viewing public. For good or bad, whether people watch CNN or Fox, *Gunsmoke* or *Deadwood*, what the public sees on the (not so) small screen often influences their opinions. Those who prefer Marshal Dillon walking the streets of Dodge see a good town and a good lawman who confronts criminals every so often. Those who like Marshal Bullock see a good man awash in the evil of a corrupt town, surrounded by criminals, a man who must sometimes resort to extreme violence to keep the peace. In between these two poles fall the other detectives and police officers, some good, some a little hard, all enforcing the rules that keep society civil. Without the Mannixes, the Barettas, the Torellos, society as we know it might not look quite the same, and Deadwood might begin to look very familiar.

Sources

Butler, Jeremy. *Miami Vice*. Museum of Broadcast Communications. http://www.museum.tv/archives/etv/M/htmlM/miamivice/miamivice.htm.
DVD Times. *Crime Story*. http://www.dvdtimes.couk/content.php?contentid=12714.
LaSalle, Mick. *Blame the Economy, the Product, the Theaters — We're Just Not Going to the Movies the Way We Used To*. San Francisco Chronicle. 7/13/2005.
NBC.com. *Law and Order*. http://www.nbc.com/Law_&_Order/about/index.html.
Rabin, Nathan. *Electra Glide in Blue*. The Onion A.V. Club. http://www.theonionavclub.com/review.php?review_id=8833 4-6-2005.
Thrilling Detective. *Joe Mannix*. http://www.thrillingdetective.com/manj.html.
Wikipedia. *Gunsmoke*. http://en.wikipedia.org/wiki/Gunsmoke.

XV

One Riot — One Ranger!

Ain't no one ever killed a Texas Ranger and lived to talk about it.*

Many tales float around about the Texas Rangers. Rough, tough, never compromising, these men have a long and sometimes controversial history. The most famous story goes something like this: A riot broke out in a town. The police and citizens couldn't stop the violence. Crime was rising, people were dying, and the town was in flames. The mayor called down to Austin and asked the governor to send them some Rangers. When the train pulled into the station, a sole Texas Ranger got off. The town asked him where the others were, and the Ranger replied, 'Well, you only have one riot." And so was born the saying "One riot — one Ranger!"†

The Texas Rangers take pride in their reputation as a force that can get things done. Rangers were first formed over 180 years ago by Stephen Austin to help protect American settlements from Indians and bandits. These colonies were legally established by the Mexican government, and the Americans in them swore allegiance to Mexico. By the eve of the Texas Revolution in 1835, the Rangers were officially formalized. But because Texas was so large, and its enemies many, from Mexico on the border and Indians within, the Rangers rode hard and fast, and had a reputation of shooting first and asking questions later. Texas did not have an army, so after the revolution the Rangers handled military and police matters. The Texas Department of Public Safety relates the following:

> During this era, the Ranger Service held a place somewhere between that of an army and a police force. When a Ranger was going to meet an outside enemy, for example, the Indians or the Mexicans, he was very close to being a soldier; however, when he had to turn to the enemies within his own society — outlaws, train robbers, and highwaymen, he was a detective and policeman.

The Rangers are organized in companies which are posted throughout the state. During the last quarter of the nineteenth century, they rid the countryside of cattle rustlers and horse thieves. Modern training for Rangers is second to none. All Rangers must have at least eight years as a Texas peace officer before they can apply. Rangers do not wear uniforms, and they often back up local departments which do not have the expertise to investigate serious crimes. These tough lawmen have made it to the screen on a number of occasions; through these films and television series, the Texas Ranger has developed a reputation as being a loner who handles things his way.

**One bandit warning another about the dangers of taking on a Texas Ranger in* Lone Wolf McQuade.
†*This is one version of the story. Another has the riot taking place because of a prize fight.*

The Texas Rangers (1951)

In the nineteenth century it wasn't uncommon for outlaws to become peace officers, and sometimes vice versa. The Rangers had a number of men who went "good" after starting off bad. In this film, set after the Civil War, the Rangers are reorganized to handle a surge in banditry and lawlessness throughout the Lone Star State. Desperado Sam Bass assembles his own version of organized crime, gathering up the cream of the criminal crop to hit banks and other lucrative targets across the country. John Wesley Hardin, Butch Cassidy, the Sundance Kid and Dave Rudabaugh, among other infamous characters, join Bass in the illegal endeavors. One outlaw not on the list is Johnny Carver, known as the fastest gun in Texas. Carver rode with the Sundance Kid, but during a bank robbery he was double-crossed and shot by the Kid. He was thrown in prison, along with his partner Buff Smith.

The Rangers know they need someone who rode with these criminals and can handle himself. Bass and his band continue to wreak havoc around the countryside, and always seem a step ahead of the Rangers. They decide to get the best "worst" bad man they can:

They recruit Carver and Smith to go after the outlaws. Carver merely wants to get free and find Sundance, but after his younger brother, a newly appointed Texas Ranger, is killed by the outlaws, Carver changes his tune and puts his fast gun to use.

Carver, and to a lesser extent his partner, are men dealing with the moral ambiguity that comes from being caught between two worlds. Being an outlaw brings fast money, good times and legendary reputations. The life of a Texas Ranger might earn you a reputation, but the money isn't coming and good times may be few and far between. The criminal life that Carver is used to is not one high on responsibility. A Ranger's responsibilities never end. Both move around a lot, and face the danger of being shot, but only the outlaw has the chance of getting rich.

After finally making his decision about which way to go, Carver begins dispatching the various outlaws, destroying Sam Bass' syndicate of criminals. However, cinema being what it is, some of those outlaws weren't around at the time depicted, or they worked other areas of the country. Still, had they actually crossed the Texas Rangers, they would have found out what John Wesley Hardin did the hard way: The Rangers get their man, sooner or later, one way or another.

As is the way in Hollywood, one good turn deserves another. The plot of *The Texas Rangers* was recycled almost 15 years later as a starring vehicle for Audie Murphy. In *Arizona Raiders* (1965), Audie plays Clint, a Confederate soldier now fighting alongside Quantrill's Raiders. They descend on a town and shoot it up, killing every man and boy in sight, and looting whatever supplies and cash they need. On their trail are a Union cavalry officer, Capt. Andrews, and a company of mounted soldiers. Quantrill is almost killed in the raid on the town, but Clint saves him. The band of outlaws takes a respite in an abandoned farmhouse to patch up their wounds and feed their horses. Capt. Andrews finds them and surrounds the barn. In the ensuing shootout, Clint and his partner Willie are betrayed by Montana, one of Quantrill's subordinates, and captured. Quantrill is killed. Clint and Willie are sentenced to years of hard labor in prison.

When Capt. Andrews musters out of the Army, the governor of the Arizona Territory asks him to form a department of Rangers, similar to those in Texas. His first task will be to hunt down the remainder of Quantrill's raiders, who are attacking army gold shipments. Andrews busts Clint and Willie out of prison and enlists their help to catch the bandits, who are led by Montana. The men find their old comrades in a village far in the desert, by the Mexican border. After Clint kills Montana, they eventually join up and foil the outlaw's raids. Most of them are killed, and those who aren't are taken by Indians helping Clint.

Like Johnny Carver, Clint begins as an outlaw. Like Johnny, he's imprisoned with his best friend. And like Johnny, he's recruited to be a Ranger, only this time in Arizona. Clint wants revenge on Montana, who stole his horse and left him and Willie to be captured by the Union. Johnny wanted revenge on Sundance for double-crossing him. Both men have doubts about being Rangers but come to the side of law after their younger brothers, who are both Rangers, are brutally murdered by the gang. And Clint's best friend Willie, like Johnny's best friend Buff, sides against him when he tries to go back on his oath and not follow through with the job.

The two films begin with an almost documentary-like feel. *The Texas Rangers* highlights the various famous outlaws plaguing Texas at the time, and the killings they've become notorious for. *Arizona Rangers* takes it a step farther, with a newspaper editor telling the whole story of Quantrill's Raiders, their atrocities and brutality. Much of it is true but a significant part is not, or is in question by historians. However, being Hollywood and not history, Quantrill is presented as almost a demon from Hades—and a good deal older than the actual Quantrill was. When the editor has finished his speech to the camera, the viewer "knows" what it should have "seen," cinema being a visual art.

Be that as it may, both *Arizona Raiders* and *The Texas Rangers* were generated by the same story, written by Frank Gruber, though the former adds political and social elements not present in the latter. Coming at the height of the Civil Rights movement, *Raiders* raises, even superficially, the issue of problems encountered by those who face disparate treatment, either institutionally by the government, or personally, by people, and what the reactions might be. After the war, Clint returned to a South where his home had been torched and his family killed. Unable to find work, he's forced to do what he must to survive—in this instance, become a bandit. Clint's plight mirrors that of the Yaqui Indians whose village the bandits have taken over. They had lived in Mexico, but were hunted down by the authorities until what few of them remained crossed into the U.S. and settled in the village, becoming Christians. The bandits do to the Indians what the Mexicans had, and what the North had done to Clint. Like Clint, they revert back to what they were before they converted, and use forms of torture on the bandits they can capture.

The oath the Rangers take is an important part of the job. In *The Searchers* (1956), when Captain-Reverend Clayton attempts to swear in Ethan Edwards as a Texas Ranger, he refuses. Immediately Clayton thinks it's because he's a wanted man. It appears bloodshed may follow, until Edwards tells the Ranger he's only good for one oath at a time—and he's sworn his to the Confederate States of America. When Clint is sworn in, he fumbles with the words. As a man of integrity, he doesn't like swearing to something he won't follow through with. He has no intention of becoming a lawman—he wants out of jail and he wants Montana. After that, it's off to Mexico. But with both Johnny and Clint, their younger brothers have taken the oath, and take it seriously. They're Rangers, and if their older brothers won't honor their word, they'll take them back to prison.

Another element of the '60s was a dash of sex and drugs. The bandits take over the Indian village and kill the priest who cares for the Indians. The chief's daughter, who speaks English, is forced to tend to the outlaws, though in a number of scenes it appears to be more than cooking they want her for. When Clint finds the village, he watches as Montana consumes a bottle of Peyote, then, overcome by lust caused by the drugs, rips the chief's daughters top. Clint steps in to prevent the rape and kills Montana in a fair fight, though the connection between illicit behavior and drugs is clearly established.

At the film's climax, the outlaws torture and kill Willie, but he doesn't give up any information. Dying like a Ranger, he is buried by the Indians with Mission's Cross as his tombstone. Clint escapes and, with Capt. Andrews, busts up the gold robbery. However, the Indians take Brady, the outlaw leader; his fate is their specialized "cactus" torture. Clint has now earned an unconditional pardon — but as he rides off with the captain, it is clear he will remain a Ranger.

The Comancheros (1961)

John Wayne plays Cutter, a Texas Ranger who says he wants to retire, but every time he does, Sam Houston calls him to take care of one thing or another. First on Cutter's plate is Paul Regret, an affable gambler wanted in Louisiana for killing a high-ranking man in a duel. Regret boards a steamer where he meets Pilar, a beautiful but mysterious woman with whom he falls in love. As the ship docks, Cutter comes aboard and arrests Regret on a fugitive warrant. They travel across country, inland, where the Ranger Company is based. Regret rides a donkey so that can't get far if he tries to escape. Along the route, Cutter comes across some settlers who have been burned out by Comanches. He knows the family — they worked for him when the ranch was his. When Cutter's wife died, he gave the family the ranch and signed up with Houston again. After Cutter buries the family, Regret smashes his head with a shovel and escapes. When Cutter rides into headquarters on the back of the donkey, the whole company gets a good laugh.

No sooner has Cutter arrived than his supervisors have another mission: flush out some Comancheros selling guns and liquor to the Indians (probably the same Indians who killed the family on Cutter's old ranch). The Rangers have locked up a Comanchero who was on his way to meet the Indians, so Cutter volunteers to take his place. He rides out to meet his partner, Crow, played by Lee Marvin. Neither man has seen the other before. Crow and Cutter jab at one another, each man trying to get the measure of the other. When they sit down to play some cards, Cutter discovers Regret sitting at the table. The gambler doesn't blow Cutter's cover, but Crow gets upset at the way the cards are falling and draws on the Ranger, who easily guns him down. Cutter thanks Regret — then promptly arrests him again!

This time Cutter takes no chances — he handcuffs Regret to an anvil. They stop at a large ranch for supplies but the Comanches attack. Regret escapes again, only this time he comes back with a company of Rangers. The men fight off the Indians and find a judge who will dismiss the charges against Regret. Now he's a Texas Ranger, too, and he and Cutter go after the Comancheros, hoping to find their hiding place. They meet with the Indians, who take them to a secret camp. Graile, the leader, doesn't trust the two men and leaves them hanging from the rocks, dying in the hot sun. It's at that moment that Pilar rides into camp — she's Graile's daughter. Now she has to decide whether to save the two Rangers or let them perish.

The Comancheros follows to a tee the notions of what a Texas Ranger is *supposed* to be. Cutter is a physically imposing presence — well over six feet tall and with bulk to back him up. He's not into adulation or hero worship, of either himself or others. He shrugs off Regret's astonishment that he (Cutter) is friends with Sam Houston. He's also cagey. He unloads Regret's Derringer and then puts it back in the gambler's bag. When Regret pulls the gun, Cutter merely slugs him. He's got the power of an ox and sends Regret reeling backward and onto the seat of his pants. Regret thinks the Ranger is incredibly brave or incredibly stupid. If Cutter was cold-blooded, he could have just shot Regret and said the

John Wayne as Texas Ranger Jake Cutter in *The Comancheros.*

gambler pulled a gun on him — and he wouldn't be lying! During the ride to the Ranger station, Cutter and Regret talk to pass time. When the conversation gets philosophical, about a man giving his word, Cutter essentially tells the gambler that words are what men live by — words they say and words they mean.

Cutter rides alone, but works with the company if they need him. He's a take-charge kind of guy. When the Indians attack the supply ranch, the Ranger immediately gets things organized. Hopelessly outnumbered, the men under Cutter's command repel the attack. When Regret returns to the ranch with a Ranger company, Cutter proves himself to be the best shot of all. In some remarkable staging, director Michael Curtiz shows Cutter, Regret and a young Ranger named Tobe whirling together in a combination and mowing down the Indians. Cutter is brave as well, if not too brave for his own good. Posing as a Comanchero is dangerous business, especially when the people you are dealing with are scum and not particularly trustworthy. Crow, the man with whom Cutter is supposed to do business, has a reputation with a gun but, much to his chagrin, his speed is no match for Cutter.

Cutter's jurisdiction is Texas—and beyond. Recorded history shows many Texas Rangers leaving the Lone Star State to bring in their man, whether they were authorized to do so or not. Even into the twentieth century, Rangers had crossed the Mexican border to dispense justice to outlaws and bandits who made the mistake of coming into Texas to cause trouble. Rangers aren't above bending the law for the good of the community. When Cutter takes Regret into custody, there's some question about whether the boat is in Texas or Louisiana. When Regret proves himself to be a man of his word, a good shot, and brave to a fault, the Rangers get together and convince a Texas judge to dismiss the charges against him—certainly a dubious proposition considering the crime was committed in the United States and not the Republic of Texas.

Cutter and Regret are helped by Pilar, who vouches for them. In the end, the Rangers raid Graile's camp of Comancheros and kill everyone—or at least everyone they can. Now Cutter has a decision to make: release Pilar or take her in for her crimes, which mean she'd no doubt dangle at the end of a rope. In typical Ranger style, Cutter lets Pilar and Regret go; however, in the middle of a desert filled with Comanches and bandits, and the Mexican border hundreds of miles away, it's a toss-up if they'll ever make it.

The Town That Dreaded Sundown (1977)

In 1946, a string of murders terrified Texarkana, Arkansas. The killer, called "The Phantom" by local newspapers, crept up on young lovers in isolated rural areas and, after extremely brutal assaults, shot and killed them. Not reported in the press or media at the time was the fact that the women were sexually assaulted. The killer left his semen at the scene but, a half-century before DNA, not much could be done with it. Serial killers, though active at the time, were not something the public knew anything about. For that matter, most police didn't either. The Phantom's first victims were the only ones who ever saw him and lived. The killer ordered them out of their car, beat the young man and then pounced on the woman, using his firearm to touch the woman's privates. The approach of another vehicle saved them. More murders followed. One couple was left in their car at the side of the road. The man was shot as he sat behind the wheel; the woman was raped and killed.

The local authorities were in over their heads. A number of agencies joined the hunt, banding together in what is nowadays called a task force. The town itself, on the border of Texas, was figuratively shutting down at sundown. Teens kept to a voluntary curfew, police heavily patrolled all lovers' lanes, and vagrants and transients were rounded up, checked and released. The online site crimelibrary.com, in the article *The Phantom Killer: Texarkana Moonlight Murders*, noted:

In the midst of the chaos, the fabled Texas Rangers made an entrance onto the scene. They came in the tall, lean form of a well-known Ranger named Manuel Gonzaullas, known as "Lone Wolf" for his ability to track down criminals and face them by himself.

In 1977, Charles B. Pierce, a low-budget independent filmmaker, produced and directed *The Town That Dreaded Sundown*, a docudrama look at the Phantom killings and famous Texas Ranger "J.D. Morales" who was sent in to stop the monster. The names of the killer's victims, the policemen and the Ranger were changed for the movie, but many of the facts presented were accurate. The description of the Phantom came from the only survivors who saw him — the kids from the first attack. The man was large, intimidating, and wore a bag-type hood with slits for eyes and mouth. He carried a small-caliber handgun and would torture his victims.

When the Ranger arrives in Texarkana, his reputation immediately puts the city at ease, and much more confident that the killer will be caught. The police set up stakeouts in lovers' lanes with male cops dressed like females, and back-up cars hidden just out of sight. Morales places patrols around the local high schools. He even speaks with a psychologist, trying to get a handle on the kind of creature they are tracking. Where Morales is hamstrung is the lack of any description; in the scene where he is speaking with the psychologist, the Phantom is in the same room, watching, and presumably listening. The Ranger's aggressive measures to prevent the killer from striking again work for a while. But, then a young couple breaks the voluntary curfew and head to a park inside the city limits. Up to this point, the killer had been striking on the outskirts. Morales' proactive stance forces the Phantom outside of his usual hunting ground.

The Phantom's final assault takes place out of town, at a farmhouse. Police pressure had completely altered the killer's routine. The Ranger and the sheriff's office also noticed that just before a murder, a car would be stolen. Officers began checking all cars they came across on the city's outskirts and rural area, hoping to find one that was stolen. Morales discovers the Phantom's car and, in a chase across a field and quarry, he wounds the killer, who disappears into a huge swamp. The murders stop, and the Ranger is credited with killing the Phantom. But he himself is not sure, and the case remains open to this day.

Though made on the cheap, *The Town That Dreaded Sundown* presents a number of truly frightening moments, all premised on the fact that the story is based on a real-life crime. Ranger Morales upholds the "lone wolf" moniker by chasing down the killer himself. While he has another officer with him, Morales is the one doing the shooting and the one closest to the Phantom — and the one under fire. Without Morales' leadership, just how long the murders would have continued is debatable. The film's ending leaves open the idea that the killer may indeed still be alive. But should he ever return, so too, shall the Texas Rangers.

Lone Wolf McQuade (1983)

Ranger Morales' modern incarnation is J.J. McQuade (played by Chuck Norris), an asocial lawman who lives in a dirty, rundown house in the middle of the desert with a wolf as his only companion. McQuade is following some horse rustlers when a state police squad busts up his stakeout and tries to take the outlaws into custody. The police are shot up, and so the Ranger has to go down and set things right. He mows down most of the bandits with a machine-gun, then uses his karate skills to take care of whoever's left. When

Texas Ranger "Lone Wolf" McQuade (Chuck Norris) gets the best of his attackers in *Lone Wolf McQuade*.

McQuade gets back to town, it's just in time for his best friend's retirement party. It never occurs to McQuade to check his personal hygiene after such difficult work, though the Rangers all around him can smell him before they see him.

McQuade's next assignment is working with the feds in busting up a major arms smuggling ring. McQuade wants to go it alone but he's assigned Kayo, one of the state police officers whose life he saved. Teaming up with an FBI agent named Jackson, they find the transport point for the guns, but the smuggler, Rawley, is waiting for them and most of the officers are killed. The three men, wounded, make it back to town. Rawley also kidnaps McQuade's daughter. Though all three men are still recovering, they confront the smuggler using massive firepower and stop the operation.

McQuade underlines the "lone," reinforcing the idea of Rangers working solitary. While Cutter would operate in company-size drills or operations, McQuade wants no partners whatsoever. Though he's assigned to work with Kayo, he ditches him at every opportunity and at every location. Only at a party thrown by Rawley, where the smuggler demonstrates his abilities as a martial arts champion, does McQuade acknowledge his partner, and that's only because Rawley's men jump Kayo. But once McQuade has cleaned the floor with the attackers, he leaves Kayo and is on the prod again. The two men only come together after McQuade's daughter is almost killed by Rawley's men during an arms shipment; McQuade seems too distracted to ditch him.

Critics like Roger Ebert liken *Lone Wolf McQuade* to a spaghetti Western and, in a sense, the film does function on such a level. The action takes place mostly in a desert setting; there are a number of bizarre characters (such as the wheelchair-bound dwarf who commands his own smuggling operation); McQuade is devastating with a gun, having machine-gunned 10 or 20 bandits in the opening scene alone; and McQuade doesn't wear a uniform — he wears jeans and a shirt while carrying his holstered gun right on his belt. When bad-asses try McQuade, like those making a move on the Man with No Name in the Eastwood films, they are either beat down or gunned down pretty quickly — sometimes both.

McQuade certainly meets the criteria set by other Rangers, shooting first and asking questions later. Without calling a warning, he fires his rifle at one of the bandits in the opening scene. When he comes back to his house, where Kayo and his retired Ranger friend are holding a prisoner, he's jumped by Rawley's men. He kills them efficiently, not leaving anyone alive to question. At the smuggler's gun transit point, the feds rush the job and blow the hook. McQuade lays back and kills as many as he can until they finally overcome him. But in typical Ranger fashion, after Rawley buries him alive in his supercharged truck, McQuade pours some generic beer on his head and runs the four-wheel drive out of the pit!

Like Cutter, McQuade doesn't care about "society" or famous people. Rawley is the past European karate champion, but when he challenges the Ranger for a money fight, McQuade shrugs him off. He doesn't need to show off. When he finally does meet up with Rawley, he beats the man literally senseless, European credentials or no. McQuade's captain is continually pushing him to show "style." McQuade can't even make it to a formal retirement celebration in decent clothes. The reason the Ranger brass wants to team McQuade with Kayo is to show a "gentler" face to the Texas Rangers. McQuade could care less about gentler — or kinder for that matter. He's just killed almost 20 men and it's not even sundown.

McQuade, even more so than Cutter, is a throwback to the old-time Rangers. The entire state of Texas is his bailiwick, but it's not quite enough. Rawley's base of operation is in Mexico, so McQuade, Kayo and Jackson head south, the Ranger not even bothering to use his own personal vehicle: His four-wheel drive has "Texas Department of Public Safety" plastered right on the side doors. When Cutter's Rangers attacked the Comancheros' camp, they used Walker Colts — this was the first practical, revolving-chamber handgun invented. The Rangers were among the first to put it to use in action. As a small force, they always relied on the best (and most) firepower available. McQuade takes this a step further, firing shoulder-launched missiles, among other weapons.

The business partner of Rawley loves McQuade. Rawley uses her to find out about McQuade, but when she helps him and his daughter, Rawley kills her. However, judging from McQuade's character, this was inevitable. McQuade, already once divorced, is incapable of close ties. Besides his best friend dying, even his wolf gets killed! McQuade remains true to himself and the Rangers. Promising to take his ex-wife and daughter to their new home in New Mexico, McQuade is summoned to handle another crime and off he goes...

Extreme Prejudice (1987)

Jack Benteen is a Texas Ranger. He works the border, interdicting drugs. His best friend is Cash Bailey, a notorious and flamboyant drug lord. Most of the time they get along, but the drugs are flooding into Texas and Jack starts putting a crimp into Cash's business. There's also Sarita, Jack's girlfriend. She used to be Cash's woman, but now she straddles the middle, torn between the way she feels about both men. In the midst of this brewing showdown enters a special unit from the military. Made up of men who have been reported dead, these "ghosts" are planning to take down Cash and stop the drugs.

Benteen, like McQuade, exemplifies the loner attitude. He prefers working by himself to the extent that he alienates most of the people he comes into contact with. His relationship with Sarita is so strained that she winds up back with Cash. When Benteen enters a crowded honky tonk filled with country boys involved in the drug trade, he makes the sheriff wait in his truck. He kills the suspect, but his actions are almost foolhardy. Later, when the sheriff and Benteen are tracking a lead, they are ambushed. The sheriff is killed but Benteen keeps returning to his truck to obtain more firepower even as the shootout continues. Like Rangers before him, he finally crosses the border into Mexico to settle the score with Cash once and for all.

While Benteen and Cash are the absolutes, the black and whites, Sarita and the military unit are wildcards bearing streaks of gray. Benteen won't budge. When Cash tries to bribe him just to stay out of his dealings, Benteen tells him that the man can always be bought but not the badge he's wearing. Cash is so laid back, he'll do anything not to kill his friend. He's a firm believer in situational ethics. Someone has to sell the drugs so it might as well be him. There's only right and wrong for Benteen, nothing in the middle. The military unit is breaking laws and killing people in America so as to better position themselves to take down Cash's operation. Clearly the end justifies the means in their eyes. They may kill a few now but that will save many later. Sarita's motives are more complex. She likes the stability of Benteen, and by extension that of America. But she likes the emotion of Cash, and the feeling of life Mexico gives her.

Extreme Prejudice was directed by Walter Hill, so an over-the-top climax was to be expected. The military unit, finding out they've been double-crossed by their leader, decides to destroy as much of the Mexican cartel as possible, knowing it's a suicide mission. With guns blazing, bodies fly everywhere. In homage to *The Wild Bunch*, the men take turns firing a large-caliber, mounted machine-gun into the crowd of Cash's henchmen, until the ghosts themselves are finally killed. Benteen and Cash then step out in the street, Old West style, and draw. Benteen wins and heads back to the U.S. with Sarita in tow. Another drug lord has taken Cash's place already, so Benteen has a new adversary.

Texas Ranger Jack Benteen (Nick Nolte) prepares for a showdown, Old West style, in *Extreme Prejudice,* as Sarita Cisneros (Maria Conchita Alonso) watches.

Texas Rangers (2002)

"King" Fisher and his bandits are laying waste to the Texas countryside, stealing cattle, raping women, looting towns. The Rangers are re-formed to put an end to the lawlessness, only Fisher isn't the easiest man to catch — or beat. This film is not a remake of *The Texas Rangers* but it does have some of the same plot elements. The Rangers, who had been off fighting for the South during the Civil War, were never formally reorganized when it was over. In the mid–1870s, however, the governor reinstates them under the command of Randall NcNeely, a former Ranger and gunfighter. McNeely begins recruiting; however, many of his volunteers are orphans or young men with no family — many in those straits because of "King" Fisher. The boys have to grow up fast, however, as McNeely's pursuit of Fisher becomes careless, and he leads them into some tight spots and ambushes. McNeely eventually catches up to Fisher and kills him. One bandit down, but many more to go.

McNeely's character is much like Carver from the film 50 years before. Both are noted gunmen, and McNeely's conduct sometimes borders on criminal. He's a dying man, having fought too much during his life, both as a Ranger and in the war, so he's willing to compromise what the Rangers stand for if it means ridding Texas of the filth that plagues them. McNeely's sickness spurs him on. He doesn't know if he'll even live until winter. The worse it gets, the harder he becomes, though unlike Cutter or Benteen, McNeely does not work alone. The Rangers ride in a company-size formation. King's bandits outnumber them, so the Rangers stay together, and with each battle, the young inexperienced boys learn their trade. When the final showdown comes, they are more than a match for the bandits.

Texas Rangers was shelved for a year or more past its intended release date. When it did finally debut, the studio didn't advertise or make it available for review. The only notice of the film was from some movie trailers shown before other features. But even that seems kind of fitting, all things considered. McNeely, like the film, was forgotten. He was recruited because of a reputation made many years prior. He delivered, like the film did, but by that time it was just too late. He passed away as the film went to video.

The Texas Rangers continue to be an organization that attracts many but chooses few. During the 1950s, television brought out *Tales of the Texas Rangers*, which was unique because it featured the same characters but each episode might be in a different time period. For example, one story would find the Rangers tracking Depression-era gangsters, while the next week the same Rangers would be back in the 1880s, shutting down cattle rustlers. Joel McCrea was the voice of the Texas Rangers on the radio show of the same name. It was ahead of its time in many respects. The crimes the Rangers investigated were brutal, and sometimes they had to go against local law enforcement which had turned bad.

Lonesome Dove (1988) was a television mini-series starring Robert Duvall and Tommy Lee Jones as retired Texas Rangers who won't stay retired. Having killed or run off all the bandits, and cleared Texas of the Indian threat, the two men pass their remaining days on a ranch with no cattle, in the middle of the desert, near a rundown town. Duvall reads his Bible or spends his time with a prostitute at the saloon. Jones works all day on the ranch (and works everyone else as well), and then goes to the river at night to clean his firearms, whether he's shot them or not. The men decide to make a cattle drive north, to Montana, which has never been done. Duvall and Jones are respected and feared throughout Texas and beyond, but a sense of futility and sadness permeates every action they take, heroic or otherwise.

Chuck Norris, whose martial arts films petered out with the collapse of Cannon in the mid–90s, starred for almost a decade in the CBS-TV series *Walker, Texas Ranger*. When he ended the show, which he co-produced with his brother, it was still a ratings getter and audience favorite, and could have continued. Probably more so than any single movie, the series portrayed the Rangers in the light that many have come to believe: fearless; intelligent; honest and unyielding. Men who get the job done, and care about the public they serve.

Sources

crimelibrary.com. *The Phantom Killer: Texarkana Moonlight Murders*. www.crimelibrary.com/serial_killers/unsolved/texarcana/beast_3

Curtis, Brandon. *Texas Rangers*. CultureDose.net. 5–2–02 www.toxicuniverse.com/review.php?rid=10003075

eFilmCritic.com. *The Town That Dreaded Sundown*. http://efilmcritic.com/review.php?movie=3977

Grost, Michael. *The Films of Phil Karlson: The Texas Rangers*. Classic Film and Television. http://members.aol.com/MG4273/Karlson.htm

Texas Department of Public Safety. *Historical Development of the Texas Rangers*. www.txdps.state.tx.us/director_staff/texas_rangers/

XVI

Walkin' the Beat ...
Cruising the Street...

*What am I? A shit magnet?**

    While the number of TV police shows increase every year, and a significant number flood the theatrical market, most modern stories involve detectives, undercover agents or feds. The actual uniform street cop really hasn't had the cinema exposure that his plainclothes brethren have. Working a uniform detail is obviously dangerous—any time one works in law enforcement, he or she takes a chance. Uniformed officers are supposed to present a deterrent to criminal activity, but the other side of the coin is that they also make a nice target. In California, just to make points with local gangsters, a wannabe gang member actually shot a CHP officer who was coming out of court. Instead, the killer got life in prison.

    And then there's the discomfort of the outfit itself. Wool shirts and slacks might be okay during the winter but the summers are another story. The ballistic vest is heavy and usually doesn't fit perfectly, and for that reason alone many officers don't wear it. The utility belt, or what is often called a "Sam Browne," is heavy, loaded down with a gun, ammunition, radio, baton, tear gas and flashlight, to name just a few things. Lower back problems are something almost all officers have to deal with during the course of their career. Twenty or thirty years of wearing the belt guarantees that.

    Hollywood tries to give the customer what they want but, in the last 50 years, with the fragmentation of an audience beyond anything the studios could ever imagine, finding a "sure thing" the customer will flock to has become almost unattainable. In response, many producers look for films which put out the simplest of narratives and a large number of special effects to try to fill as many theater seats as possible. When that translates to police films, almost always it's the plainclothes dicks on the trail of this or that. Federal agents trying to stop terrorists of every ilk. The "diehard" detective thwarting criminals taking over buildings, airports or any other place where money is readily available for the taking. Somewhere in the midst of these massive explosions and karate fights, the uniform patrol officer gets left behind. But the films about them can be brilliant, and open up a world rarely seen except by the men and women pushing a black-and-white.

Officer Orin Boyd (Steven Seagal) wondering aloud to himself before busting a gang of car burglars in Exit Wounds.

Earthquake (1974)

A tremor hits Los Angeles, swallowing the state's best seismologist inside a fault. His best student predicts that Los Angeles will soon be hit by a massive quake bigger than anything ever recorded. The best architect in the country begins an affair with the youngest and hottest-looking widow in the city, in part because he feels responsible for her husband's death. LAPD's toughest patrolman is busy crossing into sheriff's jurisdiction to catch his suspects, causing all kinds of havoc between the agencies. The world's best motorcycle daredevil is preparing for a carnival jump, hoping to attract backers to support a tour, and the state's *worst* National Guardsman is about to go on weekend duty.

This film is no different than most other films—the characters are generally special or gifted. *Earthquake*, which did battle with the same year's release *The Towering Inferno* at the Academy Awards, is the kind of high-impact entertainment most expect from big-budget studio releases. Everyone is cool and dresses hip, and the problems facing many of these people have a '70s soap opera feel to them, like casual sex versus meaningful sex, or adultery versus meaningful adultery. The earthquake hits as the student predicted, and Los Angeles is flattened, buildings crashing down everywhere. A huge dam is riddled with cracks.

How the characters work their way through the damage and the chaos afflicting the city forms the second half of the story. What's interesting, however, is that the main plot line, following architect Charlton Heston and his search for his young girlfriend, is eclipsed by the one about a street cop, played by George Kennedy, who is forced to get his act together to save the injured people lining the streets—and to confront a sexual deviant wearing a military uniform and carrying a machine-gun. Heston is eventually pulled into help him, thereby merging their storylines, but it still remains for the cop on the beat to get the job done.

Kennedy is clearly what police often term an O.G.—taken from a street term meaning "old school" or "old guard." The department has protocols and policies, but when he's after a suspect, they fly right out the window. In his opening scene he's chasing a speeder through the city streets. The traffic offender is a small fish, and Kennedy's been warned before not to trespass into the sheriff's jurisdiction without good cause. Kennedy figures the crook's a big-enough catch, though, and runs the suspect into the front yard of a house in a very exclusive area. The sheriff's officers who roll up to the scene provoke him, and he decks one of them. Later, after getting his behind reamed by his supervisors and being sent home, he sits in a bar—in uniform—and knocks back the booze. In his mid-fifties, no family, and perhaps no job, Kennedy is a man who has spent the better part of his life enforcing the law his way, only to find that the times have past him by.

Marjoe Gortner is a grocery checker at a local supermarket. He lives in an apartment filled with young men his own age, a number of whom bully him. On one occasion, the men push their way into his place and see pictures of bodybuilders lining his wall. Almost-naked men, posing in tight Speedos as they show off their muscles, seem strange to the bullies. They suggest that Gortner is homosexual, and not a real man. Gortner, called up for his weekend stint in the National Guard, ignores the bullies and heads off. He and Kennedy are on a collision course: One is too much a man, and the other not enough. The natural disaster upends the normal state of things, and suddenly Gortner is in control.

When the earthquake hits, Kennedy immediately assumes control of the street he is on. He begins organizing the uninjured to help the injured, laying out the most serious cases and flagging down transportation to get them to the city's emergency clinics on the other side of town. When drivers such as Charlton Heston are reluctant to give up their vehicles, Kennedy exercises his police prerogatives during times of national emergency and takes it. People naturally respond to Kennedy's authority and command presence. Gortner, on the other hand, is a walking nightmare. He is a milquetoast in civilian life, but once he throws on a uniform and carries a rifle he becomes a martinet with a sadist streak. With martial law declared by the mayor, the Guard spreads out across the city; looters are to be arrested or shot. When Gortner comes across a pretty young girl who patronizes his store, he arrests her for taking a donut, and keeps her prisoner in the rubble of an old building. The bullies who teased him are caught with stolen jewelry. He pretends like he's going to shoot them, makes them sweat, then tells him he's just joking. When he releases the men and they walk off, he machine-guns them.

As Heston and Kennedy are taking the last load of injured people to the clinic, they run across Gortner, who runs the checkpoint they pass through. The girl dashes out; she knows Kennedy. Gortner threatens to shoot everyone. She's his prisoner, and he's in charge — not the police. Kennedy drives up a little way, then goes back to the rubble, where he faces off with Gortner, who is trying to rape the girl. Kennedy kills him, then he and the group make it to the clinic. An aftershock has trapped a group of doctors and patients in an underground parking structure. Heston and Kennedy climb into the rubble and drill a hole, rescuing the people.

Coming in the mid–70s, when confidence in the military was at an all-time low, the film's portrayal of Guardsmen as perverts and wimps was not a surprise. The Vietnam War was still ingrained in the national psyche — the lies, deaths and the wasted money. All pointed the way to cynicism and anti-militarism among much of the public. Pro-military films didn't come back into fashion until the Reagan era a decade later. The heroism and confidence of Kennedy's beat cop, contrasted with the pathological characters in the Guard, particularly Gortner, was evident in many films of the time. Travis Bickle in *Taxi Driver* (1976), the crazed Vietnam vet driving the streets of New York City, is another example. On the other hand, the American public, fearing "rampant crime," embraced films like *Death Wish* in the very same year as *Earthquake*. No-nonsense cops like Kennedy, who took action like Dirty Harry Callahan, or everyday vigilantes like Paul Kersey placated that segment of the public that placed a high premium on safety.

Colors (1988)

Bob Hodges is a lead gang officer in LAPD's CRASH.* He's been on for a long time and is looking forward to retirement — that is, if his new partner Danny McGavin doesn't kill him first. The gang officers are placed in a difficult situation: Try to stop simmering resentment between the various factions before they shoot each other up. The goal is as simple as the solution is difficult. Too many gang members. Too few officers. A city administration which provides few resources. And overcrowded jails which release the gangsters on a revolving door basis.

The narrative evolves in a loose fashion. Hodges shows the ropes to McGavin as they patrol some of the worst parts of Los Angeles. McGavin, something of a Casanova, dates Louisa, a Hispanic girl he meets at a lunch spot Hodges frequents, though Hodges warns him

---

*Community Resources Against Street Hoodlums; pressure from elements within the city forced the name to be changed.

against the idea. The two men clash about almost everything, though Hodges bends over backward to make the partnership work, including inviting McGavin and Louisa to a barbecue at his place. On the street, a war is being fought between two gangs over a drive-by shooting, and the CRASH units are trying to capture the killers. Hodges, working on a gut-hunch, stakes out the funeral of a slain gang member. The other gang attacks, riddling the church with bullets. Hodges and McGavin pursue them, but wreck their car and cause major damage to city property. In "unofficial" discipline, CRASH supervisors provide Hodges and McGavin with an old yellow Maverick. Soon, McGavin's street name becomes Pac Man, and the gangs themselves put a hit on him for his aggressive enforcement.

Hodges and McGavin are different as night and day. The only thing they have in common is a commitment to duty. Hodges is a family man, happily married with children. He takes things slow and looks at the big picture. A big arrest later is worth a thousand small busts now. Hodges attempts to illustrate the situation with a joke. He tells McGavin that an old bull and a young one were on a bluff, overlooking a field of heifers. The young one says something like, "Let's run down and have sex with one of them." The old one replies, "Let's walk down and have sex with all of them." Hodges has been around the block. He knows that in dealing with gangs, patience is something rarely practiced and sorely needed. He even attends the community block meetings, where anti-gang counselors try to help parents deal with their problem children.

McGavin is a complete U-turn, cocky and something of a wiseass. On his first day in CRASH, the roll call supervisor tells the men it's up to them to stop the bleeding in the

Hodges (Robert Duvall) watches as his partner (Sean Penn) jacks up a drug dealer with little more than suspicion to go on, in *Colors.*

city. McGavin remarks that it sounds like they're supposed to be Kotex. The young man loves the mirror, and stops to comb his hair at almost each one he passes. When he encounters gangsters, he pushes his weight around, something Hodges never does. McGavin can be brutal — he beats one drug dealer in front of his own house, and in another instance, he spray-paints the face of Louisa's nephew when he catches him engaging in graffiti. Louisa breaks off with McGavin because of it. What she recognizes (and he doesn't) is that Hodges is someone who really wants to help the community if he can; and that he, McGavin, is someone who could not care less.

A sense of futility exists in everything the officers do. The gangs are better armed and have no rules to follow. As Hodges and McGavin drive through the community, they overlook scores of minor crimes and neighborhood nuisances so they can stay ready for serious felonies. While it makes sense to Hodges, it also dissipates respect for the law in a community which already looks at the police as occupiers and not someone they can trust. In one scene, a working woman comes out of her shop and tells Hodges to take all the gang members away. All he can do is smile and say that he's trying. During a gang roundup, CRASH fills two huge cells with dozens of Bloods and Crips. As they throw gang signs and taunt one another, it's apparent the officers have merely scraped the tip of the iceberg.

Many of the gang members feel the same sense of futility. Even if they want out — and, to be sure, most don't — there's hardly any life away from the neighborhood. Most of the young men are unemployed, have no job skills, and even if they could find work, most of them have criminal records. For many of the gangs, the only family they have is each other. McGavin, and probably most viewers, would say that these men are responsible for their own behavior, and if they break the law, then they should pay. Hodges would agree, but he'd also note that the cycle has to be broken somewhere, somehow. One group of men Hodges knows (hardly a gang like the Crips or Bloods, but a gang by their own definition) hold a certain patch of turf that no one else wants. Frog, the gang's leader, wants to keep his kid brother out of the life, but after their gang is shot up and plans revenge, the boy joins, and his life is fast-tracked to a dead end.

Colors doesn't conclude on a pleasant note. After Frog's gang retaliates against their attackers, killing a number of them, they celebrate in a park. CRASH surrounds them and takes the members into custody. As the officers begin hooking up the gangsters, Frog's little brother steps out from another area and, in a drug-induced haze, fires, hitting Hodges with a high-powered rifle bullet which shreds his ballistic vest. As his partner lies dying, surrounded by his fellow officers, McGavin finally seems to understand what the job is all about. The last scene of the film shows him training someone just like himself, only he's in the Hodges role, and the gangs are still around, everywhere he looks.

Exit Wounds (2000)

Steven Seagal disappeared from the big screen after his 1997 film *Fire Down Below*, which was released by Warners with little fanfare. His films had been steadily decreasing in box office take since his huge 1992 hit *Under Siege*, where he played a Navy SEAL turned cook who has to battle terrorists aboard a Navy battleship. In *Exit Wounds*, Seagal plays a hot-shot detective who thwarts an attack on the vice-president, whose motorcade is cut off on a bridge and attacked by an anti-government militia organization. Seagal, who comes upon the attack by chance, uses his special skills to kill almost all the attackers. Finally he throws the vice-president over the bridge and into the water, saving his life. Unfortunately for Seagal, the vice-president, who has more political ambitions, is embarrassed by the action, and Seagal is fired. The department later brings him back, only his supervisors will not return him to plainclothes or detective duty.

Seagal is given a whistle and gets a taste of directing traffic, which he doesn't much like. Eventually he's able to get his captain to transfer him to a patrol unit and, in middle age, he begins where he started so many years before. Seagal immediately suspects the officers in his division are crooked; his partner believes the same, so they investigate, and find a ring of officers dealing drugs. Seagal can only fly under the radar so long before the crooked cops discover his snooping. They attempt to kill him, but fail. He busts the group during a major drug sale and most of them are killed.

Like *Colors*, this film examines the street from the view of two officers: one a longtime veteran, the other a youngster. Seagal resembles Hodges, his counterpart, in many respects. He knows the streets; he's competent and efficient; and he's willing to deal with shady elements if it helps him do his job. Latrell, the owner of a nightclub, is also tracking the rogue cops. They have framed his brother, and he wants to get him out of jail. Rather than work without Latrell's help, Seagal takes it, even though the young man is rumored to be a criminal himself. Seagal's partner is young like McGavin, but the similarities end there. He's not egotistical, he works well with Seagal, and he's willing to learn from his more experienced partner.

The film differs from *Colors* in some salient respects: It acts as a platform to highlight Seagal's superhuman abilities, both in martial arts and firepower, whereas Hodges is just a regular guy who does a good job day in, day out. On the bridge, Seagal liquidates an entire

Officer Orin Boyd (Steven Seagal) uncovers police corruption in *Exit Wounds* with Latrell Walker (DMX), left.

squad of militia men. In the locker room he takes a full charge from a stun gun and still stands. Later, in Latrell's nightclub, he fights all the bouncers, including a huge (at least 400-pound) giant. In the film's climax he takes on the rogue cops, killing a number of them. When Hodges and McGavin wreck their regular unmarked car, they're given a clunker as a "reward." When Seagal busts up the nightclub, or wrecks cars during a chase, no one complains. In *Colors*, wearing the LAPD blue is something that Hodges, even McGavin, are proud of. In *Exit Wounds*, Seagal seems to use being a beat cop as a means to get back to detectives, never fully appreciating the positive effect a couple of honest patrol officers have on the community they serve.

XVII

END OF THE TRAIL

— Don't worry about anything. I'll take care of it. Just like you would have.
*—Hell, I know that. I always did. You just forgot it for a while, that's all.**

The work of a peace officer or federal agent has changed significantly in a hundred years, and in some ways it hasn't. It's a fact that duties are always added, laws change almost daily, and officer training is very strenuous—but the task and how the job is done remain consistent. Unlike in the "old days," most law enforcement candidates are weeded out, and out of those who make it to a police academy or federal training facility, a noteworthy number of them fall by the wayside. But the occupation itself—the wearing of uniforms, enforcing penal code sections, writing traffic citations, patrolling in automobiles and on motorcycles, standardizing booking procedures, answering radio calls—has continued decade after decade. Pensions. Health insurance. Unions and fraternal organizations dedicated to protecting peace officers everywhere. All of these are legacies of the last century. A law enforcement officer hired in 1980 wouldn't find the job so unrecognizable in 2005. But what about a peace officer in 1880? What happens to him in 1905?

A great divide has always separated the men who went out into the wilderness, fought the elements, Indians and each other to make an area safe for a society like our own—from the actual society itself. In *The Searchers* (1956), Ethan Edwards is a bitter, violent man who spent the greater part of his life battling to make Texas a place where his family could survive, first Indians, and then the North during the Civil War. Killing is natural for him. He doesn't worry about it. He just does it. He spends five years hunting Comanches to find his kidnapped niece, not only to get revenge on them, but to kill her for becoming an Indian. When he finally destroys the tribe, he comes to his senses and saves his niece, but when the family reunites, Ethan is left outside, and the front door of the house closes on him. A man like this cannot enter the civilization he has fought to achieve, any more than Moses could enter the Promised Land.

Men who shot buffalo, rode shotgun for Wells Fargo, cleaned up the streets of Wichita, or scouted for the Army ... perhaps men like these could take off their guns, work as a shopkeeper, go to a play on Saturday night and church on Sunday morning. And, then again, perhaps not. A lot changed in the last quarter of the nineteenth century. Many cities prohibited firearms within their limits, visible or concealed, and most states also passed laws banning them. Cattle ranches were fenced in, owned by large corporations. Cattle drives

---

*Gil Westrum (Randolph Scott) to Steve Judd (Joel McCrea) in Ride the High Country.

consisted of rounding up the stock and taking them to a rail station, not driving them across country. Those jobs faded away, and a cowboy might merely be someone who wore denim, a hat and sometimes rode a horse. "Cowboy's work" became harder to define — the ranch straw boss or ramrod might be an accountant now. And, by the by, automobiles replaced horses, as highways replaced trails.

At the point when the country's focus changed from reading dime novels to reading Upton Sinclair, certain men had outlived their times, and many of those men were peace officers. In 1881, the Earp brothers and Doc Holliday marched down the street and shot it out with a gang of criminals, thereby eliminating what they saw as a problem. In 1910, police would probably have waited until they had sufficient numbers, surrounded the corral, took the weapons from the gang and booked them. The municipalities and counties which hired peace officers wanted a minimum of violence, but for the men who rode the West, often alone, the badge and the violence that came with it set them apart, and for many a lawman it was too heavy a symbol to carry into the twentieth century.

The Shootist

After almost 50 years in the movie business, John Wayne made his last film, *The Shootist* (1976). Stark and original, it was among his best works, a thoughtful and at times provocative study of a dying gunman who has outlived his time. Wayne plays J.B. Books, a noted "shootist," or gunfighter, one of the last left. It is 1901, and Books rides into Carson City, Nevada, to see a doctor there, one of the few people he has ever trusted. Decades before, Books had survived a famous gunfight in which he bested a number of gunmen all by himself. The doctor in Carson City stitched him back together and Books never forgot. He had been a lawman, but the law changed, so he survives by hiring out as a gunman to rectify "problems."

Physically, Books appears strong, but inside he is being eaten up by cancer. The doctor, played by Jimmy Stewart, gives him a few painful weeks at most to live, but suggests that Books doesn't let the cancer kill him, a veiled reference to suicide by the doctor. For Books, a different path will eventually become obvious. As he rides through Carson City, Books cannot believe the changes: horse-drawn coaches for mass transit; sturdy, permanent buildings; a daily newspaper; even milk deliveries door to door! He takes up residence in a widow's boarding house, but word soon leaks out that the famous gunman is in town, and back-shooters trying to make a reputation attempt to kill him while he sleeps. Books dispatches the men, but the widow wants him out of her establishment. She and Books come to an understanding, and the gunfighter tries to mentor her son, who is standing on the line between good and bad.

Books eventually arranges a gunfight between himself and three of the town's more dubious characters. Books prevails, but is then shot in the back by a bartender hiding in another room. The widow's son rushes into the saloon and finds Books trying to pull his revolver before the bartender can reload and fire his shotgun; the boy takes Book's Colt and kills the bartender. Books dies the way he lived — bravely, and by the gun. While his death is the end of the lawman, it is the beginning of a legend, and a sign the West of old has faded with the sunset.

Books arrives in town the very day that Queen Victoria dies. An era of English history is passing, just as American history is entering a new phase. Books, like the Queen — whom he

Former lawman J.B. Books (John Wayne) in **The Shootist.**

admired — is obsolete. The police chief is a civil servant; when talking to Books about leaving town, he tells him that he (the chief) was worried the city fathers would not give his wife his pension if Books killed him. Running water and electricity will be available throughout the whole town the following year. In short, the chief tells Books, he's not wanted there, that he serves no useful purpose and should hurry up and die. After Books is ambushed, the chief calculates the shootist's value in dollars (he has to post a policeman there each day and night to prevent further bloodshed).

The film's characters might as well have no names, so close it is to a morality play. Wayne is "the shootist." There is also "the widow," "the doctor," "the sheriff," "the gambler," "the thug." A society might get along fine with all of those things, but not with a shootist. The cancer in him is a metaphor for the killing Books has done. It has grown so deep inside that the doctor cannot cut it out. When Books challenges the three men to the gunfight, not only is it a means for him to die in the only way he knows how, it also becomes an issue of supremacy, with Wayne the Western film star besting the Western television stars Hugh O'Brian (Wyatt Earp) and Richard Boone (Paladin). After the widow's son kills the bartender, he looks at the gun in his hand, then throws it away. Books nods, and then dies. The boy has chosen the "right" course, both in the sense that he will not become a killer but also that he will be a part of the modern world, a world no longer suited for the likes of J.B. Books.

Tom Horn (1979)

After almost five years away from moviemaking, Steve McQueen returned to film, *Tom Horn* being his first Western in 13 years.* Tom Horn was a true-to-life Western figure who scouted for the United States Army and eventually wound up in the Wyoming Territory the last few years of his life. This is true without question; the rest of his life has been debated fiercely. Some say he helped bring in the rebel Apache leader Geronimo while others contend that he only took credit for it. Some respected Horn, some hated him. It would be fair to conclude that most feared him, and his reputation as a tracker and rifleman was unmatched. Other facts emerge undisputed: He served as a marshal and deputy sheriff, and worked a number of years for Pinkertons as a stock detective. Horn claims to have killed 17 men during his time with the detective agency. He spent the last years of his life working as a cattle detective in Wyoming, running off homesteaders squatting on ranch land and scaring off rustlers. Horn was arrested for allegedly shooting a child, but the evidence was sketchy. He was found guilty and hung. To this day, the question of the tracker's guilt is a sore subject. In 1993, Horn received a "retrial" even though he was already dead. This time he was found not guilty, but he stayed dead.

Somewhere along the line, Horn changed from a figure of the law to an assassin. He worked for the Cattlemen's Association, and he received pay for every squatter he forced off and every rustler he killed. His M.O. was to follow the target, get the man's times down, then shoot him from long distance, never being seen. He is suspected of a number of these killings, but he took his secrets to the grave with him. His "mark" was a rock, which he would leave under the victim's head† (D.L Staley, p.6). People would know Horn was there — they just couldn't prove it. After the child was shot, a marshal tricked Horn into making a drunken confession. Based upon that — and Horn's own inability to control his boasting, particularly on the witness stand — he was convicted and hung almost two years later. Whether Horn had shot the boy or someone framed him is still a matter of conjecture. What's fairly sure is that he assassinated a number of other men, criminals mostly, and was not ashamed of his actions.

The film version has McQueen playing the tracker as a low-key, thoughtful man who recognized that he would soon be out of his element. It is fraught with historical inaccuracies and downright lies but, like the child who messes up his algebra problem yet still manages to get the right answer, the film captures the changing of the West as Horn's major problem. In the opening scene, Horn drifts into the Wyoming Territory.§ It is 1901 and he is old, weatherbeaten, and drifting to wherever some of the Old West still remains. He crashes a small get-together for "Gentleman" Jim Corbett, a heavyweight champion who is passing through the area.** His sycophants call the fighter a great man, but Horn tells him he'd have to stand on his mama's shoulders to be high enough to kiss the ass of someone as great as Geronimo. The boxer chases Horn and beats him, but this points up the changes in the West. People don't wear guns in the city. Most don't want to see them. The men are dressed fan-

---

*In 1977, McQueen did a little-seen adaptation of an Ibsen play called *An Enemy of the People*. It was not released until later and is still rarely seen.
†In Horn's drunken confession, he says this is how he identified his work so as to collect his money from the ranchers.
§Horn had actually been drifting in and out of the Wyoming Territory for years. This was the last time he would be back.
**In reality, Horn got into a saloon brawl with Young Corbett, a featherweight who broke his jaw. The fight took place in Colorado.

cily. Horn looks like he's just come off the range. They talk about things he could not care less about; he talks about things which *they* could not care less about. Horn has to fight with a man who 20 years before he could have gunned down after fair warning — and been justified.

Communication lapses like these fill the entire story. Horn prefers the solitude of the mountains and open country. He stays away from town unless he wants a drink. He romances a teacher but the relationship is ill-fated. Horn's talents have no demand, especially with tensions rising and the ranchers in hot water. She is a woman bringing education and learning to a place where Horn used to feel at home. Sometimes they have difficulty getting through to one another. Even Tom's drunken confession would have been a joke had it not cost him his life. Telling the marshal that killing the kid would have been *the best shot [I] ever made and the dirtiest trick [I] ever played*, became *it was the best shot I ever made and the dirtiest trick*. His testimony in court was just as confusing.

As cattle detective, Horn is expected to stop the problem, but stopping the problem means violence and Horn knows it. The ranchers give him a free hand and soon the body count rises. But these are men who don't want to "know" about what Horn is doing, who don't want to be connected to the blood. These are not the men who fought Indians and outlaws to establish their spreads. These are men who smoke and drink in elaborate parlors, who use money to buy influence and power; and when something comes up which they cannot handle satisfactorily, they pay an anachronism like Horn to do what he does best, then desert him when things get hot.

The film is clearly pro–Horn. His gunfights are in the open, man-to-man shootouts— whereas the real stock detective had become an invisible killer whom many of the locals

Horn (Steve McQueen) at the end of the trail in ***Tom Horn***.

Gil Westrum (Randolph Scott) and Steve Judd (Joel McCrea) head into the mountains for one last job in *Ride the High Country*.

began to despise. Eventually the ranchers get together with the marshal, hoping to rid themselves of Horn — he is bringing too much negative attention. So, Hollywood history has Horn framed, and McQueen's version of the tracker is a man looking for a West that is disappearing so fast that even the mountains he professes to love will soon be filled with people and industry. However, unlike the fictional J.B. Books, who outlived his time but hadn't realized it, Horn seems to know his days are numbered, even before he was arrested and convicted. Chip Carlson, who has written a number of books on Horn and is recognized as an expert on the subject, notes that Horn was a transitional figure, not capable of moving forward from the past century, perhaps because he chose not to. Ironically, his path follows the Apaches, whose lifestyle he was so instrumental in ending.

Tom Horn remains a cult-like figure even now, his death being what many historians key in on. However, his execution can certainly be viewed as the transition from the Old West to modern times. Questions of Horn's guilt or innocent in the child killing remain unanswered, but even had he been acquitted, where would he go and what would he do? The Indians he tracked were penned up on reservations. The police were using telegraphs and mug shots to find criminals. Within a few years, the rustling and squatting problem would be controlled. The blood spilled by Horn's Winchester was so great that no one wanted to deal with him, let alone hire him. What does one do when his legend precedes him, but his infamy surrounds him? For the real Tom Horn, as well as his celluloid double, the end of a rope seemed just as good a way out as any other.

Ride the High Country

Sam Peckinpah was a writer-director whose talent was only surpassed by his own self-destructiveness, and his ability to anger every studio head with whom he had to work. In 1962, Peckinpah signed on to direct *Ride the High Country*, a low-budget MGM Western starring Randolph Scott and Joel McCrea. The story was as simple as it was elegiac, and highlighted the themes of obsession, trust and standing up despite the futility, which Peckinpah later became famous for. Many believe it was the director's greatest work. Some hold it as the finest Western ever made. Whatever the case, it was a beautiful film about men who find themselves obsolete, and how they struggle to retain their self-respect and dignity in an indifferent and changing world.

Steve Judd is an ex-lawman who has come to town looking for a job transporting gold to a local bank from a miner's settlement in the mountains. The offer from the bank indicates the amount of gold is unusually high, and Judd looks forward to the challenge. As he rides down the street, a gathering of people on both sides cheer. Judd thinks the greeting is for him—for taking on the dangerous assignment. He is then rudely rushed off the street by a uniformed police officer to clear the way for a horse race. Judd goes to the bank and gets his assignment, but finds he will have to hire another man to help him. That man is Gil Westrum, an ex-lawman who was partnered with Judd years before. Westrum's young partner Heck is also hired and the trio set off for the mining camp.

The men pick up a stowaway, the young daughter of a farmer whose barn they had slept in. The girl insists on going with the men to the camp, where she will marry one of Hammond, a miner she hardly knows, mostly to get away from her harsh father. During the entire trip, Gil and Heck secretly plot to steal the gold. Westrum hints to Steve that the money is owed to them for all the danger they faced in times past, but Judd would rather do the job right, honestly. When Gil tries to take the gold, Judd stops him, and when the miner and his brothers want the girl traveling with the three men, the two old lawmen must rise to the occasion.

Peckinpah only agreed to do the film if he could re-write the script (Cinebooks, n.p.). From the very first scene, the parameters of the old and new, of tradition and modernity, are set. A former marshal, Judd is run off the street by a policeman wearing a newfangled uniform who tells him he's in the way. Later, he is almost hit by an automobile. The bankers tell him they thought he'd be younger, and advise that the day of steady business is at hand. When reading the contract, Steve goes into the bathroom, where there is running water and a flush toilet. He puts on spectacles, which he doesn't want the bankers to see.

Gil, Steve's former partner, isn't doing much better. He works in a carnival shooting gallery, dressed up in an outrageous costume and proclaiming to be the Oregon Kid. The guns that Westrum's customers use are rigged, and the earlier race on the street, pitting Heck on a camel against another man on a horse, was a set-up as well—camels can easily beat horses at short distances. Both Westrum and Judd have fallen upon hard times, yet Steve has maintained some dignity and professionalism. Gil is more practical, and will do what it takes to survive. Steve points out to Gil the deceptions of the carnival, and the hoax of "The Oregon Kid." Gil shirks it off as necessary historical embellishment.

In some ways, the men are doubles. Their clothes are old, frayed a bit at the cuffs. The men have made mistakes in their lives, and continue to do so out on the trail, mostly because of age, like forgetting to load the rifles. They have sunk to places where they never thought they'd be — Judd remembers how he was a bouncer, a stickman, anything to make some money to stay alive. One glimpse at "The Oregon Kid" tells where Westrum landed. Both want to keep their dignity, their pride, and gain the respect of others like they had years before. Judd sees the path as doing honest work, gaining back their reputations. Gil thinks heisting the money and living high on the hog is a fitting revenge against a society which turned on them after they'd given the best years of their lives making it safe. Heck is in the middle. Westrum is his mentor, but he begins to appreciate the quiet poise of Judd, who remains unshakable, almost obsessed in his commitment to getting the job done right and above board.

Their conduct in the mining camp demonstrates the two men's ways of thinking. Steve and Gil want to be rid of the girl, so they send Heck to drop her off. Heck finds her husband-to-be and his brothers a white trash nightmare. The wedding is held in a bordello. When the other Hammond brothers try to force themselves on the girl, Steve immediately breaks in and rescues her. The bridegroom, his brothers and Steve agree to let a miners' court settle the matter of whether the girl was legally married. Gil gets to the heart of the matter — he sticks the barrel of his revolver up to the justice of the peace's head and tells him what to say when the court convenes. Though Judd knows what will happen to the girl if the court rules against him, he cannot go against the law he once served. Westrum is more pragmatic: Saving the girl is a little more important than following some miners' rules — especially if it will help him get the gold.

Steve Judd and Gil Westrum are clearly remnants of the past, while the bankers they serve are the future; they as much as tell Steve so. Simply stated, the two lawmen have clearly outlived their time. But the likes of the Hammond brothers continue with different names in different times in different places, and if the lawmen are on one side of a coin, the Hammonds are the other. As in so many of Peckinpah's films, two groups stand opposed to one another, and what separates one from the other is a code the men live by . In *The Wild Bunch* (1969), the Bunch are stone killers, but they side with each other, protect one another, to the very end. The bounty men chasing them have no code — they are a sickness with no redeeming qualities whatsoever. Though the Bunch has sometimes not lived up to their ideals, at the end they take on the whole Mexican Army for one of their own, dying to gain back their honor.

Similarly so in *Ride the High Country*, though the differences are more conventionally cast. The Hammonds are killers and back-shooters. They attempt to gang-rape their brother's wife on the wedding night. When confronting Steve and Heck (who Judd has untied for the fight), they retreat once they see the men are better shots than they are. Instead they ride ahead quickly, murder the girl's father, and set up an ambush, which Steve rides into. Judd and Westrum, though having their differences, are the same at the core. They will not back-shoot — Steve gives Gil a chance for a fair draw against him when he catches him trying to steal the gold. They protect the girl, though it would be easier to give her up. And most importantly, at the end, when Heck is wounded and Steve completely outgunned, Gil rides up to back his old friend. They goad the Hammonds into coming out for a fair-and-square showdown. In the ensuing gunfight, the Hammonds are killed and Judd is mortally wounded.

Earlier in the story, when Gil was trying to turn Steve's mind toward stealing the gold,

Judd tells him that all he wants is to enter his house justified. (This was a favorite saying of Peckinpah's father, which the director included in the film.) As Judd lies dying, Gil tells him that he will deliver the gold, just like Steve would have. The old friends say goodbye, and Steve takes one more look at the mountains and sunshine, then leans out of frame to die, worthy of the respect he worked so hard to get back. The ending here was a little unconventional: Gil's character was supposed to die, redeeming himself, but Peckinpah thought Steve should; *that* way, he could enter his house justified. Both Randolph Scott and Joel McCrea thought it was a fantastic change.

In examining the element of men out of their time, *Ride the High Country* was unparalleled. Not only were the characters of Steve Judd and Gil Westrum anachronisms of the nineteenth century still breathing in the twentieth, but so, too, in a different way, were Randolph Scott and Joel McCrea. Both men had long and distinguished movie careers, but for the last ten years had been doing almost exclusively Westerns. Neither man's films were large moneymakers, though Scott's Ranown productions were quite intense and critically praised. The actors' fans were older, and the '60s would begin changing things before their very eyes. *Ride the High Country* would be the last straight Western ever directed by Sam Peckinpah, who was at the start of a brilliant career. Scott immediately retired; McCrea semi-retired. Both knew it was the best work they had ever done.

In promising to deliver the gold shipment to the bank, Gil Westrum will complete the job he signed on for. But for Heck and the girl, who are clearly in love, the lawmen's ways are not their ways. They have a farm they can work. Perhaps someday kids to send to school, kids who will take their place in the new century. Steve Judd has died the way he always lived — bravely, with a sense of dignity, and honor. But what about Gil Westrum? Does he just ride off into the sunset like so many old cowboys and lawmen did? Maybe die in a cheap flophouse like Doc Holliday, where no one knows his name or what he did to make the towns and cities safe places to live? McCrea was originally designated to play Gil, while Scott was supposed to be Steve. Both wanted to change their characters, and though Judd is the one most people remember, Westrum is the one still out there, the celluloid lawman, perhaps riding with Ethan Edwards, looking for a time and place of his own.

Sources

Carlson, Chip. *Tom Horn: Misunderstood Misfit*. thehistorynet.com. www.thehistorystorynet.com/we/b1gunfightermostmisunderstood/.
Ride the High Country. Cinebooks. CD-Rom. 1994.
Sam Peckinpah's West. Starz Encore Entertainment. The Western Channel. 5–26–05.
Staley, D.L. *Horn vs. Hollywood*. leverguns.com. www.leverguns.com/articles/staley/horn_vs_hollywood.html.

FILMOGRAPHY

Above the Law. Directed by Andrew Davis. Screenplay by Steven Pressfield, Ronald Schusett and Steven Seagal. A hard-boiled detective takes on corrupt police and federal agents attempting to kill a senator. Starring Steven Seagal. Warners, 1988. 99 min.

Arizona Raiders. Directed by William Witney. Screenplay by Alex Gottlieb, Mary Willingham, and Willard Willingham. A member of Quantrill's Raiders is sworn in as an Arizona Ranger to rid the territory of the rest of the gang. Starring Audie Murphy. Columbia, 1965. 88 min.

Bad Lieutenant. Directed by Abel Ferrara. Screenplay by Zoe Lund and Abel Ferrara. A corrupt police detective investigates the rape of a nun, only to find out some things about himself during the process. Starring Harvey Keitel. Bad Lts. Film, 1992. 98 min.

The Big Gundown. Directed by Sergio Sollima. Screenplay by Sergio Sollima. A bounty hunter crosses the border after a child molester. Columbia, 1968. 107 min.

Big Jim McLain. Directed by Edward Ludwig. Screenplay by James Edward Grant, Richard English and Eric Taylor. Investigators for HUAC battle with Communists in Hawaii. Starring John Wayne. Warners, 1952. 90 min.

The Big Sleep. Directed by Howard Hawks. Screenplay by William Faulkner, Jules Furthman and Leigh Brackett. Philip Marlowe investigates a general's promiscuous daughter. Warners, 1946. 114 min.

Blade Runner. Directed by Ridley Scott. Screenplay by Hampton Fancher and David Peoples, based upon the Philip K. Dick story *Do Androids Dream of Electric Sheep?* A bounty hunter tracks down androids hiding in a Los Angeles of the future. Starring Harrison Ford. Warners, 1982. 118 min.

The Blue Dahlia. Directed by George Marshall. Screenplay by Raymond Chandler. An ex-vet looks for his wife's killer. Starring Alan Ladd. Paramount, 1946. 99 min.

The Bounty Hunter. Directed by Robert Ginty. Screenplay by Robert Ginty and Thomas Baldwin. A bounty hunter journeys to a small town to find his best friend's killers. Starring Robert Ginty. Action International Pictures, 1989. 90 min.

Bounty Hunters. Directed by George Erschbamer. Screenplay by Jeremy Barmash and Michael Ellis. Two competing bounty hunters team up to take on the Mafia. Starring Michael Dudikoff. Dimension Video, 1997. 98 min.

Bounty Hunters 2: Hardball. Directed by George Erschbamer. Screenplay by Jeremy Barmash and Michael Ellis. Two competing bounty hunters team up again to take on the Mafia. Starring Michael Dudikoff. Dimension Video, 1997. 97 min.

Bounty Tracker. Directed by Kurt Anderson. Screenplay by Caroline Olson. An East Coast bounty hunter comes to L.A. to find his brother's killers. Starring Lorenzo Lamas. Ascot Video, 1993. 86 min.

Chinatown. Directed by Roman Polanski. Screenplay by Robert Towne. A detective finds himself over his head when he takes on an adultery case and it turns into murder. Starring Jack Nicholson. Paramount, 1974. 131 min.

Chisum. Directed by Andrew V. McLaglen. Screenplay by Andrew J. Fenady. A powerful rancher goes up against a corrupt conglomerate trying to take over the New Mexican Territory. Starring John Wayne. Warners, 1970. 111 min.

Cobra. Directed by George P. Cosmatos. Screenplay by Sylvester Stallone. A rogue detective takes on a Satanist gang trying to kill a prosecution witness against them. Starring Sylvester Stallone. Cannon, 1986. 87 min.

Colors. Directed by Dennis Hopper. Screenplay by Michael Schiffer. Two gang officers ride the streets of Los Angeles trying to keep an uneasy peace between the gangs. Starring Robert Duvall. Orion, 1988. 120 min.

Comanche Station. Directed by Budd Boetticher. Screenplay by Burt Kennedy. A bounty hunter rescues a woman from Indians, then has to get her back safely to her home. Starring Randolph Scott. Columbia, 1960. 74 min.

The Comancheros. Directed by Michael Curtiz. Screenplay by James Edward Grant and Clair Huffaker. Texas Rangers break up a gang of Comancheros attacking settlers. Starring John Wayne. 20th Century–Fox, 1961. 107 min.

Crash. Directed by Paul Haggis. Screenplay by Paul Haggis. Police and the public deal with racism on an everyday basis. Starring Matt Dillon. Bull's Eye Entertainment, 2005. 113 min.

Dark Blue. Directed by Ron Shelton. Screenplay by James Ellroy and David Ayer. A dirty LAPD detective goes up against his even corrupter boss, shaking the department to its foundations. Starring Kurt Russell. United Artists, 2002. 118 min.

Death Wish. Directed by Michael Winner. Screenplay by Wendell Mayes. A man turns into a vigilante after his wife is murdered and his daughter raped. Starring Charles Bronson. Paramount, 1974. 93 min.

Death Wish 3. Directed by Michael Winner. Screenplay by Michael Edmonds. A vigilante returns to New York City to help the police clean up a neighborhood gang. Starring Charles Bronson. Cannon, 1985. 90 min.

Demolition Man. Directed by Marco Brambilla. Screenplay by Daniel Waters, Robert Reneau, Peter M. Lenkov and Jonathan Lemkin. A police officer is taken out of cryogenic freeze to take on a marauding criminal. Starring Sylvester Stallone. Warners, 1993. 115 min.

Destry Rides Again. Directed by George Marshal. Screenplay by Felix Jackson, Henry Myers and Gertrude Purcell. A sheriff tries to clean up a dangerous Old West town without using firearms. Starring James Stewart. Universal, 1939. 94 min.

Devil in a Blue Dress. Directed by Carl Franklin. Screenplay by Carl Franklin. A black detective investigates a mysterious woman. Starring Denzel Washington. TriStar, 1995. 102 min.

Dirty Harry. Directed by Don Siegel. Screenplay by Harry Julian Fink, Rita M. Fink and Dean Reisner. "Dirty" Harry Callahan lays down the law his way in San Francisco. Starring Clint Eastwood. Warners, 1971. 102 min.

Doc. Directed by Frank Perry. Screenplay by Pete Hamill. Doc Holliday journeys to Tombstone to see his friend Wyatt Earp. Starring Stacy Keach. United Artists, 1971. 96 min.

Double Indemnity. Directed by Billy Wilder. Screenplay by Billy Wilder and Raymond Chandler. A woman and her lover plot to murder the woman's husband to collect from his insurance policy. Starring Barbara Stanwyck. Paramount, 1944. 106 min.

Earthquake. Directed by Mark Robson. Screenplay by George Fox and Mario Puzo. A massive earthquake destroys Los Angeles. Starring Charlton Heston. Universal, 1974. 129 min.

Easy Street. Directed by Charlie Chaplin. Screenplay by Charlie Chaplin. A tramp is appointed to be a policemen in a troubled neighborhood. Starring Charlie Chaplin. Mutual Film Corporation, 1917. 19 min.

Eight Legged Freaks. Directed by Ellory Elkayen. Screenplay by Jesse Alexander. Giant spiders try to take over a town, and only the sheriff and her deputy can stop them. Starring Kari Wuhrer. Village Roadshow Productions, 2002. 99 min.

El Diablo. Directed by Peter Markle. Screenplay by Tommy Lee Wallace and John Carpenter. Bounty hunters go after a kidnapped schoolgirl. Starring Anthony Edwards. HBO, 1990. 115 min.

El Dorado. Directed by Howard Hawks. Screenplay by Leigh Brackett. A gunfighter backs his best friend, a drunken sheriff, in a fight with a powerful rancher trying to take over the town. Starring John Wayne. Paramount, 1967. 126 min.

Electra Glide in Blue. Directed by James William Guercio. Screenplay by Robert Boris and Michael Butler. A highway cop is promoted to detective and investigates a murder. Starring Robert Blake. United Artist, 1973. 113 min.

The Empire Strikes Back. Directed by Irvin Kershner. Screenplay by Leigh Brackett and Lawrence Kasdan. A smuggler runs from Imperial ships chasing him, as well as a bounty hunter. Starring Harrison Ford. 20th Century–Fox, 1980. 124 min.

End of Days. Directed by Peter Hyams. Screenplay by Andrew W. Marlowe. An ex-cop tries to protect a woman from Satan as the Devil tries to sire an Anti-Christ. Starring Arnold Schwarzenegger. Universal, 1999. 121 min.

Exit Wounds. Directed by Andrzej Bartkowiak. Screenplay by Ed Horowitz. A tough cop patrols the streets and uncovers a secret drug operation. Starring Steven Seagal. Warners, 2000. 101 min.

Extreme Prejudice. Directed by Walter Hill. Screenplay by Deric Washburn. A Texas Ranger bands together with a secret military squad to bust a drug operation in Mexico. Starring Nick Nolte. TriStar, 1987. 104 min.

Falling Down. Directed by Joel Schumacher. Screenplay by Ebbe Rowe Smith. A man wanders through the streets of a city, at times being victimized and other times victimizing those he comes across. Starring Michael Douglas. Warners, 1993. 115 min.

Farewell My Lovely. Directed by Dick Richards. Screenplay by David Zelag Goodman, based on the story of the same name by Raymond Chandler. A detective tries to track down an elusive woman for a very strange — and large — client. Starring Robert Mitchum. AVCO Embassy, 1975. 97 min.

A Fistful of Dollars. Directed by Sergio Leone. Screenplay by Sergio Leone, based on the film *Yojimbo*. A bounty hunter plays two feuding families against one another in a small town. Starring Clint Eastwood. Constantine Film Produktion GmbH., 1964. 96 min.

For a Few Dollars More. Directed by Sergio Leone. Screenplay by Luciano Vincenzoni. Two bounty hunters cooperate to bring down a notoriously savage outlaw. Starring Clint Eastwood. Constantin Film Produktion GmbH., 1965. 130 min.

The Glove. Directed by Ross Hagen. Screenplay by Julian Roffman and Hubert Smith. A bounty hunter goes after a huge convict killing people with a monstrous glove. Starring John Saxon. Pro International Pictures, 1979. 91 min.

The Good, the Bad, and the Ugly. Directed by Sergio Leone. Screenplay by Luciano Vincenzoni and Sergio Leone. Three bounty vicious bounty hunters fight over a treasure, killing anyone in the way to get it. Starring Clint Eastwood. Constantine Film Produktion GmbH., 1966. 161 min.

Gunfight at the O.K. Corral. Directed by John Sturges. Screenplay by Leon Uris. The Earps and Doc Holliday clean up Tombstone, shooting it out with the Clantons. Starring Burt Lancaster. Paramount, 1957. 122 min.

Gunsmoke: *One Man's Justice.* Directed by Jeremy Jameson. Screenplay by Harry and Renee Longstreet. Matt helps a young man track the bandits who killed his mother. Starring James Arness. CBS, 1994. 91 min.

Gunsmoke: Return to Dodge. Directed by Vincent McEveety. Screenplay by Jim Byrnes. Matt has to face a psychotic gunfighter just released from prison. Starring James Arness. CBS, 1987. 100 min.

Gunsmoke: The Last Apache. Directed by Charles Correll. Screenplay by Earl W. Wallace. Matt searches for a daughter he never knew he had, kidnapped by the Apaches. Starring James Arness. CBS, 1990. 100 min.

Gunsmoke: The Long Ride. Directed by Jerry Jameson. Screenplay by Bill Stratton. Matt is framed for murder and goes after the real killers. Starring James Arness. CBS, 1993. 94 min.

Gunsmoke: To the Last Man. Directed by Jerry Jameson. Screenplay by Earl W. Wallace. Matt finds himself caught up in the middle of a very bloody range war. Starring James Arness. CBS, 1992. 100 min.

Hang 'Em High. Directed by Ted Post. Screenplay by Leonard Freeman and Mel Goldberg. A rancher is wrongly lynched, but survives, then tracks down the men who did it. Starring Clint Eastwood. United Artists, 1969. 114 min.

Hard to Kill. Directed by Buce Malmuth. Screenplay by Steve McKay. A cop investigating corruption is attacked and lays in a coma. Recovering, he goes after the men who wronged him. Starring Steven Seagal. Warners, 1990. 95 min.

Heat. Directed by Michael Mann. Screenplay by Michael Mann. An obsessed police detective goes after a heist gang. Starring Al Pacino. Warner, 1995. 171 min.

High Noon. Directed by Fred Zinneman. Screenplay by Carl Foreman. A sheriff protects a cowardly town from outlaws, though the town doesn't want him there. Starring Gary Cooper. United Artist, 1952. 84 min.

The Hired Gun. Directed by Ray Nazarro. Screenplay by David Lang, Bucky Angell. A gunmen is hired to bring back a fugitive from the New Mexican Territory. MGM, 1957. 63 min.

Hour of the Gun. Directed by John Sturges. Screenplay by Edward Anhalt. The Earps and

Doc Holliday stand trial for the shootout at the OK Corral, then kill the rest of the Clanton gang after they are released. United Artist, 1967. 100 min.

The Hunter. Directed by Buzz Kulik. Screenplay by Ted Leighton, Peter Hyams. A bounty hunter makes his living picking up bail jumpers and fugitives. Starring Steve McQueen. Paramount, 1980. 97 min.

I, Robot. Directed by Alex Proyas. Screenplay by Jeff Vintar, Akiva Goldsman. A detective tries to prove a robot committed murder, which is said to be a physical impossibility. Starring Will Smith. 20th Century–Fox, 2004. 115 min.

In the Heat of the Night. Directed by Norman Jewison. Screenplay by Stirling Silliphant. A small town white sheriff and a big city black detective have to work together to solve a high profile murder. Starring Sidney Poitier. United Artists, 1967. 109 min.

An Innocent Man. Directed by Peter Yates. Screenplay by Larry Brothers. A man is railroaded into prison and has to fight to stay alive. Released, he goes after the crooked cops who put him there. Starring Tom Selleck. Touchstone, 1989. 113 min.

Internal Affairs. Directed by Mike Figgis. Screenplay by Henry Bean. A dirty cop is investigated by IA, only he always stays a step ahead of them — until they break the rules, too. Starring Richard Gere. Paramount, 1990. 117 min.

Invasion USA. Directed by Joseph Zito. Screenplay by James Bruner and Chuck Norris. Terrorists make a beach landing in Florida and begin attacking all over the state. Starring Chuck Norris. Cannon, 1985. 107 min.

Jesse James. Directed by Henry King. Screenplay by Nunnally Johnson. The James boys become outlaws after the railroad runs them off their land. Starring Tyrone Power. 20th Century–Fox, 1939. 105 min.

Joe Kidd. Directed by John Sturges. Screenplay by Elmore Leonard. A bounty hunter tracks, then assists, a Mexican revolutionary trying to obtain justice. Starring Clint Eastwood. Universal, 1972. 88 min.

Judge Dredd. Directed by Danny Cannon. Screenplay by William Wisher and Steven E. De Souza. A future lawman is framed and must break back into society to clear his name. Starring Sylvester Stallone. Cinergi Pictures Entertainment, 1995. 91 min.

Kindergarten Cop. Directed by Ivan Reitman. Screenplay by Murray Salem, Hershel Weingrod, Timothy Harris. A hard edge police detective teaches kindergarten as a cover while looking for the wife of a fugitive. Starring Arnold Schwarzenegger. Universal, 1990. 111 min.

Kinjite: Forbidden Subjects. Directed by J. Lee Thompson. Screenplay by Harold Nebenzal. A detective investigates the kidnapping of a Japanese worker's daughter. Starring Charles Bronson. Cannon, 1989. 97 min.

Lady in the Lake. Directed by Robert Montgomery. Screenplay by Steve Fisher, Raymond Chandler. Marlowe looking for a young girl's killer. Starring Robert Montgomery. MGM, 1946. 103 min.

Loaded Weapon I. Directed by Gene Quintano. Screenplay by Don Holland, Gene Quintano. Two detectives parody police buddy films as they unravel a mystery. Starring Samuel Jackson. New Line Cinema, 1993. 83 min.

Logan's Run. Directed by Michael Anderson. Screenplay by David Zelag Goodman. Police bounty hunters go after people trying to escape a domed city where life is terminated at 30. Starring Michael York. MGM, 1976. 120 min.

Lone Wolf McQuade. Directed by Steve Carver. Screenplay by B.J. Nelson. A Texas Ranger goes after a gun smuggler flying in weapons from Mexico. Starring Chuck Norris. Orion, 1983. 107 min.

Lonesome Dove. Directed by Simon Wincer. Screenplay by William D. Wittliff. Television mini-series about two Texas Rangers crossing thousands of miles on a cattle drive no one has ever attempted. Starring Robert Duvall. CBS, 1988. 384 min.

The Long Goodbye. Directed by Robert Altman. Screenplay by Leigh Brackett. Philip Marlowe investigates the disappearance of his friends. Starring Elliot Gould. United Artists, 1973. 112 min.

The Maltese Falcon. Directed by John Huston. Screenplay by John Huston. Sam Spade goes after his partner's murderer. Starring Humphrey Bogart. Warners, 1941. 100 min.

Marabunta. Directed by Jim Charleston and George Manasse. Screenplay by Linda Palmer and Wink Roberts. A legion of soldier ants invades a rural Alaskan village. Starring Eric Lutes. Irwin Meyer Productions, 1998.

Midnight Run. Directed by Martin Brest. Screenplay by George Gallo. A bounty hunter has to work overtime to bring his captive back to Los Angeles. Starring Robert DeNiro. Universal, 1988. 122 min.

Mildred Pierce. Directed by Michael Curtiz. Screenplay by Ranald MacDougall. A divorcee opens a successful restaurant chain, only to be ruined by those around her. Starring Joan Crawford. Warners, 1945. 109 min.

Moving Target. Directed by Damian Lee. Screenplay by Kevin McCarthy and Mark Sevi. A bounty hunter has to survive the Russian mob. Starring Michael Dudikoff. Royal Oaks, 1997. 106 min.

My Darling Clementine. Directed by John Ford. Screenplay by Samuel G. Engel and Winston Miller. Wyatt Earp faces off against the Clantons in Tombstone. Starring Henry Fonda. 20th Century–Fox, 1946. 97 min.

Naked Gun. Directed by David Zucker. Screenplay by Jerry Zucker, Jim Abrahams, David Zucker and Pat Proft, A parody of police films. Starring Leslie Nielsen. Paramount, 1988. 85 min.

Naked Gun 33⅓. Directed by Peter Segal. Screenplay by Pat Proft, David Zucker and Robert LoCash. The third of the trilogy of police parody films. Starring Leslie Nielsen. Paramount, 1994. 82 min.

Naked Gun 2½. Directed by David Zucker. Screenplay by David Zucker and Pat Proft. A parody of police films with the same cast as its predecessor. Starring Leslie Nielsen. Paramount, 1991. 85 min.

Nemesis. Directed by Albert Pyun. Screenplay by Rebecca Charles. Tough cop of the future battles cyborgs bent on world domination. Starring Olivier Gruner. Imperial Entertainment, 1993. 94 min.

Once Upon a Time in the West. Directed by Sergio Leone. Screenplay by Sergio Leone and Sergio Donati. A railroad enforcer tries to kill a widow to stop her from building on land the company wants. Another man is out to stop the enforcer. Starring Charles Bronson. Paramount, 1968. 165 min.

Out of the Past. Directed by Jacques Tourneur. Screenplay by Daniel Mainwaring. A private eye is entangled in a gangsters scheming, and undermined by the gangster's beautiful girl. Starring Robert Mitchum. RKO, 1947. 97 min.

Outland. Directed by Peter Hyams. Screenplay by Peter Hyams. A federal marshal fights hit men trying to stop his investigation into illegal drug sales on the moon Io. Starring Sean Connery. Warner, 1981. 109 min.

The Outlaws Is Coming! Directed by Norman Maurer. Screenplay by Elwood Ullman. The Three Stooges help a tenderfoot clean up a lawless town. Starring The Three Stooges. Columbia, 1965. 89 min.

Paradise Canyon. Directed by Carl Pierson. Screenplay by Robert Emmett Tansey. A federal agent goes undercover to break up a counterfeiting gang. Starring John Wayne. Lone Star, 1935. 52 min.

Pink Cadillac. Directed by Buddy Van Horn. Screenplay by John Eskow. A bounty hunter goes up against some neo–Nazi types. Starring Clint Eastwood. Warners, 1989. 122 min.

Rainbow Valley. Directed by Robert N. Bradbury. Screenplay by Lindsley Parsons. A federal agent busts up a gang trying to take over an isolated valley. Starring John Wayne. Lone Star, 1935. 52 min.

Return of the Jedi. Directed by Richard Marquand. Screenplay by Lawrence Kasdan and George Lucas. A gunrunner–rebel hero escapes from bounty hunters who have him captured and frozen him. Starring Harrison Ford. 20th Century–Fox, 1983. 133 min.

Ride Lonesome. Directed by Budd Boetticher. Screenplay by Burt Kennedy. A bounty hunter uses his captive as a means to get bigger quarry. Along the way he's joined by three companions, none of whom he desires. Starring Randolph Scott. Columbia, 1959. 73 min.

Ride the High Country. Directed by Sam Peckinpah. Screenplay by N.B. Stone, Jr. Two ex-marshals reunite to transport gold from a mining camp high in the mountains. One wants to do the job — the other wants to steal the gold. Starring Joel McCrea. MGM, 1962. 94 min.

Rio Bravo. Directed by Howard Hawks. Screenplay by Jules Furthman and Leigh Brackett. A sheriff tries to hold a prisoner in his jail while the prisoner's powerful brother wants to get him out. Starring John Wayne. Warners, 1959. 141 min.

Rio Diablo. Directed by Rod Hardy. Screenplay by Frank Q. Dobbs and David S. Cass, Sr. A bounty hunter goes after a murderous gang. Starring Kenny Rogers. CBS, 1993. 92 min.

Rio Lobo. Directed by Howard Hawks. Screenplay by Leigh Brackett and Burton Wohl. A man hunting a traitor from the Civil War helps a town throw off a corrupt sheriff. Starring John Wayne. National General, 1970. 114 min.

The Running Man. Directed by Paul Michael Glaser. Screenplay by Steven E. De Souza. A framed police officer is placed in a futuristic death game for the amusement of the public. Starring Arnold Schwarzenegger. 20th Century–Fox, 1987. 100 min.

Salt of the Earth. Directed by Herman Biberman. Screenplay by Michael Wilson and Michael Biberman. A corrupt lawman tries to bully strikers picketing a mine. Starring Will Geer. International Union of Mine, Mill and Smelter Workers, 1953. 94 min.

The Searchers. Directed by John Ford. Screenplay by Frank S. Nugent. A man searches years for his niece, who was kidnapped by Indians. Starring John Wayne. Warners, 1956. 119 min.

The Shootist. Directed by Don Siegel. Screenplay by Miles Swarthout and Scott Hale. A former sheriff turned gunmen dying of cancer tries to do so in peace. Starring John Wayne. Paramount, 1976. 99 min.

Showdown at Boot Hill. Directed by Gene Fowler, Jr. Screenplay by Louis Vittes. A bounty hunter finds it hard to collect his money. Starring Charles Bronson. 20th Century–Fox, 1958. 72 min.

Silent Rage. Directed by Michael Miller. Screenplay by Joseph Frayly. Small town sheriff has to take on a scientifically engineered killer who won't stay dead. Starring Chuck Norris. Columbia, 1982. 105 min.

Soylent Green. Directed by Richard Fleisher. Screenplay by Stanley A. Greenberg. A police detective from the future finds that a food conglomerate is using people as a supplement. Starring Charlton Heston. MGM, 1973. 100 min.

Star Packer. Directed by Robert N. Bradley. Screenplay by Robert N. Bradley. A federal agent goes undercover to break up a secret land-grabbing gang. Starring John Wayne. Lone Star, 1934. 53 min.

Sunset. Directed by Blake Edwards. Screenplay by Blake Edwards. Wyatt Earp tries to solve a Hollywood murder in the waning days of his life. Starring James Garner. TriStar, 1988. 107 min.

SWAT. Directed by Clark Johnson. Screenplay by David Ayer and David McKenna. A Special Weapons and Tactic team handles big capers in the city. Starring Colin Farrell. Columbia, 2004. 117 min.

Ten to Midnight. Directed by J. Lee Thompson. Screenplay by J. Lee Thompson. A police detective turns vigilante to nail a serial killer. Starring Charles Bronson. Cannon, 1983. 100 min.

Texas Rangers. Directed by Steve Miner. Screenplay by Scott Busby and Martin Copeland. A ranger company is formed to fight outlaws rampaging through post–Civil War Texas. Starring Dylan McDermott. Dimension, 2002. 90 min.

The Texas Rangers. Directed by Phil Karlson. Screenplay by Richard Schayer. Rangers parole a gunfighter to help them rid the state of bandits. Starring George Montgomery. Columbia, 1951. 74 min.

Them! Directed by Gordon Douglas. Screenplay by Ted Sherdeman and Russell Hughes. Mutant giant ants terrorize the American Southwest. Starring James Whitmore. Warners, 1954. 94 min.

Timecop. Directed by Peter Hyams. Screenplay by Mark Verheiden. A police officer patrols the time zone keeping violators from changing history. Starring Jean Claude Van Damme. Moshe Diamont, 1994. 99 min.

Timecop 2. Directed by Steve Boyum. Screenplay by Gary Scott Thompson. Time police try to stop a criminal from changing the course of history. Starring Jason Scott Lee. TE Encore Films, 2003. 81 min.

Tom Horn. Directed by William Wiard. Screenplay by Thomas McGuane and Bud Shrake. The famous tracker and lawman hunts down rustlers at the turn of the century, only to find himself charged with murder. Starring Steve McQueen. Warners, 1980. 98 min.

Tombstone. Directed by George P. Cosmatos. Screenplay by Kevin Jarre. The Earps and Doc Holliday take on the Clantons in Tombstone. Starring Kurt Russell. Cinergi Pictures, 1993. 128 min.

Total Recall. Directed by Paul Verhoeven. Screenplay by Ronald Schusett, Dan O'Bannon and Gary Goldman. A government agent's desire for an implanted vacation memory unleashes a revolution on Mars. Starring Arnold Schwarzenegger. Carolco, 1990. 109 min.

Touch of Evil. Directed by Orson Welles. Screenplay by Orson Welles. A crooked cop frames a Mexican drug agent. Starring Orson Welles. Universal, 1958. 93 min.

The Town that Dreaded Sundown. Directed by Charles B. Pierce. Screenplay by Earl E. Smith. A famous Texas Ranger goes after a serial killer in 1946 Arkansas. Starring Ben Johnson. Charles B. Pierce Productions, 1977. 90 min.

True Confessions. Directed by Ulu Grosbard. Screenplay by John Gregory Dunne and Joan Didion. A cop pursues a woman's sadistic killer. Starring Robert Duvall. United Artists, 1981. 108 min.

Two Rode Together. Directed by John Ford. Screenplay by Frank S. Nugent. A marshal tries to rescue some captives being held by the Comanche. Starring James Stewart. Columbia, 1961. 109 min.

Unforgiven. Directed by Clint Eastwood. Screenplay by David Webb Peoples. Bounty hunters go after two men for mutilating a prostitute in nineteenth century Wyoming. Starring Clint Eastwood. Warners, 1992. 127 min.

Walking Tall. Directed by Phil Karlson. Screenplay by Mort Briskin. Sheriff Buford Pusser takes on the syndicate which terrorizes his family. Starring Joe Don Baker. Cinerama, 1973. 125 min.

Wanted: Dead or Alive. Directed by Gary Sherman. Screenplay by Michael Patrick Goodman, Gary Sherman and Brian Taggert. An ex–CIA operative turned bounty hunter is called back by his partners to help track a terrorist. Starring Rutger Hauer. New World Pictures, 1987. 104 min.

The Wild Bunch. Directed by Sam Peckinpah. Screenplay by Walon Green and Sam Peckinpah. The railroad sends its agents after an infamous gang in Mexico. Starring William Holden. Warners, 1969. 142 min.

Witness. Directed by Peter Weir. Screenplay by Earl W. Wallace, William Kelley and Pamela Wallace. A cop hides out with an Amish family until he recovers from an ambush laid by dirty colleagues. Starring Harrison Ford. Paramount, 1984. 112 min.

Wyatt Earp. Directed by Lawrence Kasdan. Screenplay by Lawrence Kasdan and Don Gordon. Wyatt Earp, from early teen to Tombstone marshal, is covered in this biopic. Starring Kevin Costner. Warners, 1994. 195 min.

Young Guns. Directed by Christopher Cain. Screenplay by John Fusco. Young cowboys are appointed special deputies during the range wars in the New Mexico Territory. Starring Charlie Sheen. 20th Century–Fox, 1988. 107 min.

Sources

Ball, Larry D. *The United States Marshals of New Mexico and Arizona Territories, 1846–1912.* Albuquerque: University of New Mexico Press, 1978.

Brandt, James. *What Defines Human?* www.brinsight.com/display.php?contents=article.009&cat=ANALYSI.

Buford Pusser. www.talentondisplay.com/pusserabout.html.

Butler, Jeremy. *Miami Vice.* Museum of Broadcast Communications. http://www.museum.tv/archives/etv/M/htmlM/miamivice/miamivice.htm.

Carlson, Chip. *Tom Horn: Misunderstood Misfit.* www.thehistorystorynet.com/we/b1gunfightermostmisunderstood/.

Carroll, Noel. *The Philosophy of Horror.* New York: Rutledge, Chapman, and Hall, 1990.

Cavagna, Carlo. *Blade Runner.* www.br-insight.com/display.php?contents=article.011&cat=ANALYSI.

Cook, David A. *A History of Narrative Film.* New York: W.W. Norton, 1990.

Cook, Pam. *Authorship and Cinema. The Cinema Book.* Ed. Pam Cook. London: BFI, 1985.

Corrigan, Timothy. *A Cinema Without Walls.* New Brunswick, NJ: Rutgers University Press, 1991.

Cross, Robin. *The Big Book of B Movies.* New York: St. Martin's, 1981.

Curtis, Brandon. *Texas Rangers.* www.toxicuniverse.com/review.php?rid=10003075.

Dirks, Tim. *High Noon.* www.filmsite.org/high.html.

DVD Times. *Crime Story.* http://www.dvdtimes.couk/content.php?contentid=12714.

Easy Street. Moviediva.com. www.moviediva.com/MD_root/reviewpages/MDChaplinShorts.html.

Ebert, Roger. *An Innocent Man.* http://rogerebert.suntimes.com/apps/pbcs.dll/article?AID=/19891006/REV.

_____. *Doc.* Rogerebert.com.

_____. *Falling Down.* Roger Ebert's Video Companion. CD-Rom. 1994.

_____. *Part Two: Walking Tall.* http://rogerebert.suntimes.com/apps/pbcs.dll/article?AID=/19750101/REV.

_____. *Wanted: Dead or Alive.* http://rogerebert.suntimes.com/apps/pbcs.dll/article?AID=/19870116/REV.

Ford, Greg. *Mostly on Rio Lobo. Movies and Methods: Volume I,* ed. Bill Nichols. Berkeley, CA: UCB Press. 1976.

Gramstad, Thomas. *Humans and Technology, What Separates Them?* www.br-insight.com/display.php?contents=article.010&cat=ANALYSI.

Grost, Michael. *The Films of Phil Karlson: The Texas Rangers.* Classic Film and Television. http://members.aol.com/MG4273/Karlson.htm.

Hanson, Hal. *Sunset.* washingtonpost.com.

Harrington, Richard. *Wanted: Dead or Alive.* www.washingtonpost.com/wp-srv/style/longterm/movies/videos/want.

Heilman, Jeremy. *The Hunter.* http://apolloguide.com/mov_fullrev.asp?CID=3434&Specific=4134.

Hinson, Hal. *Midnight Run.* www.washingtonpost.com./wp-srv/style/longterm/movies/videos/midn.

Hollywood Ten. Baseline Encyclopedia of Film. Baseline, CD-Rom. 1996.

James, Ken. *End of Days.* www.christiananswers.net/spotlight/movies/pre2000/endofdays.html.

Jameson, Frederic. *The Geopolitical Aesthetic.* Bloomington: Indiana University Press, 1992.

Joe Mannix. http://www.thrillingdetective.com/manj.html.

Johnson, Gary. *Thirty Great Westerns.* http://imagesjournal.com/issue10/infocus/ridelonesome.html.

Johnston, Claire. *Double Indemnity. Women in Film Noir,* ed. Ann Kaplan. London: BFI, 1994.

Jung, Carl, M-L von Franz, Joseph Henderson, Jolande Jacobi, and Aniela Jaffe. *Man and His Symbols.* New York: Dell, 1964.

Kael, Pauline. *Dirty Harry. 5001 Nights at the Movies.* Microsoft CD, 1996.

LaSalle, Mick. *Blame the economy, the product, the theaters — we're just not going to the movies the way we used to.* San Francisco Chronicle. July 13, 2005.

Lavender, Catherine. *Salt of the Earth.* www.library.csi.cuny.edu/dept/history/lavender/salt.html.

Law and Order. http://www.nbc.com/Law_&_Order/about/index.html.

Litwack, Leon F., Winthrop D. Jordan, et al. *The United States.* Englewood Cliffs, NJ: Prentice Hall, 1985.

Logan's Run. www.geocities.com/oscarmovs/logansrun.html.

Lott, M. Ray. *The American Martial Arts Film.* Jefferson, NC: McFarland, 2004.

Maloney, Frank. *Blade Runner.* http://imdb.com/REVIEWS/15/1524.

Maltese Falcon, The. Cinebooks. CD-Rom. 1994.

Maltin, Leonard. *Movie and Video Guide.* New York: Penguin, 1995.

McLaglen, Andrew. *Chisum Interview.* The Western Channel. May 16, 2005.

Merritt, Greg. *Celluloid Mavericks.* New York: Thundermouth Press. 2000.

Musser, Charles. *The Emergence of Cinema: The American Screen to 1907.* Los Angeles: University of California Press, 1990.

My Darling Clementine. Cinebooks. CD-Rom. 1994.

Nusair, David. *Timecop 2.* www.reelfilm.com.

Pfeiffer, Lee. *The John Wayne Scrapbook.* New York: Citadel Press, 1989.

The Phantom Killer: Texarkana Moonlight Murders. www.crimelibrary.com/serial_killers/unsolved/texarcana/beast_3.

Place, J. A. *The Western Films of John Ford.* New Jersey: Citadel Press, 1974.

Platt, Richard. *Film.* New York: Alfred E. Knopf, 1992.

Rabin, Nathan. *Electra Glide in Blue.* http://www.theonionavclub.com/review.php?review_id=8833, April 6, 2005.

Ray, Robert B. *A Certain Tendency of the Hollywood Cinema, 1930–1980.* Princeton, NJ: Princeton University Press, 1985.

Real Police. *History of Police and Law Enforcement.* http://realpolice.net/police_history.html.

Sam Peckinpah's West. Starz Encore Entertainment. The Western Channel. May 26, 2005.

Schechter, Harold, and Jonna Gormely Semeiks. *Discoveries: Fifty Stories of the Quest.* New York: Oxford University Press, 1992.

Soylent Green. www.geocities.com/moviecritic.geo/reviews/s/soylentgreen.html.

Soylent Green. www.tvguide.com/Movies/database/ShowMovie.asp?MI=21373.

Staley, D.L. *Horn vs. Hollywood.* www.leverguns.com/articles/staley/horn_vs_hollywood.html.

Texas Department of Public Safety. *Historical Development of the Texas Rangers.* www.txdps.state.tx.us/director_staff/texas_rangers/.

Total Recall. Cinebooks. CD-Rom. 1996.

The Town That Dreaded Sundown. http://efilmcritic.com/review.php?movie=3977.

Turner, Graeme. *Film as Social Practice.* London: Routledge, 1994.

US Marshals Service. Microsoft Encarta. CD-Rom, 1995.

Warren, Jason. *Soylent Green.* www.scifilm.org/reviews/soylentgreen.html.

Wikipedia. *Gunsmoke.* http://en.wikipedia.org/wiki/Gunsmoke.

Wyatt Earp. Microsoft Encarta. CD-Rom, 1995.

INDEX

Above the Law 135
Academy Award 9, 13, 63, 143
American International Pictures (AIP) 42
Arizona Raiders 176–177
Arness, James 38, 45, 162, 164, 166
Autrey, Gene 29

B movies 9, 26, 29, 55, 79
Bad Lieutenant 139
Baker, Joe Don 126
Baretta 166–167
The Big Gundown 81, 82, 85
Big Jim McLain 28, 39, 40, 63
The Big Sleep 104
Biograph 8
Birth of a Nation 8
Blade Runner 22, 51, 60, 93–95
Blake, Amanda 163, 165
Blake, Robert 166–167
The Blue Dahlia 98
Boetticher, Budd 74
Bogart, Humphrey 36, 98
The Bounty Hunter 89–90
Bounty Hunters 2 90
Bounty Trackers 88
Boyd, William 29
Bronson, Charles 16–17, 73, 112, 127–128

Calhoun, Rory 73
Campbell, Eric 10
Campbell, Joseph 151, 153
Chaplin, Charles 10–12
Chapman, Duane "Dog" 72
Cheadle, Don 14, 16
Chinatown 107–109
Chisum 82–84
Cinematograph 6
Cleef, Lee Van 78, 79, 80
Cobra 142, 147
Cold War 34
Colors 189–191, 192, 193
Comanche Station 75–76
The Comancheros 177–179
Connors, Mike 166
Cooper, Gary 9, 36–38, 40, 63–67
Costner, Kevin 157–159
Crash 14–16
Crime Story 170–171
Curtis, Ken 163

Dark Blue 139–140
Dawson, Richard 50
The Dead Pool 122
Deadwood 172–173
Death Wish 121, 127, 128
Death Wish 3 127, 142
Defiance 121
Demolition Man 53–54, 56
De Niro, Robert 87, 171
Destry Rides Again 145–147
Devil in a Blue Dress 107–109
El Diablo 84
Dickson, William K.L. 5
Dillon, Matt 14–16
Dirty Harry 120–121, 124
Doc 155–157
El Dorado 67–69
Double Indemnity 99–101
Douglas, Kirk 97, 153
Dudikoff, Michael 88–90, 185
Duvall, Robert 17, 18

Earthquake 188–189
Eastman, George 5
Eastwood, Clint 43, 78, 79–81, 87, 95, 120, 125, 150
Easy Street 10–12, 17, 19
Edison, Thomas 5, 6, 7
Editing 7
Eight Legged Freaks 59–60
Electra Glide in Blue 167
The Empire Strikes Back 92
End of Days 58–59
The Enforcer 122
Exit Wounds 191–193
Extreme Prejudice 183–184

Falling Down 17–19
Farewell My Lovely 104
Film shot (placement) 6, 7
A Fistful of Dollars 78
(Flexible) Film stock 5
Fonda, Henry 33, 36, 112, 151
For a Few Dollars More 78
Ford, Harrison 133
Ford, John 26, 76–77, 151–153

Garner, James 155
Geer, Will 40
Ginty, Robert 87–88
The Glimmer Man 135
The Glove 85

The Good, the Bad, the Ugly 78, 79
The Great Depression 9, 26–28, 34
The Great Train Robbery 7
Griffith, D.W. 7, 8
Gunfight at the OK Corral 153, 155
Gunsmoke 162–165, 172, 173
Gunsmoke: One Man's Justice 166
Gunsmoke: Return to Dodge 164–165
Gunsmoke: The Last Apache 165, 166
Gunsmoke: The Long Ride 166
Gunsmoke: To the Last Man 166

Hang 'Em High 79–80
Hard to Kill 135
Hauer, Rutger 86
Hawks, Howard 63–70
Heat 171
Heston, Charlton 20, 130, 188, 189
High Noon 9, 36–38, 40, 63–67, 121
Hill, Walter 183
The Hired Gun 73, 85
Hour of the Gun 155
HUAC 9, 34–38, 40, 63
The Hunter 85

I, Robot 60–62
In the Heat of the Night 12–13, 17
An Innocent Man 136–137
The Inside of the White Slave Traffic 8
Internal Affairs 137–138, 139
Intolerance 8
Invasion USA 149

Jesse James 111–112
Joe Kidd 80
Johnson, Ben 79
Johnson, Don 169
Jones, Tommy Lee 185
Judge Dredd 56–57

Kennedy, George 142, 188, 189
Kindergarten Cop 144–145, 147
Kinjite: Forbidden Subjects 16–17

Lady in the Lake 104
Lamas, Lorenzo 88
Lammele, Carl 8
Lancaster, Burt 153
Law and Order 171–172

213

Lawrence, Florence 8
Leone, Sergio 78, 155
Life and Legend of Wyatt Earp 153–155
Loaded Weapon I 143
Logan's Run 92–94
Lone Wolf McQuade 180–183
Lonesome Dove 185
The Long Goodbye 104–107
Lucas, George 92
Lumière, Auguste 6
Lumière, Louis 6

Magic lanterns 5
Magnum Force 122, 125
The Maltese Falcon 98–99
Mann, Michael 170
Mannix 166
Marabunta 57–58
Marked for Death 135
Marshal Plan 34
McCrea, Joel 9, 185, 200, 202
McQueen, Steve 85, 86, 197–198, 200
Miami Vice 169–170
Midnight Run 87
Mildred Pierce 101–104
Mitchum, Robert 68, 97, 104
Motion Picture Patents Company 8
Moving Target 88–89
Murder My Sweet 104
Mutual Corporation 10
My Darling Clementine 151–153

Naked Gun 143
Naked Gun 33 1/3 142–143
Nemesis 21–24
Nielson, Leslie 142
Norris, Chuck 48, 180, 186

O'Brian, Hugh 153–155
Once Upon a Time in the West 112–113
180 degree rule 7
The Organization 13
Out for Justice 147–149
Out of the Past 97–98
Outland 46–48
The Outlaws Is Coming 142

Pacino, Al 171

Paradise 154
Paradise Canyon 31–33
Peace Officers Standards and Training (P.O.S.T.) 4
Peckinpaugh, Sam 114, 117, 164, 200–202
Peel, Robert 4
Pierce, Charles B. 180
Pink Cadillac 87
Poitier, Sidney 13
Police Academy 142
Porter, Edwin S. 7
Powell, Dick 104
Power, Tyrone 112
Praetorian Guard 3
Purviance, Edna 10

Rainbow Valley 29–31, 33
Return of the Jedi 92
Ride Lonesome 74–75, 78
Ride the High Country 9, 200–202
Rio Bravo 63–67
Rio Diablo 84–85
Rio Lobo 63, 69–71
Rogers, Roy 29
Roosevelt, Franklin D. 28
The Running Man 49–51
Russell, Kurt 139–140, 157

Salt of the Earth 39
Saxon, John 80, 85
Schwarzenegger, Arnold 49–53, 58, 144–145, 147
Scott, Randolph 9, 74–75, 77, 78, 200–202
Seagal, Steven 135, 147–148, 191–193
The Searchers 176–177, 194
Selleck, Tom 136
Shire-reeve 3
The Shootist 150, 195–196
Showdown at Boothill 73–74
Silent Rage 48–49
Smith, Will 60–62
Soylent Green 20–21
Stallone, Sylvester 49, 56, 142, 147
Star Packer 9, 29–30, 32, 33
Steiger, Rod 13
Stewart, James 76, 77, 145, 195
Stone, Milburn 163
Sudden Impact 122
Sunset 155

Svenson, Bo 125
SWAT 168–169
SWAT (TV show) 167–168

Tales of the Texas Rangers 185
Ten to Midnight 127–128
Terminator 55
The Texas Rangers 175–176
Texas Rangers (film) 185
Them! 43–46, 57, 59, 60
They Call Me MISTER Tibbs! 13
Thomas, Philip Michael 169
Time Cop 54–56
Time Cop 2 55–56
Tom Horn 197–200
Tombstone 157–159
Total Recall 51–53
Touch of Evil 129–130
The Town That Dreaded Sundown 179–180
Traffic in Souls 8
True Confessions 130–132
Two Rode Together 76–77

Unforgiven 72, 80–81, 84, 150
United States Marshal's Service 4

Van Damme, Jean-Claude 55–56
Vitagraph 8
Vitascope 7

Walker, Texas Ranger 186
Walking Tall 124
Walking Tall (2004) 126
Walking Tall II: Part 2 125–126
Walking Tall III 126
Wanted: Dead or Alive 86
Wayne, John 29–33, 38, 39, 40, 48, 63–71, 82, 114, 150, 177, 195
Welles, Orson 129–130
West, Adam 142
White Line Fever 121
Whitmore, James 43
Widmark, Richard 77
The Wild Bunch 113–117, 155, 164, 183, 201
Willis, Bruce 155
Wyatt Earp 157–159
Wyatt Earp: Return to Tombstone 154

Young Guns 84